ASPEN PUBLI:

MW01688029

# ESI HANDBOOK

## Sources, Technology and Process

Adam I. Cohen
G. Edward Kalbaugh

Wolters Kluwer
Law & Business

AUSTIN BOSTON CHICAGO NEW YORK THE NETHERLANDS

This publication is designed to provide accurate and authoritative information in regard to the subject matter covered. It is sold with the understanding that the publisher is not engaged in rendering legal, accounting, or other professional services. If legal advice or other professional assistance is required, the services of a competent professional person should be sought.

—From a *Declaration of Principles* jointly adopted
by a Committee of the American Bar Association
and a Committee of Publishers and Associations

© 2009 Aspen Publishers. All Rights Reserved.

Cover Photo: Guy Crittenden, Getty Images

No part of this publication may be reproduced or transmitted in any form or by any means, electronic or mechanical, including photocopy, recording, or any information storage and retrieval system, without permission in writing from the publisher. Requests for permission to reproduce content should be directed to the Aspen Publishers website at *www.aspenpublishers.com*, or a letter of intent should be faxed to the permissions department at 212-771-0803.

Printed in the United States of America

1 2 3 4 5 6 7 8 9 0

Library of Congress Cataloging-in-Publication Data

Cohen, Adam I., 1968-
ESI handbook : sources, technology, and process / Adam I. Cohen, G. Edward Kalbaugh.
p. cm.—(Law & business)
Includes bibliographical references and index.
ISBN 978-0-7355-6267-7 (alk. paper)
1. Electronic discovery (Law)—United States. 2. Electronic records. 3. Electronic data processing. I. Kalbaugh, G. Edward. II. Title.

KF8902.E42C65 2008
347.73′72—dc22

2008042041

# About Wolters Kluwer Law & Business

Wolters Kluwer Law & Business is a leading provider of research information and workflow solutions in key specialty areas. The strengths of the individual brands of Aspen Publishers, CCH, Kluwer Law International and Loislaw are aligned within Wolters Kluwer Law & Business to provide comprehensive, in-depth solutions and expert-authored content for the legal, professional and education markets.

**CCH** was founded in 1913 and has served more than four generations of business professionals and their clients. The CCH products in the Wolters Kluwer Law & Business group are highly regarded electronic and print resources for legal, securities, antitrust and trade regulation, government contracting, banking, pension, payroll, employment and labor, and healthcare reimbursement and compliance professionals.

**Aspen Publishers** is a leading information provider for attorneys, business professionals and law students. Written by preeminent authorities, Aspen products offer analytical and practical information in a range of specialty practice areas from securities law and intellectual property to mergers and acquisitions and pension/benefits. Aspen's trusted legal education resources provide professors and students with high-quality, up-to-date and effective resources for successful instruction and study in all areas of the law.

**Kluwer Law International** supplies the global business community with comprehensive English-language international legal information. Legal practitioners, corporate counsel and business executives around the world rely on the Kluwer Law International journals, loose-leafs, books and electronic products for authoritative information in many areas of international legal practice.

**Loislaw** is a premier provider of digitized legal content to small law firm practitioners of various specializations. Loislaw provides attorneys with the ability to quickly and efficiently find the necessary legal information they need, when and where they need it, by facilitating access to primary law as well as state-specific law, records, forms and treatises.

Wolters Kluwer Law & Business, a unit of Wolters Kluwer, is headquartered in New York and Riverwoods, Illinois. Wolters Kluwer is a leading multinational publisher and information services company.

## ASPEN PUBLISHERS SUBSCRIPTION NOTICE

This Aspen Publishers product is updated on a periodic basis with supplements to reflect important changes in the subject matter. If you purchased this product directly from Aspen Publishers, we have already recorded your subscription for the update service.

If, however, you purchased this product from a bookstore and wish to receive future updates and revised or related volumes billed separately with a 30-day examination review, please contact our Customer Service Department at 1-800-234-1660 or send your name, company name (if applicable), address, and the title of the product to:

**ASPEN PUBLISHERS**
**7201 McKinney Circle**
**Frederick, MD 21704**

---

**Important Aspen Publishers Contact Information**

- To order any Aspen Publishers title, go to *www.aspenpublishers.com* or call 1-800-638-8437.
- To reinstate your manual update service, call 1-800-638-8437.
- To contact Customer Care, e-mail *customer.care@aspenpublishers.com,* call 1-800-234-1660, fax 1-800-901-9075, or mail correspondence to Order Department, Aspen Publishers, PO Box 990, Frederick, MD 21705.
- To review your account history or pay an invoice online, visit *www.aspenpublishers.com/payinvoices.*

Wolters Kluwer
Law & Business

# TABLE OF CONTENTS

# ABOUT THE AUTHORS

**Adam I. Cohen**

Adam I. Cohen is a senior managing director in the New York office of FTI's Technology Consulting practice. Mr. Cohen is a nationally recognized expert in electronic discovery and electronic information management policy issues. Mr. Cohen advises on planning and implementation issues associated with every phase of electronic discovery in litigations and investigations as well as electronic information management policies and practices, including, for example, proactive litigation readiness and regulatory compliance, complying with electronic preservation obligations and avoiding spoliation sanctions, crafting and responding to discovery requests targeting electronic information, and cost containment strategies.

Prior to joining FTI, Mr. Cohen was a litigation partner at Weil, Gotshal & Manges, LLP, where he represented major corporate clients in complex litigation involving computer and Internet-related issues. He is co-author (with Weil partner David J. Lender) of the treatise Electronic Discovery: Law and Practice (Aspen Publishers), which already has been cited as authority in several landmark electronic discovery opinions by federal courts.

Mr. Cohen is co-chair of the Electronic Discovery committee of the New York State Bar Association's Federal and Commercial Litigation Section, a member of the Advisory Board of the Georgetown Law Center E-Discovery Institute, and a member of the board of Volunteer Lawyers for the Arts. He is admitted to practice in the courts of the State of New York, as well as the United States District Courts for the Southern and Eastern Districts of New York. He holds a B.A. from Wesleyan University and a J.D. from Duke University School of Law.

**G. Edward Kalbaugh**

G. Edward Kalbaugh is senior managing director of Allegent Consulting Group, a consultancy that advises companies on strategies and application of information technology to achieve business objectives, including governance, risk management, and compliance programs.

Mr. Kalbaugh has led and participated in numerous major national and international engagements involving assessments, strategies, policies and implementation procedures dealing with regulatory compliance, corporate governance, information systems migrations, and enterprise risk management.

Prior to Allegent, Mr. Kalbaugh held senior management positions in banking, where his responsibilities included operations and information systems and membership on the regulatory and risk management steering committees. Mr. Kalbaugh began his career with the Space Division of Rockwell International, where he completed the company's six-year management development program and was director of engineering extended space operations.

Trained as an industrial engineer, Mr. Kalbaugh has been a frequent writer and speaker on business transformation through leverage of information systems. He has formed and sold three technology companies.

# ACKNOWLEDGMENTS

We would like to thank the professionals and staff at FTI Consulting, Inc., in particular the members of the Technology segment and especially David Remnitz, Stephen O'Malley and Adil Dharssi. Without their experience, expertise, dedication and support the consulting practice in electronic discovery compliance that inspired this book would never have taken flight.

We would also like to thank Adam's former partners at the law firm Weil, Gotshal & Manges LLP for supporting Adam's journey down the path of eDiscovery enlightenment, and in particular David Lender, the leader of the firm's electronic discovery practice and Adam's co-author on the legal treatise Electronic Discovery: Law and Practice, for his continued professional collaboration and friendship.

Adam would especially like to thank his family—his parents for instilling academic discipline, intellectual curiosity and a love of books, and his wife, Lori, and children, Zachary, Charlotte and Logan, for their continued love and support for his professional pursuits.

Edward would especially like to thank his wife Christine for her continuous support and encouragement, and Richard Hershman, Senior Managing Director of FTI's Global Insurance Practice for his professional insights, counsel and friendship.

# FOREWORD

In 2004, Adam Cohen and David Lender co-authored the book, ***Electronic Discovery: Law and Practice***, as a guide for litigators involved in e-discovery.

The book focused on the details of case law to illustrate the practical application of real-world e-discovery, primarily under U.S. federal law.

The book has been cited in several major decisions and federal court opinions. It has had several major supplements and remains without peer as an authoritative case law treatise on the subject.

This new book, ***ESI Handbook: Sources, Technology and Process***, expands on chapter 9 of the original by focusing on information technology, especially as it relates to electronic discovery of electronically stored information under the amendments to the Federal Rules of Civil Procedure adopted in December 2006.

This book is intended to provide non-technical litigators, judges, other practitioners, and corporate e-Discovery teams with a practical guide to the information systems infrastructure and the various technology components that support electronic discovery as sources of ESI.

# DISCLAIMER

This book is intended to provide a broad range of information to inform and educate, and is not intended to offer legal advice. Information in this book is derived from multiple published and unpublished sources, including the authors' personal files, reference books, articles, vendor literature, and Web sites. Accordingly, while the authors believe the statements contained herein are based on accurate and reliable information, they cannot warrant that each topic is complete, up to date, or error free. References to specific vendors are for informational purposes only, and do not imply endorsement by the authors. Any brands, products, or service names are, or may be, trademarks or service marks and are used solely to identify products or services of their respective owners.

Part I

# INTRODUCTION AND OVERVIEW

## CHAPTER 1

# INTRODUCTION

Discovery of electronically stored information (ESI), even under optimum circumstances, is a complex, dynamic, and difficult process. It is also a collaborative process requiring a mix of legal, business, and technical knowledge and skills combined with an increasing reliance on technology to facilitate the process.

These imperatives are being positively addressed by the courts through evolving interpretations of the Federal Rules of Civil Procedure and the December 2006 Amended Rules, resulting in several major themes that are important for litigation and discovery practitioners to understand.

Foremost is the requirement for counsel to demonstrate best efforts to achieve a cooperative and efficient approach for accomplishing cost-effective ESI discovery. Inherent in this requirement is the desire of the courts to be unburdened from involvement in resolving capricious discovery issues resulting from lack of diligence and good-faith effort on the part of counsel.

These requirements point to the unquestionable need for counsel to understand ESI sources and information technology, including the software tools that facilitate discovery and litigation. It is also important for counsel to understand how the ESI discovery process works within the framework of corporate governance and technology issues.

These imperatives are made more urgent as the absolute volume of information continues to increase and litigators are obliged to forego "game theory" approaches in favor of strategic cooperation in order to effectively contain discovery costs and protect the client's position. Seeking all relevant information will give way to seeking the best relevant information.

This will require use of sophisticated discovery tools—concept and contextual searching, artificial intelligence, statistical sampling, and relationship mapping—that help automate the discovery process, reduce costs, and enhance process and information integrity.

As noted, these efforts take place within the framework of law. In that regard, there is considerable detailed material available covering the Federal Rules of Civil Procedure and the December 2006 Amended Rules, including compendia of related case law. Accordingly, this book does not attempt to repeat that body of information.

Instead, this book is designed to provide discovery and litigation practitioners with an easy-to-read introduction and reference source for understanding ESI sources and underlying information technology, the functional components of the discovery process, and the discovery technology that supports that process. The book is organized into five Parts:

- Introduction to the ESI discovery lifecycle and the information technology systems likely to be encountered
- Explanations and discussions of the major sources of ESI
- "Walkthrough" of the e-discovery lifecycle processes
- Information on how to be better prepared for e-discovery in the future
- Additional reference information

Each chapter provides information to educate the reader concerning the various topics covered, and concludes with a summary of issues and concerns that may need attention, as well as recommendations that may be helpful to practitioners in addressing those issues.

In using this book it is important to keep in mind the constant and rapid pace of change that takes place within information systems organizations and in the systems and software tools used by those organizations.

This dynamic aspect of information systems makes it extremely difficult even for specialists in the field to keep current with emerging technology, especially its impact on systems already in place within the organization (legacy systems).

To gain a thorough understanding of any particular information technology would require intensive study of large volumes of information on the subject. Such an effort is impractical and beyond the ordinary scope of most practitioners in the legal profession. However, counsel must understand information technology well enough to meet the intent of the Amended Federal Rules and to adequately represent the best interests of their client.

This book addresses this challenge by focusing on the fundamental characteristics and intent of the applicable technology, not on the arcane details of any particular technology. By taking this approach, the reader is equipped with sufficient information to know what questions to ask, what person in the organization might have the answers, and whether the answers are sufficient to satisfy the particular issue or requirement.

To achieve these objectives, the book is organized to enable easy reading and quick reference to topics, while minimizing dependence on footnotes, endnotes, and other cumbersome annotations.

The Appendix contains sample material that helps make the content of the book more meaningful by illustrating how selected components of the e-Discovery process have, or might be implemented in actual practice.

Finally, the authors recognize that most organizations face budgetary and other resource constraints that impose limitations on their practical ability to implement some of the recommendations set forth in this book. This does not mean that the recommendations should not be considered where resource constraints exist. On the contrary, in all situations, the recommendations should be viewed as incremental objectives that can move the organization forward in terms of achieving effective e-Discovery capabilities. Accordingly, each organization should consider the recommendations, set priorities, and establish plans for selective implementation that optimize that organization's respective capabilities.

## CHAPTER 2

# OVERVIEW OF THE ELECTRONIC DISCOVERY PROCESS

## § 2.01 INTRODUCTION

ESI discovery takes place within a lifecycle framework of components comprising governance, processing, and technology that guide and facilitate the activities of all parties involved. Accordingly, it is important for practitioners to understand this lifecycle and its components, so they can function effectively in achieving ESI discovery objectives.

The electronic discovery process is a dynamic and iterative process that may vary somewhat in any particular situation depending on a number of factors, including the size of the enterprise, the scope of discovery, and the methodology and technology tools used in any given circumstance. In any case, the overview that follows provides a typical approach that serves to illuminate the process as background for material in chapters that follow.

## § 2.02 FORMS OF ESI

Essentially ESI is any digital information[1] generated by a computer or computer-aided device and stored in a form retrievable by a computer or computer aided device. Common ESI types include emails, instant messages, Web pages, word processing files, spreadsheet files, databases, calendars, digital faxes, animation, video, and audio. ESI exists in three forms—native files, metadata, and images.

See Chapter 4, Introduction to Sources of ESI, for more detailed discussions on forms of ESI.

### [A] Native Files

A native file is the original form in which a document or file is created by a software application. Two good examples are spreadsheets and word processing documents. Native files contain the content that users see, such as text and spreadsheet numbers, and information (metadata) about the document that users normally do not see, such as author and creation date.

### [B] Metadata

Metadata is information describing a variety of characteristics about a document, including, for example, the creation date, author, modification dates, file size, and file type. Metadata is a major source of intelligence regarding ESI.

### [C] Image Files

The intent of creating static images such as Tagged Image File Format (TIFF) and Portable Document Format (PDF) of paper or electronic documents is to provide standardized, printable and non-modifiable versions that enable review of all document content. When a TIFF or PDF is created, a separate image file may also be created for inclusion of information, such as metadata that was not readily visible to users in the original document.

These images are arranged into a "load file" that can be uploaded into a software program for reviewing the various documents. (See § 2.03[E] and § 2.03[F] for further discussion of load files.)

While paper documents are not considered ESI in their paper form, paper documents converted to digital or image format are considered ESI. Some paper documents are converted to digital form using Optical Character Recognition (OCR) software. Other paper or electronic documents may be converted to images such as TIFF and PDF.[2]

---

[1] In conformance to the intent of the Amended Rules, we have chosen to use the term "information" as opposed to the term "data" throughout the book, except in specific instances where "data" is traditionally used, and where use of "information" would be awkward.

[2] Xerox has applied for a patent for its printing technology, dubbed "Erasable Paper," that creates images lasting approximately 16 to 24 hours. Xerox perceives application for emails and documents that are printed for immediate viewing and then discarded. According to Xerox, this category accounts for 40 percent of office printing.

## § 2.03 ELECTRONIC DISCOVERY PROCESS LIFECYCLE

To be achieved cost-effectively, electronic discovery must be conducted under an orderly methodology that takes into account and answers key questions related to several fundamental issues.

- **Federal Rules of Civil Procedure and other legal and regulatory requirements:** What is the intent and implication of each applicable Federal Rule? How have these rules been interpreted by the courts? Can the parties meet the requirements of each rule? How do other legal and regulatory requirements impact discovery?
- **Polices governing information systems:** Are policies reliable and enforced? How have these policies affected information content and retention? Do the policies constrain or enhance the discovery of ESI?
- **Information technology infrastructure:** What are the sources of information? Can relevant information be identified and retrieved? Can the scope of discovery be defined?
- **Software and methodology used to conduct and manage the electronic discovery process:** Can the process be conducted and managed effectively? Is the process beneficial to the parties? Does the process maintain quality controls to ensure there is no spoliation? Does the process preserve security and chain-of-custody requirements? Does the process achieve desired discovery results?
- **Key participants in the electronic discovery process:** Who are the key players? What are their roles? How will they contribute?

The Electronic Discovery Process Lifecycle model, shown in Figure (1) below, is designed to illustrate how these elements relate and interact within the discovery process flow. In addition, Figure (1), briefly discussed on the following pages and covered in detail in Part Three, Performing Electronic Discovery, provides a context for discussions that take place throughout the book.

**Note:** The Electronic Discovery Process Lifecycle illustrated in Figure (1) is similar to, but provides more detail than, the Electronic Discovery Reference Model (EDRM), a widely-recognized depiction of the e-Discovery process developed by Socha Consulting LLC and Gelbmann & Associates for use as a reference by participating members to promote a better understanding of e-Discovery.

There are six phases to the e-Discovery Process Lifecycle. These phases typically involve an iterative, overlapping process as both parties strive to satisfy the Federal Rules and other laws and regulations, and to achieve their respective objectives.

**FIGURE (1) ELECTRONIC DISCOVERY PROCESS LIFECYCLE**

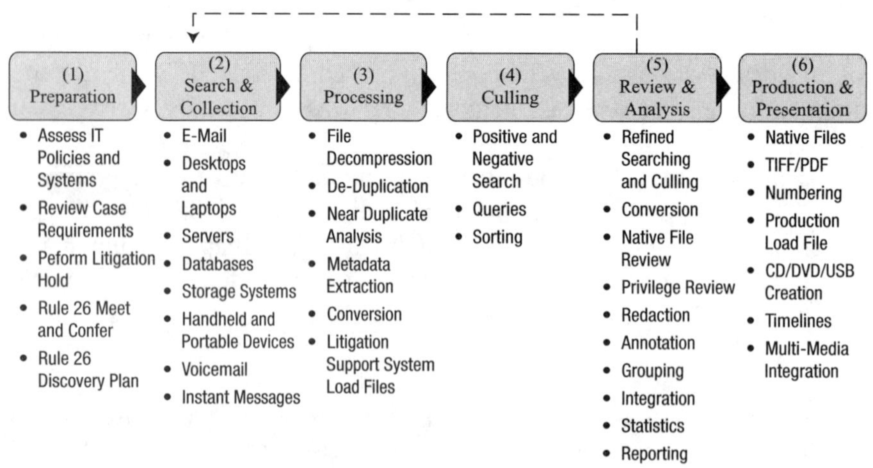

### [A] Phase 1: Preparation

Phase 1 typically involves an initial assessment of a potential or actual legal or regulatory matter to determine the potential severity of the issue, whether it could result in litigation, whether it will be handled by in-house and/or outside counsel, and what next steps should be taken.

These considerations are driven by requirements set forth in the Federal Rules of Civil Procedure, other laws, and regulations, and take into account the company's existing information management policies, records and content management systems, IT infrastructure, and those requirements applicable to the specific legal case being addressed.

Once a determination is made that the matter is subject to actual or potential litigation, relevant documents are initially identified and a "Legal Hold" order must be issued to responsible parties within the organization in order to preserve evidence.

Once a legal hold is issued, opposing counsel must meet in accord with Amended Rules 26 (f) and 16 in order to make best efforts to reach agreement on a mutually acceptable Discovery Plan.

### [B] Phase 2: Search and Collection

The initial "scope of discovery," defined under the Rule 26 conference referred to in Phase 1 above, forms the basis for the execution of initial searches across all sources of potentially relevant ESI. Searches are designed to filter information according to a variety of parameters that are relevant to the discovery matter, including, for example, key words or phrases, key persons, date and time, and chain-of-custody. As noted in Figure (1), Phases 2 through 5 may comprise an iterative process.

Information is collected (extracted) from identified sources of ESI and is normally placed in a central repository that provides security, protection, and access by authorized parties.

### [C] Phase 3: Processing

The purpose of processing is to decompress files, extract metadata from files, eliminate duplication, and prepare the collected information for loading into a document review software tool. This may include creating image files such as TIFF and PDF and text files from scanned images using OCR software.

### [D] Phase 4: Culling

Culling is basically a process of refined searches, filtering, and queries used to reduce the volume of ESI and create a set of potentially responsive documents for detailed review. While culling is most heavily focused during Phase 4, culling also takes place during Phases 2, 3, and 5.

### [E] Phase 5: Review and Analysis

One of the most difficult tasks in discovery management is the organization of information so that it can be reviewed and acted on by the discovery team in an efficient, cost-effective manner. Accordingly, litigation teams use a variety of document review software tools or "review platforms" to facilitate the review process. Documents for review are uploaded to the respective document review platform by means of a review load file. The review load file is structured in conformance with the specific requirements of the applicable review platform. The review platform enables review teams to perform various functions, such as native file analysis, redaction, annotation, privilege review, document grouping and integration, and reporting in a collaborative manner within LAN or Web-based environments.

### [F] Phase 6: Production and Presentation

Most litigation support systems leave the original files intact, but convert the files to TIFF or PDF while applying the appropriate redactions, annotation, Bates stamps, headers, and footers. The pages may be printed or stored on a hard drive in a folder structure. Once all document pages have been created, a production load file is generated. The production load file typically includes page and metadata information and may include reference to native files containing embedded metadata. The load file outlines how the individual pages are connected together as documents. In addition, collections of multimedia materials are integrated to create trial presentations. The collection of files typically is placed on a CD, DVD, or USB hard drive for production or presentation. Phase 6 also includes production of statistics and reports created throughout the discovery process.

## § 2.04 ISSUES AND CONCERNS

It should be expected that opposing counsel will do whatever is ethically possible to serve the interests of their client, including taking advantage of any weaknesses in the information retention and ESI discovery capabilities of the opposition. Positioning for advantage usually takes place early in the discovery process when vulnerabilities are exposed and capable of being leveraged by opposing counsel. Some of these vulnerabilities could include:

- Inadequate or poorly enforced retention policies and procedures
- Untimely, inadequate, or poorly enforced litigation holds
- Preservation issues
- Chain-of-custody issues, internally or through non-parties
- Antiquated information storage systems
- High turnover or relatively new information systems personnel
- Weak knowledge of information systems
- Exposure of potential privileged or work product information
- Weak ESI discovery capability, both personnel and technology

## § 2.05 RECOMMENDATIONS

Most companies give no second thought to the need for "fire drills" as part of disaster planning. The drills expose vulnerabilities and help improve the evacuation process. It should be no different with discovery.

Companies need to conduct electronic discovery readiness reviews that expose vulnerabilities and provide recommendations for remediation. These reviews should exercise the complete electronic discovery lifecycle process, with sufficient documentation to enable development of constructive remediation plans.

In many cases, an effective electronic discovery readiness review may require working in conjunction with third-party experts capable of providing objective and informed assessments and recommendations.

CHAPTER 3

# OVERVIEW OF THE INFORMATION TECHNOLOGY INFRASTRUCTURE

## § 3.01 INTRODUCTION

As mentioned earlier in the discussion of the electronic discovery lifecycle, each party is required to understand the other party's information technology infrastructure in order to use best efforts in facilitating the ESI discovery process.

This chapter provides an overview of the information technology infrastructure to help guide discovery practitioners in what to look for and ask for as they attempt to facilitate the discovery process.

As illustrated in Figure (2), an information technology infrastructure essentially comprises the computers and related equipment, communications networks, systems and application software, and the organization (people and operating policies, procedures and methodologies) that support the creation, access, application, and storage of information shared among users.

**FIGURE (2) THE INFORMATION TECHNOLOGY INFRASTRUCTURE**

| Hardware and Software Components ▶ | Connected in a Communications Network ▶ | Arranged into Functional Systems ▶ | Managed and Operated by People |
|---|---|---|---|
| • Bridges/Routers | • Broadband | • Business Apps | • Unit Heads |
| • Client Computers | • DSL | • Client Systems | • Business Unit Heads |
| • Firewalls | • ISDN | • Data Warehouses | • Data Administrator |
| • Hubs/Switches | • Local Area | • Databases | • Information Officer |
| • Modems | • Metro Area | • File Systems | • Network Aministrator |
| • Operating Software | • Wide Area | • Performance Mgmt | • Security Officer |
| • Printers | • Wired | • Security Mgmt | • System Aministrator |
| • Servers | • Wireless | • Server Systems | • Technology Officer |
| • Storage Devices | | • Storage Systems | |

Today, those users might be in the same room connected by a simple copper cable or at different locations worldwide, connected by wired and wireless networking technology, including the Internet.

## § 3.02 NETWORKS AND COMPONENTS

Networks comprise the wired or wireless communication structure and the components that connect to that structure. The graphic in Figure (3) below is constructed to illustrate various devices that might comprise a network. It is not intended to depict an actual network configuration, which can range in size and scope from two computers connected to a printer, to thousands of devices connected from hundreds of locations around the world.

The networks of very large companies, such as Internet service providers like AOL, Google, and Yahoo that each connect thousands of 100-plus large-scale server-clusters worldwide, are very large and complex, and require equally complex IT infrastructures. Regardless of size and complexity, however, networks consist of certain basic components.

These components are available from a large number of vendors, and are arranged in various configurations and sizes depending on purpose and scope of operation.

Network components operate and interact with the network though a special class of software that runs specific processes that, for example, enables clients and servers to share applications, files, and devices such as printers, across the network. Although much of the systems' software is vendor-proprietary, most system software relies on common standards to achieve interoperability.

Components residing on the various network configurations include three main groups—peripherals, clients, and servers.

### [A] Network Peripherals

These are devices that contain their own processors and network connections so that they are not required to be directly attached to computers. (Some peripherals, such as large routers and firewalls, however, may contain powerful special-purpose computers.) Examples of commonly found peripherals include printers, modems,

FIGURE (3) ILLUSTRATION OF NETWORK COMPONENTS

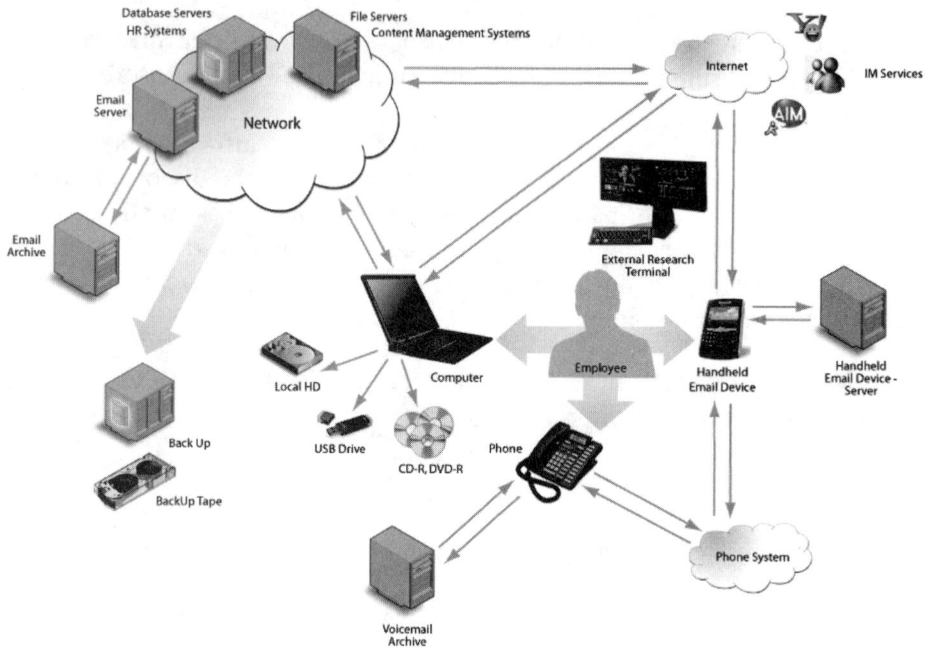


hubs/switches, bridges/routers, and firewalls. These peripherals are not a direct source of ESI. However, information flowing through a peripheral such as a router, for example, can be captured by network performance or security management systems and subsequently used to help map information flows.

## [B] Clients

There are two types of clients—"thick" clients and "thin" clients. Traditional desktop and laptop computers are referred to as thick clients because they have powerful computing and information storage capability and are capable of standing alone, independent of the network. (In some network configurations, desktop and laptop computers can also function as servers.)

Thin clients on the other hand, refer to those devices that rely on communication with servers in order to perform their functions. There are two types of thin clients. One is a desktop computer configured with a sealed case, no hard drive, no CD-ROM, and no USB ports, with constraints on the operating system and with limited processing capability. The other type of thin client is a handheld device. Examples of such devices include Web-based cell phones, PDAs, and devices for recording inventory, to name a few. Handheld devices rely on special servers that manage information in forms compatible with the slower connections, limited power, small screens, and small keyboards of these handheld devices.

## [C] Servers

These are special-purpose computers that perform specific functions in support of "clients." There are essentially six types of servers—application servers, file servers, database servers, print servers, storage servers, and Web servers. Application servers can be dedicated to one application, such as email or accounting, for example, or can support multiple applications for multiple users. File servers essentially function as active file processing devices and come in a wide range of capability and configurations, from a small hard drive to vast arrays of remotely located storage drives. Database servers are specialized for managing databases. Print servers provide access by large work groups to the capabilities of expensive, specialized printers. Storage servers are designed to optimize backups and archiving of information for temporary or long-term storage. Web servers aggregate functions specific to the Internet to enable greater efficiency in processing, especially where e-commerce functions are performed.

**Note:** Routers are sometimes referred to as communications servers, but we have chosen to include routers under the category of peripherals. Web servers are sometimes thought of as a combination of application server and file server, but we have chosen to refer to Web servers as a separate category for clarity and because of their increasing importance in the discovery process.

## § 3.03 TYPES OF NETWORKS

Various network schemes are used within the information technology infrastructure to connect network components, including those components providing sources of ESI. Although an in-depth understanding of these network schemes is not essential to understanding sources of ESI, it is useful in discussions with information technology staff to be acquainted with the primary types of networks deployed within the organization.

### [A] Local Area Networks

Networks supporting small offices or groups of buildings are typically arranged in a configuration of copper cabling spanning less than 1,000 feet. These local area networks consist of one or more switches, a router, various peripherals and computers, and potentially, a modem for connection to the Internet. Because of their short networking distance, LANs are able to use high-speed switched Ethernet or Wi-Fi technology. LANs can link to other networks, including other LANs, metropolitan area networks, and wide area networks.

### [B] Metropolitan Area Networks

Metropolitan area networks, as the name implies, are usually located in cities. MANs use a combination of fiber-optic cable and microwave antennas to link buildings. LANs within buildings connected by MANs can usually connect to the MAN through a fiber-optic "backbone" that spans floor-to-floor in the building.

### [C] Wide Area Networks

Wide area networks include those networks that link across local boundaries to span broad areas, including across international boundaries. WANs link other networks together and link networks to the Internet, the largest and most widely known WAN. Some WANs are constructed using dedicated leased lines for the private use of a particular organization.

WANs require use of high-bandwidth connections because they span large distances, and because they usually support text and a variety of multimedia such as animations, graphics, sound, and video that require high-speed connectivity and that create very high traffic volumes.

Bandwidth is a term roughly denoting the amount of network transmission throughput, expressed as bits-per-second or bps. The high-bandwidth connections required by multimedia content and the Internet are referred to as broadband connections. There are four types of broadband connections.

#### [1] Integrated Services Digital Network (ISDN)

ISDN is an all-digital telephone service with a connection of 128Kbps using existing telephone wiring. Because it has the lowest bandwidth of the broadband services, ISDN is used primarily only in sparsely populated areas where higher bandwidth connections are not available.

#### [2] Digital Subscriber Line (DSL)

DSL is also an all-digital telephone service using existing telephone wiring. DSL can achieve connection speeds as high as 1.5Mbps to the computer (downstream) and 256Kbps from the computer (upstream). DSL is considered a cost-effective connection to the Internet where there are a limited number of simultaneous users on the DSL connection.

#### [3] Internet/TV Cable

Internet cable services run on the same cable as cable-TV, which was originally developed as an entertainment technology. Internet cable service providers claim throughput somewhat higher than DSL. However, because cable-TV is shared with other subscribers on the local network, throughput of the Internet cable connection may become degraded.

#### [4] Fiber-Optic Cable

Fiber-optic cables have a higher throughput than other broadband services, achieving speeds of over 100Gbps. However, because they are inherently expensive and difficult to install, fiber-optic cables are usually limited to use as the "backbone" cabling in buildings connecting LANs to the Internet, and to connecting buildings within relatively small geographic areas. New techniques by telephone companies to install fiber-optic cables on top of traditional telephone cables strung between poles will help reduce the cost and help expand the usage of fiber-optic cables.

## § 3.04 FUNCTIONAL SYSTEMS

Functional systems comprise the hardware and software platforms that help users create, access, apply, and store information in support of business objectives. While this includes a wide range of systems, of primary importance to discovery practitioners are those related to sources of ESI, which are discussed in detail in the following Part 2, Sources of Electronically Stored Information.

## § 3.05 INFORMATION TECHNOLOGY ORGANIZATION

### [A] Introduction

All companies are organized differently, with the same titles often conveying different functions within different companies, so it is important to go beyond titles to understand who has essential knowledge of the IT infrastructure, as well as who has direct responsibility for providing access to information.

In addition, in large companies there are a number of positions and roles involved. Therefore, the practitioner must determine who, with what title in the organization, performs the duties listed below. We have used standard titles with a brief statement of the typical duties and responsibilities for the key information technology positions.

### [B] Chief Information Officers (CIO)

CIOs perform a governance and oversight role, providing strategic direction, policy, and review. CIOs are focused on the high-level "what and why" of information systems. CIOs probably do not have in-depth operating knowledge concerning ESI, but should be useful in lending support to discovery initiatives.

### [C] Chief Technology Officers (CTO)

CTOs are responsible for selecting, designing, and developing technology components and solutions in support of technology strategies, goals, and objectives. CTOs are focused on the "what and how" of information systems. CTOs are in a good position to provide direct operating knowledge of sources of ESI, as well as providing support for discovery initiatives.

### [D] Chief Security Officers (CSO)

CSOs are responsible for ensuring that the IT infrastructure and information residing therein are protected from external and internal threats. In fulfilling their role of protecting information systems, CSOs by default have a good understanding of sources of ESI.

### [E] Network Administrators

Network administrators are responsible for ensuring that network performance is optimized, that protection schemes are working, and that all users are satisfied. A network administrator's knowledge of sources of ESI is usually limited to his or her segment of the network, so discussions must include all network administrators in order to be inclusive of the overall corporate network.

### [F] Data Administrators

Data administrators are responsible for designing and maintaining effective capabilities to store and access information. Data administrators work closely with business units and other IT staff, and have in-depth knowledge of sources of ESI specific to their area of responsibility. Discussions must include all data administrators to be inclusive of the overall organization. The term "data administrator" may also refer to or include "database administrator," a role that is primarily focused on the internal issues related to databases.

### [G] Email Administrators

Email administrators are responsible for performance and security of email and collaboration systems, adding and deleting users, managing information related to each user account, such as password, user name, and email alias, and maintaining logs and reports concerning system activity. There may be separate email administrators for each specific email/collaboration system in use within the organization.

### [H] System/Application Administrators and Developers

System/application administrators and developers are responsible for designing, developing, and maintaining systems and business applications in support of goals and objectives of corporate offices and business unit heads. Systems and application staff work closely with business units and other IT staff, and may only have knowledge of sources of ESI specific to their particular application. Discussions must include all systems and applications administrators to be inclusive of the overall organization.

### [I] Records Administrators

Records administrators are responsible for coordinating with company counsel, IT management, and business unit heads to define and implement a comprehensive records retention program across the enterprise. Records administrators are essential participants in helping craft electronic discovery plans under Amended Rule 26, and should be members of the discovery team. In large organizations, there may be a number of records administrators reporting to a central authority.

### [J] Business Unit Heads

Business unit heads are responsible for applying the information technology systems and business applications that support their respective business unit goals and objectives. Business unit heads are focused on the "what and why" of information systems for their respective units, and may not have in-depth operating knowledge of sources of ESI. In some organizations, business units have their own independent IT infrastructure and personnel.

In many companies, some of these IT roles may be combined, or they may not exist. In all cases, it will most likely require discussions starting from the top down to determine the correct people to speak with. Therefore, it is important to obtain an organization chart as early as possible to facilitate this process.

## § 3.06 ISSUES AND CONCERNS

There are certain common characteristics of IT organizations that make gaining insight into operations difficult. The negative influence of these characteristics will vary among organizations, so attention must be given equally to each in order to discern their impact.

- Technical people use terms specific to their particular discipline and that have meaning within a particular context. Unfortunately, technical terms sometimes confuse instead of enlighten. Accordingly, interviewers must probe to find the true meaning behind these terms.
- Technical people tend to think and speak in literal terms. The specificity of the question dictates the specificity of the answer—no more and no less. This is compounded when one does not know what questions to ask in order to obtain meaningful answers.
- Current, complete, accurate, and easy-to-follow technical documentation, policies, and procedures are often viewed as a luxury, not a necessity, and may not be readily available.
- IT organizations are always resource constrained and under critical deadlines, so access to personnel is limited.
- IT organizations are always in a state of transformation as systems are tuned and reconfigured and newer technology replaces older technology. This very often includes turnover of key personnel.
- Responsibility for corporate information is dispersed throughout the enterprise. There is usually no supreme information custodian.

## § 3.07 RECOMMENDATIONS

Achieving an understanding of complex IT infrastructures can be a daunting task, even for those technology professionals specializing in this area of operations. The following recommended steps will help in initiating a dialogue with colleagues and opposing counsel.

1. Obtain organization charts that define roles and responsibilities. Look for those people that may be involved in sources of ESI within the IT organization and throughout the enterprise, and obtain their contact information. Get permission to speak with them directly.
2. Obtain records retention policies and procedures, and detailed requirements for specific classes and categories of records, the records custodians, retention periods, storage devices and mediums, retrieval methods, volume of information, costs, and any issues, concerns, or constraints related thereto.
3. Obtain network diagrams that indicate where computers (mainframes, centralized computers, desktops, and portable computers) and information stores are located. Have someone circle or identify the applicable equipment on the network diagrams. Include network management devices, such a routers and security management consoles, that may contain their own information.
4. Obtain functional descriptions of the applicable equipment identified above—what the equipment does, what format the information is stored in, what is required to extract relevant information.
5. Identify and obtain descriptions of applications related to content management and retention, along with flow charts and pointers to information sources.
6. Obtain a list of all custodians of potentially relevant information and seek to develop a preliminary map of these to related sources of ESI.
7. Obtain any procedures or instructions that might facilitate information identification and collection.
8. Armed with this preliminary information, begin defining your discovery strategies and scoping rough ideas of the amount of effort involved so that you can be in a reasonable position to refine your planning, preparation, and negotiations with opposing counsel while you gain more information and insight as the process moves forward.

# Part II

# SOURCES OF ELECTRONICALLY STORED INFORMATION

## CHAPTER 4

# INTRODUCTION TO SOURCES OF ESI

The last chapter presented an overview of the information technology infrastructure as an introduction for understanding the context in which the sources of ESI exist. This chapter addresses the sources of ESI in detail in relation to the electronic discovery process.

ESI is generally categorized as being structured or unstructured, based on certain characteristics. Structured information refers to computer-generated information that can be organized into logical entities readable by machine. Unstructured information refers to information that has no logical data structure or that is not easily readable by machine.

In essence, these definitions imply that all structured information is capable of being placed in a database, and all unstructured information is not capable of being placed in a database, and is placed in file systems as indicated in Figure (4).

**FIGURE (4) CATEGORIES OF INFORMATION**

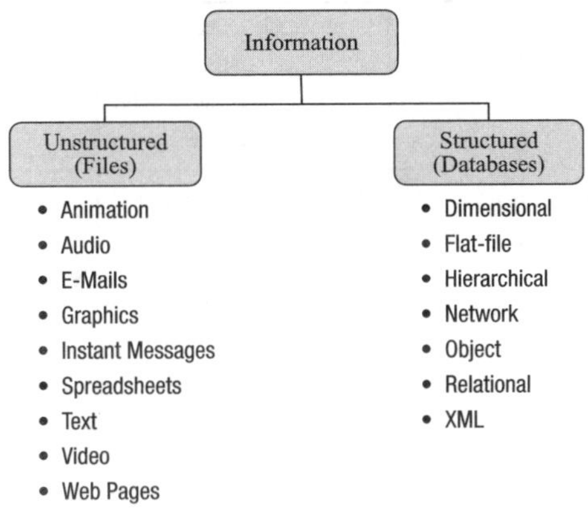


Under this definition, over two thirds of business information could be classified as unstructured. However, regardless of whether information is structured or unstructured, or where it resides, discovery technology has enabled the search, extraction, and analysis of almost all information in digital form, including email, Web applications, animation, graphics, and video.

Figure (5) below provides summary information regarding these primary sources of ESI—their native application, type of content, file systems, storage devices, and short-term and long-term storage methods. The table is intended to provide a common and simple frame of reference for further discussion of these topics.

## FIGURE (5) TABLE OF ESI SOURCES

| ESI Category | Native Application | Type of Content | File System | Physical Storage Device | Short-Term Storage System/Media | Long-Term Storage System/Media |
|---|---|---|---|---|---|---|
| Email | Email System | Text<br>HTML<br>Attached Documents | Network File System<br>Distributed File System | Desktop<br>Laptop<br>PDA<br>Cell Phone<br>MP3 Player<br>File Server | Disk Drive<br>Disk Array<br>SANs<br>NAS<br>Flash Memory<br>CD<br>Disk/Tape Hybrids | Tape Drive<br>Tape Array<br>Disk/Tape Hybrids |
| Documents | Word Processor | Text<br>Graphics | | | | |
| | Spreadsheet | Text<br>Formulae | | | | |
| | Presentation | Text<br>Graphics | | | | |
| Instant Messaging | Instant Message System | Text | | | | |
| Audio | Voice Mail<br>Rich Media | Sound | | | | |
| Video | Video System | Video | | | | |
| Web Pages | Web Browser | HTML<br>Rich Media | | | | |
| Databases | Database System | Structured Information | Database File System | Desktop<br>Laptop<br>Database Server | | |
| Transactional Files | Transaction System | Structured Information | Transactional File System | Transactional File Server | Disk Array<br>SANs<br>NAS | |

CHAPTER 5

# OVERVIEW OF FILE AND STORAGE SYSTEMS

IT organizations deploy a myriad of file and storage components and systems in various configurations in an effort to balance the objectives of security, performance, compliance, and cost. While no two IT organizations pursue their objectives in the same way, they all deploy some combination of the systems covered in the following overview.

One of the major considerations regarding file systems is the amount of storage capacity available. Figure (6) below provides a summary of the terms and related values for computer storage.

**FIGURE (6) COMPUTER STORAGE CAPACITIES**

| Root Value | Result Value | Computer Term | Numberical Term |
|---|---|---|---|
| $1000^1=10^3$ | 1,000 | Kilobyte | Thousand |
| $1000^2=10^6$ | 1,000,000 | Megabyte | Million |
| $1000^3=10^9$ | 1,000,000,000 | Gigabyte | Billion |
| $1000^4=10^{12}$ | 1,000,000,000,000 | Terabyte | Trillion |
| $1000^5=10^{15}$ | 1,000,000,000,000,000 | Petabyte | Quadrillion |
| $1000^6=10^{18}$ | 1,000,000,000,000,000,000 | Exabyte | Quintillion |
| $1000^7=10^{21}$ | 1,000,000,000,000,000,000,000 | Zettabyte | Sectillion |
| $1000^8=10^{24}$ | 1,000,000,000,000,000,000,000,000 | Yottabyte | Septillion |

## § 5.01 FILE SYSTEMS

The term "file system" generally refers to the method or characteristics that distinguish one type of storage approach from another. All file systems use some form of media such as a disk, tape, CD, or static memory on which to store information. The following file systems are of primary importance for the majority of ESI.

### [A] Network File Systems

A network file system supports sharing of files, printers, and other resources and provides persistent storage over a computer network. The file server function provides file services to clients. The client interface for the file service provides access to primitive file operations, such as creating a file, deleting a file, reading from a file, and writing to a file. The essential hardware components that a file server controls are local secondary-storage devices on which files are stored or retrieved according to requests from clients.

### [B] Database File Systems

This form of file management, in addition to a hierarchical structure of information management, identifies files by their characteristics, such as file type, topic, author, or similar descriptive information. Databases typically consist of tables, with the columns containing descriptive characteristics (name, business, address, phone, etc.) and with rows containing the individual records.

### [C] Transactional File Systems

This type of file system is designed to log events or transactions to files. Operations performed by users may involve changes to a number of different files and disk structures that are related, which means the operations must be executed simultaneously. Transactional file systems are designed for fault tolerance and high availability, with the ability to dynamically rebuild transactions by re-synchronizing the transactions on the fly. In addition, transactional file systems save all transactions to create complete and continuous records.

### [D] Distributed File Systems

In a distributed file system, the clients, servers, and storage devices are dispersed among the machines within a distributed system or the Intranet. Service activity occurs across the network. Instead of a single centralized information repository, the system uses multiple and independent storage devices. The distinctive feature of a distributed file system is that the system has many autonomous clients and servers.

## § 5.02 STORAGE SYSTEMS

Essentially there are four primary categories of information storage—computer memory, secondary storage, offline removable media, and online mass storage devices. Storage devices can range in size from several megabytes to multiple petabytes of storage capacity.

Mass storage devices are connected to the computer's central processing unit (CPU) through input/output channels, and can be attached directly to the computer creating the information, or can be separate from the computer, communicating with the computer via wired or wireless networking.

### [A] Computer Memory

Computer memory is the solid state (electronic with no moving parts), temporary storage of information within the computer that is creating the information. Computer memory includes registers, cache memory, and main memory. Computer registers are part of the CPU and contain information needed by the CPU to perform its current instruction. Cache memory is a special type of internal memory to increase CPU performance. Main memory, commonly referred to as random access memory (RAM), contains the programs and the information being processed. RAM is directly connected to the CPU by two devices referred to as a memory bus and a data bus. While computer memory was not traditionally considered a source of ESI, under certain circumstances, applications of computer forensics can uncover pointers within computer memory to sources of ESI. In addition, recent legal developments suggest that such memory may be considered a relevant source of ESI under the right circumstances.

### [B] Secondary Storage

Secondary storage typically refers to the hard disk attached to the computer. The hard disk operates as temporary support for main memory processing functions, and as permanent storage for information generated by applications. A hard disk stores digitally encoded information on rapidly rotating, non-removable platters with magnetic surfaces.

### [C] Removable and Offline Storage Media

Removable and offline storage media includes a number of permanent storage devices such as USB hard drives, optical drives, memory cards, flash memory devices, MP3 players, floppy disks, Zip disks, and magnetic tapes.

### [D] Online Mass Storage

Online mass storage comprises devices designed to hold large volumes of information for continuous processing. Online mass storage devices can store information permanently, or temporarily pending offline archival. There are five primary types of online mass storage devices: Redundant Array of Independent Drives, Network Attached Storage, Storage Area Network, Tape Drives, and Disk/Tape Hybrids.

#### [1] Redundant Array of Independent Drives (RAID)

RAID refers to information storage using multiple hard drives in a single logical unit to share or replicate information among the drives. RAID is typically used on server computers, but is also available in more advanced desktop computers. The benefit of RAID is to increase information integrity, fault-tolerance, throughput, and capacity, as compared to single drives. The distribution of information across multiple drives can be managed either by dedicated hardware or by software, or via hybrid RAIDs that are partially software and partially hardware.

A hardware implementation of RAID requires a special-purpose RAID controller. On desktop systems, this could be combined with the computer hardware or contained in a PCI expansion card.[1] In larger applications, the controller and drives are provided as a stand-alone enclosure. Hardware implementations provide guaranteed performance, add no overhead, can support various operating systems, and enable hot swapping, which allows failed drives to be replaced while the system is running, with no loss of information.

### [2] Network Attached Storage (NAS)

RAIDS are often a component of Network Attached Storage (NAS), a dedicated information storage technology that can be connected directly to a computer network to provide centralized information access and storage to heterogeneous network clients. The NAS operating system and other software are limited in functionality to information storage and access.

NAS removes the responsibility of file serving from other servers on the network and can be deployed using integrated units or using standard computers running NAS software. NAS units enable use of multiple file transfer protocols for use with multiple disks configured as RAIDs. NAS is deployed using commercial embedded units or using standard computers running NAS software.

### [3] Storage Area Network (SAN)

A SAN is network architecture for enabling attachment of remote storage devices, such as disk arrays, tape libraries, and CD arrays, to servers so that the storage devices appear as locally attached devices. Accordingly, SANs are capable of providing large numbers of computers with storage capacity over a network. SANs are connected via special Gigabit Ethernet cabling called a Fibre Channel, which can be copper wire or fiber-optic cable.

SANs are highly suited to transactional information, such as information from email servers, databases, and high usage file servers that require high speed access to hard drives. SANs are often deployed to replace clusters of storage RAIDs that are locally attached to particular application servers, since such RAIDs would have to be backed up over the network, and the servers upgraded when application information exceeded the maximum amount storable by the individual server.

The primary difference between NAS and SAN is that NAS presents and manages file systems to client computers. SAN provides access to disks while the attached system manages information or file systems.

### [4] Tape Drives (May be offline or online)

A tape drive is an information storage device that writes and reads on a magnetic tape in a sequential mode, as opposed to a hard disk, which writes and reads information onto a magnetic platter in random access mode. Accordingly, tape drives have comparably fast information write rates, but comparably slow information retrieval rates.

Tape drives can be standalone or arrayed in clusters. Accordingly, tape systems can range in capacity from a few megabytes to many hundreds of gigabytes. Tape systems are primarily used for archival storage (primary copy) and backup storage (secondary copy) of information obtained from hard drives. Tape media generally costs less than other media and has long archival stability if handled and stored properly. If not handled and stored properly, tapes can become brittle and break.

[1] PCI (Peripheral Component Interconnect) is a small printed circuit board that can be inserted into an expansion slot of a computer motherboard to add functionality to a computer system.

#### [5] Disk/Tape Hybrids

The continuous reduction in cost of disk drives has created storage systems using disks that emulate tape arrays, allowing higher speed backups and full redundancy, with faster, more flexible retrieval capabilities. The devices are capable of being used with fixed and removable disks across WANs via NAS and SAN connectivity. These systems are typically deployed using a two-tier approach, with the first tier accomplishing fast backup to reduce downtime, and the second tier backing up the first tier for disaster recovery and limited archiving.

### [E] Storage Virtualization

Storage virtualization is a centrally managed capability that enables physical storage devices dispersed throughout a network to appear as one storage device. Virtualization software manages the mapping of the user's logical information storage space with the actual physical device location. Storage virtualization is primarily used with SANs.

## § 5.03 ISSUES AND CONCERNS

Organizations use a mix of file and storage systems in an attempt to balance cost, storage capacity, minimum operational disruption, ease of use, legal and regulatory requirements, and the requirements of specific applications. Larger enterprises tend to employ more sophisticated (and complex) configurations of NAS, SAN, and tape array archival systems. Smaller organizations tend to employ less complex NFS and standalone tape archival systems.

Regardless of the size and complexity of the enterprise however, the primary objective for discovery practitioners is to gain an understanding of what information is where. This objective is constrained by specific issues related to each individual file and storage system. However the central issues common to understanding all file and storage systems in most organizations is the lack of a clear definition of the chain-of-custody of ESI and lack of any "information mapping" that defines the flow of information within the organization.

## § 5.04 RECOMMENDATIONS

The lack of adequate chain-of-custody identification and information mapping suggests that third-party resources and tools may be required to achieve the preliminary ESI objective of knowing what information is where. These third-party search and collection tools are discussed in Part 3, Performing Electronic Discovery, and Part 4, Chapter 29, e-Discovery Technology and Tools.

CHAPTER 6

# NATIVE FILES AND METADATA

## § 6.01 NATIVE FILES

Native files refer to files as they were originally created by the particular application. Within Microsoft applications, popular examples would be Word, Excel, and Outlook files that end in ".doc," ".xls," and ".pst" respectively. Native files usually require the software in which the files were created and stored in order to view and/or manipulate the files. However, there are special software programs that enable viewing, editing, and converting files without launching the native file application.

Native files may contain attendant information such as metadata, embedded data, and attachments not available in paper or common image file formats, such as TIFF or PDF. A good example underscoring the need to retain the native format is preservation of formulae in spreadsheets, which would not be visible if the spreadsheet were converted to TIFF or PDF.

When a file is saved using a certain program, the file is often saved in a proprietary format only recognized by that program. When the command "Save As . . ." is used, the file may be saved in another format, such as saving a Microsoft Word document as a plain text file (.txt) or rich text file (.rft). In these two examples, the text formatting added in Microsoft Word will be removed, but the metadata remains when opened in Microsoft Word.

## § 6.02 METADATA

Metadata may provide information about sources—origins, usage, authenticity, and characteristics that provide additional meaning and context, and accordingly may be discoverable if relevant.

The definition of metadata can vary, depending on the context in which it applies. Metadata can be created automatically by the application or manually by the user as the document is created or modified. Metadata can be hidden from the user, or it can be visible depending on the kind and purpose of the metadata. In addition, metadata can be printable or non-printable. Also, information can be data and metadata at the same time, as is the case with the headline of an article, which is both its title (metadata) and part of its text (data).

ESI metadata, while not easily defined, generally fits into two categories—application metadata and system metadata. Application metadata is embedded in, and stays with the file it describes, such as with Microsoft Word documents. System metadata, on the other hand, resides in the computer's file system separately from the file itself. System metadata may be highly complex and difficult to identify and extract. In any case, application and system metadata may provide valuable evidence, either individually or in conjunction.

Metadata from other sources may also be stored externally in a database, which enables more efficient searching. However, care must be taken to ensure that the metadata is linked to its data.

A simple example of the value of metadata is when the characters "11797" (the data) are appended with the term "Zip Code" (the metadata), making the number meaningful. When structured into a hierarchical arrangement within a database, metadata is referred to as a schema, which describes "what exists" for some purpose or to enable some action. Therefore, metadata is what makes the database useful.

Other good examples of the diversity of metadata can be found in Microsoft Word document files. Some examples of metadata automatically generated and available via the Microsoft Word "File Properties" dialog box include:

- Version of the software used to create the file
- Name and file path of document location on the computer or the network
- File size
- Dates the file was created, last modified/saved, and printed
- Number of revisions to the document
- Time spent editing the document

- Information about the document, such as the title, subject, author, company, category, keywords, comments, hyperlinks, and the template used to create the document
- Name of the person who last saved the document

In addition, two user-enabled features are also sources of metadata. The "Change Tracking" feature provides information regarding all changes by all users. This feature is usually hidden from view in the final document by the document owner, but is often inadvertently left active when the owner transmits the file to others. The "Version Tracking" feature, if enabled, provides metadata such as a subset of the document, changes made, the author of the changes, and the date and time the changes were made.

The diversity of ESI has and will continue to result in the creation of various forms of metadata that will require identification, extraction, and analysis. Examples of some other forms of ESI not mentioned above where the separation of metadata is more complex include:

**Voice Mail**—This can be recorded as analog or digital, or converted to text, with separate metadata providing information such as date, time, length of recording, caller ID, and mailbox ID.

**Animation**—This can be embedded in many forms of communication vehicles, including computer-based presentations, videos, Web pages, and mobile devices.

**Video**—This can be analog or digital and can be compressed or parsed, and contain overlays of information providing additional intelligence, including object tracking, alerts, composite views, associated database information, dates, times, record length, location, and camera ID, to name a few.

## § 6.03 ISSUES AND CONCERNS

The primary issue with native files is that the act of accessing the native file may change the file content and the metadata associated with the file, which may destroy evidence or compromise the evidentiary integrity of the file. These changes can be made at any time by either party, either inadvertently or with intent. Such inadvertent or intentional compromise or spoliation of metadata can occur by actions such as:

- Turning on or off a computer
- Opening, transferring, or closing a file
- Searching a dataset with a search tool that is not specifically designed to preserve metadata
- "Cutting and pasting" portions of one document to another document

Other issues with production of native files and revelation of metadata are the potential for inadvertent disclosure of privileged or confidential information, or other information having potentially negative impact for the disclosing party.

From a logistics perspective, native file format precludes the ability to redact and assign Bates numbers to documents. Verifying the authenticity of native files may prove cumbersome under the dynamic circumstances of a trial or hearing.

Notwithstanding the above issues, e-Discovery technology is capable of enabling review and production of native files while preserving metadata. In addition, production in native file format eliminates conversion costs involved in processing native files into more "workable" formats. Because of the above, native file format is being accepted as a preferred method of production in many cases.

## § 6.04 RECOMMENDATIONS

Dealing with native files and metadata is a tactical issue for both parties. On the one hand, there is the desire to see as much as possible of the other party's native files and metadata, and on the other hand there is the need to protect client information and avoid the unnecessary review of irrelevant information. To be in the best defensive position possible, it is important to consider the following.

1. Among the universe of documents or ESI that needs to be produced, determine which portions of this universe might be suited to production in native format, and which portion might more appropriately be provided as image files.
2. After copies of the native files have been properly segregated and preserved, the documents identified for production are ready to undergo further processes to protect against disclosure of attendant electronic information that is not intended to be part of production to a third party. For those documents that are to be produced as native files or PDF files:
   a. Disable "Track Changes" in Word files and eliminate any residual changes to the document.
   b. Ensure that there are no other versions of the document in storage.
   c. Ensure that the file is redacted properly.
   d. Using the File/Properties menu, ensure that no proprietary or otherwise confidential information is displayed.
   e. Using the Tools/Options/Security Tab, select the option to "Remove Personal Information from File Properties on Save." This must be done for *each* document.
   f. When converting to PDF, be sure to disable the options to "convert document information" and "attach source file." Also, be sure to turn password protection on and assign a password to the document.
3. For those files that are to be produced in native format, it is also worth considering creation of an image file of the native file and a separate image file of the metadata for later verification purposes.
4. Consider use of a database for metadata linked to imaged files to facilitate searching.
5. Consider use of File Viewers that enable viewing without the native application. Be sure to limit the viewer to the "View Only" option so that any editing capability is disabled.
6. Assure file integrity by using a hashing function such as "MD5 Hashing," an industry standard algorithm used to "Fingerprint" individual files.[1] Also see Chapter 19, Forensic Considerations, for more information on hashing.
7. Consider upgrading to the latest Acrobat software from Adobe for creating PDF files. Acrobat 8 and later versions contain features designed to assist electronic discovery. Some of these features include Bates numbering, redaction, removing metadata, combining multiple documents into a single file, online conferencing using Adobe Flash, and the ability to fill in fields and save changes using the free PDF viewer, Adobe Reader.

## § 6.05 MORE INFORMATION

The process associated with assessing, collecting, review, production, and presentation of metadata is discussed in Part 3, Performing Electronic Discovery.

---

[1] In "hashing," the content of a file is put through a hashing function, such as MD5, which yields a very large unique number. Any change in the content, even at the byte level, yields a different number. If two files yield the same number, they are always exact duplicates. By adding file metadata and that of parent and attached files, another unique number can be created called a "Family MD5 Hash."

CHAPTER 7

# EMAIL AND COLLABORATION SYSTEMS

## §7.01 STANDARD EMAIL SYSTEMS

Email is a method of composing, sending, storing, and receiving messages, with or without attachments, over electronic networks. It has become one of the most ubiquitous and important forms of communication because of its ease of use and its ability to convey attached documents. Important components of an email system are the client component to compose, store, and send the email, the host component to receive, store, and forward the email, and the messaging system to transport the email.

There are many different email systems, but the most prevalent corporate email systems are Microsoft's Outlook and Outlook Express, and IBM's Lotus Notes. The most popular Web-based email systems are Yahoo, Google, MSN, and AOL. Email systems may differ somewhat, but they essentially provide the same basic functions that enable users to:

- Display a list of email headers containing the sender, subject, date and time, and size
- Select and read content of emails
- Open attachments
- Reply and create new emails by selecting one or more recipients, creating content, and optionally adding attachments
- Save emails, including attachments, that are received and sent

Email can be stored on the client, on the server, or in both places. With most systems, messages are exchanged between servers using the Simple Mail Transfer Protocol (SMTP) for outgoing mail, and the Post Office Protocol (POP3) or the Internet Mail Access Protocol (IMAP) for incoming mail.

Most corporate internal email systems are client/server messaging systems. The server acts as the "post office" (storing files and routing messages). The client workstation originates and accesses messages. Larger organizations scale their email systems by grouping servers into domains.

Emails reach destinations on the Internet through an Internet Service Provider (ISP) using domain names such as XYZ.com for example, and the recipient name, such as John Doe for example. When emails are transmitted, SMTP servers use software called "Sendmail" that handles message queues and communication back to the sender if the message is delayed or is undeliverable.

Virtually all Internet email is transmitted via SMTP in the Multipurpose Internet Mail Extensions (MIME) format. MIME is an Internet standard that supplements the email formatting rules to allow non-English text in both email headers and bodies, and defines a mechanism for including non-textual attachments in email bodies. (Microsoft Exchange and Lotus Notes Servers, discussed later in this chapter, use proprietary protocols.)

Email messages consist of two major sections—the header and the body. The header includes at minimum the:

- Email address of the sender, and optionally the sender's name
- Email addresses of the receivers, and optionally the names of the receivers
- Subject, which is typically a brief summary of the contents of the message
- Local time and date when the message was originally sent

Other information in the header includes who is copied, the tracking information generated by mail servers that have previously handled a message, and information about how the message has to be displayed.

The body contains the message, and possibly an optional signature block. The header and body are separated by a blank line.

POP3 servers maintain a text file for each email account. Incoming messages for the account are appended to the bottom of the account file. Users log in to their account with an account name and password, and the

POP3 servers enable retrieval of the emails. The retrieved email may be deleted or retained on the server, depending on the preferences set by the account administrator.

With the IMAP protocol, emails remain on the email server, but users can copy emails to their local machine for storage and access at any time from an Internet connection.

Both plain text and HTML are used to convey email. Text is more common, but HTML-based email is gaining in popularity since it enables richer graphic content. Advantages of HTML include the ability to include links and images, set apart previous messages in block quotes, wrap naturally on any display, use emphasis such as underlines and italics, and change font styles. HTML emails often include an automatically-generated plain text copy as well, for compatibility reasons.

Email messages can be converted to text or word processing files and saved as separate files. Attachments are normally opened and saved in their native application and format.

With Microsoft email products, the messages, calendar, and other items are delivered to and stored locally in a Personal Folders file, with the extension pst, for "Personal Information Store." It is worth noting that .pst files are easily corrupted and extremely difficult to repair, especially if they are close to their maximum capacity, which varies depending on the particular release version.

## § 7.02 MICROSOFT EXCHANGE SERVER

Deployed primarily in large enterprises using Microsoft Infrastructure Solutions, Microsoft Exchange Server is a messaging and collaborative software product offering electronic mail, calendaring, contacts and tasks, support for mobile and Web-based access, and information storage. The 2007 release also offers unified messaging that allows users to receive voice mail, email, and faxes in their mailboxes, and lets them access their mailboxes from cell phones and other wireless devices. Voice commands can be given to control and listen to email over the phone. Messages, calendar, and other items are delivered to and stored on the server in personal folders file.

Exchange Server provides a large database engine for mail storage and includes two important features that enhance data recovery and auditing.

- Replicates the database continuously so that the secondary database takes over immediately if there is a problem with the primary database
- Records system and user transactions to logs for subsequent auditing and problem resolution

The Exchange database engine (Extensible Storage Engine or ESE) is specialized and tuned for use with hierarchical information such as mailboxes, folders, message items, message bodies, and attachments. ESE is neither a fully relational database, nor a structured query language (SQL) database, nor a simple Access database, but a combination of these. The ESE database engine provides Exchange Server with a robust database platform that can perform extremely well even under large loads, survive server failures, and enable disaster recovery.

Microsoft Exchange Server was designed primarily to be used by a Microsoft Outlook client, and uses a proprietary protocol with an application programming interface (API) as the only documentation for use by third-party developers. Email hosted on an Exchange Server can be accessed using POP3 and IMAP with clients such as Mozilla and Lotus Notes.

## § 7.03 LOTUS NOTES

Lotus Notes is IBM's client-server and collaborative application for accessing email, calendars, and applications on an IBM Lotus Domino server. Lotus Notes provides blogs, wikis, RSS aggregators, Customer Relationship Management, Help Desk systems, group calendaring and scheduling, SMTP-based email, instant messaging, and a full text search capability.

Lotus Notes is commonly deployed as an end-user email client in larger organizations, but the Domino server also supports POP3 and IMAP mail clients, with support for Microsoft Outlook clients, and use of email and calendaring through Web access using Internet Explorer and Firefox browsers.

In addition, Lotus Notes enables rapid development of databases consisting of forms that allow users to create documents and views that display selected document fields in columns. Using Domino Designer, Lotus Notes can also be a platform for developing customized client-server and Web workflow applications comprising complex information routing and approval processes.

A Lotus Notes database differs from a relational database. Some of the differentiating characteristics include a document centric architecture, multiple values in fields, no required schema, built-in document-level access control, and storage of rich text data. This structure closely mimics the paper-based workflows that Lotus Notes is typically used to automate.

Newer versions of the Domino server support IBM's DB2 database as an alternative store for Notes databases. A Notes database can be mapped to a relational database using tools designed for that purpose.

## §7.04 INSTANT MESSAGING

Instant messaging (IM) is a form of real-time communication between two or more people based on typed text conveyed via computers connected over a network. IM requires an instant messaging client that connects to an instant messaging service.

IM enables communication using multiple media among a number of parties at the same time. For example, participating parties may be using Web cameras while simultaneously talking and typing text into the computer.

Enterprise Instant Messaging (EIM), as provided in large companies with Lotus, Microsoft Exchange or Jabber platforms, may be federated with public IM networks, enabling employees to use a single interface for the internal EIM system and the external systems offered by AOL, MSN, Google, and Yahoo!. IM text messages can be logged and saved in a local file or archived in the database of the respective EIM server.

## §7.05 ISSUES AND CONCERNS

Emails, collaboration, and instant messaging systems present unique problems for discovery of ESI, because of their volume combined with the lack of a unified, central method for managing their retention.

A typical thousand-person company may have hundreds of millions of messages stored across a thousand workstations, and hundreds of servers and tapes in many different locations. Accordingly, compliance with electronic discovery obligations may be costly and fraught with complexities without a centralized email archive and sophisticated tools for electronic search and retrieval.

Many companies still do not have a comprehensive strategy to centrally administer messages in a dedicated, special purpose repository. While email servers can store large amounts of information, they are not designed to archive email for long periods of time. Therefore, most companies use a variety of storage systems, such as disk, RAID arrays, and tape arrays, to satisfy retention requirements. However, these storage systems are typically designed to restore the status of a system, and are not optimized to enable precise location of specific pieces of information buried in terabytes of email archives. Additionally, they are not designed to index email and related information, and do not enable retrieval of information from multiple data and document formats.[1]

Unlike most files stored on the client hard disk, once fully deleted, emails do not leave any residual data on the disk. This is because most email systems continuously compress files, which purges deleted files and eliminates such residual data. However, an email must be manually deleted from the incoming message folder and the sent message folder, and from the "Deleted" items folder in order to be entirely deleted from the client system.

[1] Indexing is a technique used in information systems to enable faster and more efficient search and retrieval of information in files and databases. Although vendors use a variety of indexing techniques, an index typically consists of a separate file or database of key data elements (dates, names, keywords, etc.), parsed from a source, with pointers to the original source. For example, the indexing software may index the content of every email, attachment, and file on a business user's hard drive, including network drives that appear on the desktop. The index, stored separately on the hard drive, enables users to find information they know exists without having to know how or where it is stored.

Because email and instant messaging systems have become more integrated with collaboration systems, there is an increased connection among the various communications embedded in these systems. Essentially these various systems were designed to optimize initial communication, not storage or retrieval. In addition, the mix of protocols and sheer volume make discovery from such systems more complex and difficult.

One way enterprises attempt to deal with the issues of complexity and volume associated with email and collaboration systems is to outsource all or part of these systems to a Web-based hosting service.

However, Web-based email, whether used for personal or business purposes, can expose companies to less control over distribution of email, and less control over preservation and retrieval of emails.

Third-party hosting services raise significant concerns for their clients seeking to comply with ESI preservation and discovery obligations. Retention policies of third-party hosting services may result in deletion of emails, or storage techniques may make retrieval extremely difficult and expensive. Very often, parties do not think about their data held by these services until it is too late; courts, prosecutors, regulators, and litigation adversaries are not apt to be sympathetic to such lapses.

## § 7.06 RECOMMENDATIONS

In most organizations, email is centrally administered by a person or group within the IT organization. As noted earlier, that person or group is responsible for performance and security of the systems, adding and deleting users, managing information related to each user account, such as password, user name, and email alias, and maintaining logs and reports concerning system activity.

In interviewing or deposing email administrators, it is important to cover the following items. These recommendations also apply to third parties that may be involved in hosting or supplying services related to email and collaboration systems.

1. Listing of all email, messaging, and collaboration systems in use within the company, including Web-based systems.
2. Description of each email, messaging, and collaboration system, containing at minimum the following information:
   a. List of all users falling within the ESI time frame, including name, title, and role,
   b. Locations of all sources of ESI—client workstations, servers, and online and offline information stores, both onsite and offsite,
   c. Description of the media, storage formats, and retrieval methods in use for all sources of ESI, including requirements for conversion from non-responsive media such as tape to responsive media such as disk,
   d. Copies of User and Administrator policies and procedures, including system operation and maintenance, and information backup, archival, retention, and retrieval, and
   e. Copies of system logs, maintenance operations, problem reports, and repair, including software patches and upgrades.
3. Methodology for restoration of emails that ensures integrity of the original, maintains chain-of-custody, and ensures authenticity of recovered information.
4. Identification of any third-party hosting or service providers that have access to email or other records, with copies of contracts and service agreements.

As a practical matter, the preponderance and complexity of issues related to retrieval of email, collaboration, and instant message information is often beyond the scope of the internal IT resources available. Such potential internal resource constraints may require consideration of vendors that can perform collection into centralized systems that provide the capabilities required for discovery.

CHAPTER 8

# DATABASES

Databases are designed to create a structure for information and to enable operations to be performed on that information. There are essentially six active database models—Flat, Hierarchical, Network, Object, Dimensional (Data Warehouse), and Relational.

## § 8.01 FLAT DATABASE

A flat database is similar to a spreadsheet table in which information in the cells in a particular column have similar values, and information in the cells in a particular row are related. An example would be a flat database containing a column "Name" and a column "PhoneNumber." Each row would contain a particular person's name and phone number. Accordingly, flat databases are primarily used for lists.

## § 8.02 HIERARCHICAL DATABASE

In a hierarchical database, information is organized into a one-to-many parent/child tree structure, where each parent can have many children, but each child can have only one parent. The hierarchical model is not usually found in contemporary databases, but is common in other forms of storing information, such as file systems, XML documents, and the Windows registry, where content is nested and capable of being sorted on a particular record field.

## § 8.03 NETWORK DATABASE

The network database can be considered a bridge between the hierarchical database model and the relational database model. It is a flexible way of representing objects and their relationships, with each record having multiple parent and child records. The network database model comprises two main elements—records and sets—that enable records to own any number of sets and be a member of any number of sets. Network databases use pointers that directly address the location of a record, thus providing exceptional retrieval performance.

## § 8.04 OBJECT DATABASE

The object database represents a marriage of database models and programming models in an attempt to optimize the capability to manage complex information types. Object databases have adopted Structured Query Language (SQL) and often use the navigational technique found in network databases to achieve very fast retrieval rates.[1] There are several different approaches used for object databases. However, the use of multiple approaches has limited interoperability between products and caused limited application across the commercial sector. Accordingly, object databases have been primarily limited to the scientific and engineering communities.

## § 8.05 DIMENSIONAL DATABASE

The dimensional database, a database structure commonly used for data warehouses, is an adaptation of the relational database model (see § 8.07) that enables information to be easily summarized using OLAP (On Line Analytical Processing) queries to achieve complex analytical and ad-hoc queries with rapid execution. A dimensional model comprises a single large table of facts described using measures and dimensions. A measure is a quantity describing the fact. A dimension provides the context for a fact and is used in queries to group related facts together. Dimensions tend to be discrete and are often hierarchical. Typically there is one table containing facts (and their measures) and many tables containing dimensions.

In an OLAP query, dimensions are chosen and the facts are grouped and added together to create a summary. The output of the query is displayed in a matrix format, with dimensions forming the row and column of the matrix and measures representing the values.

---

[1] SQL is a standard structured language for querying and modifying data and managing relational databases, including retrieval, insertion, updating, and deletion of data.

## § 8.06 DATA WAREHOUSE

The data warehouse is a special form of database. They are typically large, centralized repositories of corporate information used to feed information to various functional units for analysis and decision-making. Data warehouses, as noted earlier, are structured under a dimensional model that is optimized for reporting and analysis. The structure of a data warehouse provides a cohesive organization for information, with attributes that include: linkage of information elements relating to the same events, automatic recording of changes to information, information that is read-only and retained, information that is integrated from across the enterprise, and information that is consistently represented.

## § 8.07 RELATIONAL DATABASES

A relational database manages information about real-world entities in multiple tables that contain information elements in columns and rows, similar to a spreadsheet. Columns contain identifiers, such as "FirstName" for example. Rows in the database make up individual records comprising one or more columns. The record for "Jane Doe," for example, could contain information elements from the columns, FirstName, LastName, Address1, State, PostalCode, and Phone1.

Tables in the database may be "related" by a key information element shared by two or more tables. Therefore, the record above for Jane Doe may be expanded to include information elements from a "Telephone Bill" table related by Jane Doe's unique phone number contained in both tables.

Most relational databases minimize the need for application programs to contain information about the physical storage of the information they access, and strive to isolate programs from the information structures. This is done through SQL, which enables users to retrieve, insert, update, and delete data, and database administrators to maintain the database, such as creating new tables.

However, relational databases may also include processing and computational logic that can be highly complex. The results of database processing and computational logic may populate tables in the database with new information that may be permanent or transitional, depending on the database design.

## § 8.08 ISSUES AND CONCERNS

Information resides in databases as discrete "data elements" contained in a highly structured and relatively rigid framework, and is usually only meaningful when organized by database software into reports conveying answers to specific queries. Many such reports are prepared in advance and generated automatically in anticipation of business information needs. Other reports are generated on an ad hoc basis. Not all such reports are retained.

In addition, the discrete information elements within a database may be relatively dynamic, changing significantly over time. This means that certain information may bc lost if not contained in reports that are retained, or if the database elements are not properly retained in storage.

Also, databases are constantly being tuned to achieve improved performance. This "tweaking" of databases by programmers often results in changes to table structures, information elements, and reporting capabilities; thus impacting the integrity of information continuity.

## § 8.09 RECOMMENDATIONS

The following steps are designed to help discovery practitioners quickly gain insight into the scope of database ESI and any issues related thereto, as preparation for a systematic discovery effort.

1. Obtain a list of all potentially relevant databases in use within the enterprise.
2. Match each database to a particular business function.

3. Determine who has direct responsibility for changes to the database structure, what those changes were within the discovery period, and what impact the changes had on the database.
4. Determine how data is input to the database, and what controls exist over the input process.
5. Obtain a list and description of all reports for each database, with sample copies of reports determined relevant to discovery.
6. Determine where and how the database and database reports are stored, and what issues are related to retrieval of database information via reports and/or export of information from the database.

CHAPTER 9

# FILE SERVERS

## §9.01 DESCRIPTION

Most desktop computers have several thousand files on the hard disk. The files are organized in folders by a file system created by the operating system when the hard disk was initialized. The file system established a root directory and subsequent directories beneath it, an arrangement that allows users to add new files and folders to different parts of the directory tree on the hard disk.

On desktop computers, there are separate folders for programs, documents, pictures, music, and movie files. Within these folders, there are other folders that further organize the files. There are also folders that the computer's operating system uses to store system files, such as startup data and system preferences. Some of these folders are invisible to the user, but are recognized by the computer's file system. All the folders are organized by the computer's file system.

Non-system files are the constructs of computer users applying individual computer application software programs to create and represent meaningful information such as emails, spreadsheets, word processing documents, graphic images, audio clips, animations, videos, or lines of executable code.

More formally, the file system is a set of abstract information types that are implemented for the storage, organization, manipulation, navigation, access, and retrieval of information. File systems share some characteristics in common with database technology, but are not classified as databases.

The term "File Server" refers specifically to a computer on which a user can map or mount a disk drive or directory so that the directory appears to be on the machine at which the user is sitting. Additionally, on this type of file server, the user can read or write a file as though it were part of the file system of the user's computer.

Computer files are stored by means of the file system so that the files are easier to find and access. File systems may use information storage devices to maintain the physical location of the files, or provide access to information on file servers by acting as clients for a network protocol, or they may be virtual and exist only as an access method for virtual information.

Most applications enable users to create and manipulate files, and store them at locations chosen by the user. File systems typically have directories that associate file names with files, and files are typically accessed using their respective file names. In some operating systems, the name is associated with the file itself. In others, the file is pointed to by links that have names. Filenames use special characters to uniquely identify the file or the directory in which the file is stored. Directories may contain files or links to files. Different operating systems impose different restrictions regarding certain characters and number of characters used for filenames. A filename could include one or more of:

- Unique name of the file (Bplan1.doc)
- Directory or path (C:\Documents and Setting\All Users\Application Data\Bplan1.doc)
- Type of file (.doc)
- Device (C:)
- Host or network ID (\\C:)
- Access method (http)

Files are typically organized in hierarchies using folders, directories, or catalogs, which can contain any number of subsets and any number of files, resulting in tree-like structures ranging from very simple to highly complex. In the preceding paragraph, the path C:\Documents and Setting\All Users\Application Data\Bplan1, identified the Microsoft Word file Bplan1.doc in the subfolder Application Data, in the subfolder All Users, in the folder Documents and Settings, on the device C, which is the desktop computer hard disk.

File servers generally offer some form of system security to limit access to files to specific users or groups. In large organizations, this is a task usually delegated to functions known as "Directory Services," such as Microsoft's Active Directory. File servers work within a hierarchical computing environment that treats users, directories, computers, applications, and files as distinct but related entities on the network, and grant access based on user or group credentials. In large organizations, directory services can span hundreds of file servers—often referred to as "Server Farms."

File servers are designed for continuous updating of files under dynamic interaction with users and applications. The methods used by file servers to maintain integrity of file information vary, but all have some form of logging or journaling system that enables synchronization of files for recovery in case of an interruption, such as a power failure.

File servers are not intended for long-term storage, and are usually backed up to storage devices on an incremental, tiered cycle that includes daily, weekly, and monthly backups. Monthly backups are archived for longer-term storage.

## § 9.02 ISSUES AND CONCERNS

The primary issues faced in ESI discovery with file servers is usually related to the disparate mix and quantity of servers combined with the variety of backup and archival methods in use. This can appear to be a chaotic environment if there is no clear description that provides guidance for information retrieval.

## § 9.03 RECOMMENDATIONS

As mentioned earlier, network diagrams can be an important tool for the discovery practitioner. Accordingly, it may be useful to obtain a current network diagram that identifies all the file servers in use within the company. File servers are often grouped within geographical boundaries or categories such as business unit or particular application served, which may match discovery scope. Accordingly, practitioners should:

1. Identify each file server and related storage device with potentially relevant information, and the particular individuals, business units, functional groups, or applications served by a particular file server or group of file servers.
2. Obtain a detailed description of how the file server and its related backup and archival storage device stores information and how that information can be retrieved.
3. Interview and/or depose the Network Administrator, Data Administrator, and Records Administrator to obtain the above information.
4. As with other information technology, server technology is replete with buzzwords, acronyms, and arcane jargon that can confuse more than enlighten. Ensure that all terms are explained and mutually understood.

CHAPTER 10

# ENTERPRISE STORAGE SYSTEMS

## § 10.01 INTRODUCTION AND BACKGROUND

As discussed briefly by way of introduction in Chapter 5, Overview of File and Storage Systems, storage is accomplished on various mass storage devices based on the type of the storage required. These requirements comprise three functional categories—operational, backup, and archival—which address the specific storage requirements associated with the major ESI repositories of files, online transaction processing, data warehouses, and databases. Operational may be considered as active ESI, archives as primary copies of ESI, and backups as secondary copies of ESI.

- **Operational Storage** refers to the day-to-day storage associated with normal business transactions and the work of individuals throughout the organization. Operational storage requirements range from small portable USB drives holding a few gigabytes to large-scale, modular storage appliances with capacities in the petabyte range.
- **Backup Storage** is usually for the retention of information in support of disaster planning and recovery. Backup storage can also be for temporary retention of information in support of operational needs, such as equipment replacement for example, with an expectation that it will need to be accessed in the near term. Long-term backup storage has traditionally been on tape, but in many enterprises hard disks are replacing tape as the preferred media. Temporary backup storage is usually on hard disks. Backup storage may involve equipment with hundreds of terabytes of capacity.

  Backups to tape usually involve tape recycling, a process of overwriting tapes with new data, usually on a fixed schedule involving tape rotation such as, for example daily backups being overwritten in a seven-day sequence after a weekly backup, weekly backups being overwritten in sequence following at least two monthly backups, and monthly backups being overwritten no sooner than before the end of the second year. Also see § 10.11, Tape-Based Storage, for additional information.
- **Archival Storage** is for the long-term retention of information generally not expected to be frequently accessed. Therefore, information to be archived is usually stored on tape systems. However, as with backups, hard disks may eventually be replacing tape as the preferred media. Because of its long term nature, archival storage may involve many petabytes of storage capacity.

Many of the storage approaches used for these requirements are influenced by a number of factors—legacy issues, technology convergence, availability of open-source products and solutions; and innovative solutions such as application fabrics, storage virtualization, deduplication, information lifecycle management, and Web-based storage.

In addition, management is requiring more focus on strategic objectives, ensuring that storage and retrieval are effectively responsive to business, regulatory, and litigation ESI discovery requirements.

## § 10.02 STRATEGIC ISSUES

Results of thousands of assessments worldwide by Sun Microsystems (and StorageTek) reveal that 30 percent of disk drive information is referenced routinely for business, 40 percent is related to business but referenced infrequently, and the remainder is a mix of orphan information, e.g., the owner no longer exists, non-company personal information such as audio and video files, and space reserved for applications and operating systems.[1]

This storage inefficiency partly explains the difficulty in effectively meeting regulatory requirements and discovering relevant ESI. But a more important hindrance is the lack of inherent interoperability among products and systems. Often, even different products from a single vendor do not work together, and products

[1] "Managing Enterprise Storage," Information Week, Oct. 22, 2007.

from different vendors seldom work together without significant additional effort towards integration. The understandable desire on the part of technology vendors to protect their intellectual property may be in tension with the long term strategic imperatives of corporate storage requirements.

Accordingly, some enterprises are moving away from proprietary solutions, and embracing newer technology that includes openness, flexibility, scalability, and a unified architecture that provides storage and retrieval efficiency.

## § 10.03 STORAGE CONVERGENCE

Storage systems are particularly heavily dependent on other software and hardware technologies, especially as it relates to performance and management capabilities. Many of these supporting technologies have been converging to impact storage solutions.

Generally, technology convergence refers to the inclusion of multiple technological capabilities into one hardware device or solution suite. For example, the mobile phone, once designed exclusively for voice communication, now may include the ability to perform a wide variety of functions—such as taking photos and videos for example—that are distinct from voice technology but complementary to wireless communication among individuals.

Storage has been undergoing the same kind of convergence. Storage systems are incorporating additional functions distinct from data recording technology but complementary to information management. Much of this convergence is enabled by increases in device storage capacity, innovative software, and improvements in data transmission speeds across networks, combined with decreases in price-per-gigabyte of storage. A few examples are provided below.

### [A] 10 Gigabit Ethernet (10GbE)

10GbE, the highest speed for Ethernet, operates in seven media types designed for use in either local or wide area networking. This provides the 10GbE system with the flexibility needed to operate in local area networks, metropolitan area networks, regional area networks, and wide area networks. This flexibility enables the enterprise to more cost effectively use existing infrastructure to deploy advanced storage devices that combine better and simpler features with higher performance, but that require higher speed networks.

### [B] Serial Attached SCSI (SAS)

The SAS advancement enables the enterprise to use multiple disk drive interfaces (SATA, SATA2, and iSCSI) without having to lock into one particular technology. SAS offers higher bandwidth, dual-port options, and port expansion.[2]

### [C] Internet SCSI (iSCSI)

Internet SCSI enables SCSI drives to be used with the Internet, thus providing a lower-cost alternative to Fibre Channel SAN.

### [D] High Capacity Solid State Drive (hSSD)

Standard SSDs are primarily found in mobile devices because of the requirement to retain a small form factor. They usually have capacities not exceeding a few megabytes. However, hSSDs are appearing in laptops

[2] A disk drive interface is a data transmission device that manages the exchange of data between a hard disk drive and a computer. Often linked by cables, interfaces use various physical configurations, implemented in hardware with microprocessor chips on the motherboard, adapter boards, or on the drives themselves.

that stress small size and lower weight, as well as in specialized environments subject to harsh handling conditions—military and airborne systems, time-critical video and audio servers, telecommunication systems, high-availability computing systems, and factory automation systems. The capacity range of hSSDs is from a few gigabytes to hundreds of gigabytes.

### [E] RAM Hard Disk

A RAM hard disk is a combination of a standard hard disk with rotating media and a solid state disk. The solid state disk is used to cache frequently accessed information, with the result of providing instant information access, less disk wear, and lower power consumption.

## § 10.04 OPEN SOURCE STORAGE PRODUCTS

No longer viewed as illegitimate, open source solutions are now recognized as valid choices offering attractive price performance value. Accordingly, a number of storage alternatives are provided by the open source community, and are incorporated into the products offered by major vendors. The following represents a small sampling of these types of open-source products.

### [A] Amanda

Amanda (Advanced Maryland Automatic Disk Archiver) is a backup and archiving system originally developed at the University of Maryland Computer Science Department, and now maintained by SourceForge, an open-source development site. Amanda enables users to set up a master server to backup and/or archive to a wide range of tape, disks, and optical devices—tape libraries, optical jukeboxes, RAID arrays, and NAS. Amanda can backup to disk and other storage media simultaneously, making ESI immediately available online for disaster recovery and offsite for archiving. ESI that has been stored using Amanda can be recovered using the native utility of the recovery device, regardless of whether Amanda is installed on that device.

### [B] FreeNAS

FreeNAS is an open-source network attached storage server that includes support for a wide range of protocols. It uses less than 32MB and can be installed via a USB drive, CD, or hard drive, or executed online without installing on the computer.

Another network attached server is NASLite, a product designed to extend the life of older computers through special software that bypasses the operating system and accesses hard drives directly. It also fits on a USB drive and supports Windows, Mac OS X, and Linux.

### [C] Areca Backup

Areca is a file backup system offering a number of management features such as ZIP formats, encryption, and filtering—extension, subdirectory, regular expression, size, data, status, or usage. It enables backup automation as well as providing general administration functions.

### [D] ZFS

ZFS (Zettabyte File System), introduced by Sun Microsystems and subsequently made available to the open-source community, uses a pooled storage model that eliminates some of the older constructs such as partitions, provisioning, stranded storage, and dedicated bandwidth. ZFS's common storage pool can include thousands of file systems, each taking only as much space as it needs, with the combined bandwidth available to all file systems. ZFS is self-healing in RAID configurations, detecting a damaged copy and automatically using another copy to repair it.

### [E] Lustre

Lustre is a scalable, secure, robust, highly-available cluster file system, designed, developed, and maintained as open-source. Lustre runs on many of the largest Linux clusters in the world, and is included as a core component of cluster offerings such as HP's StorageWorks SFS, and the Cray XT3 and XD1 supercomputers. Lustre scales down as well as it scales up, and runs in production on clusters as small as 4 and as large as 25,000 nodes. It is designed to provide petabytes of storage, and move hundreds of gigabytes per second within a state-of-the-art security and management infrastructure.

### [F] Samba

Samba is an open-source software suite that enables non-windows systems—Unix, Linux, IBM system 390, Open VMS, and others—to provide file and print services for a wide range of clients, including Microsoft Windows. Some of its attractions are that it provides network administrators with flexibility and freedom in terms of setup, configuration, and choice of systems and equipment.

### [G] OpenAFS

OpenAFS is a distributed file system, pioneered at Carnegie Mellon University and acquired and made available as open-source by IBM. OpenAFS offers client-server architecture for federated file sharing and replicated read-only content distribution, providing location independence, scalability, security, and transparent migration capabilities. AFS is available for a broad range of heterogeneous systems including UNIX, Linux, MacOS X, and Microsoft Windows.

## § 10.05 HYBRID AND BRIDGING SYSTEMS

At the same time that innovative products are fueling convergence, the need for storage flexibility and capacity continues to increase, driven in large part by regulatory and business requirements, including an increased focus on e-Discovery readiness. Two approaches meeting this demand are "hybrid" and "bridge" systems.

Hybrid systems can, for example, combine any number of disk arrays, from tens of disks to thousands of disks, and can operate in a wide variety of network configurations, including SAN and NAS. Hybrid systems can even emulate tape arrays. Many hybrid systems are centrally managed modular storage systems that are small enough to cost effectively meet the needs of small to medium size enterprises requiring a few hundred gigabytes, but that can also scale to meet the needs of very large enterprises requiring hundreds of terabytes of storage.

Bridging products help span the gap between outdated legacy storage systems and more modern storage solutions. Bridging systems are available that help track and manage ESI regardless of what hardware it resides on. Companies are employing bridging software to help manage large diverse networks of storage systems as if they were one homogenous system. Many of these deployments use open-source components mentioned earlier.

## § 10.06 DEDUPLICATION

Deduplication technology fundamentally changes the role of disk in backup. It gives users a cost effective way to retain their backup information on disk for weeks or months, making their file restores fast and easy and increasing the number of available recovery points.

Disk-based backup appliances that use deduplication technology provide a combination of advantages, including ease of use, extended retention, fast restoration, and cost savings. They can also make replication of backup information over WANs a practical tool for providing off-site protection for backup information.

Deduplication technology is used to reduce ESI redundancy and the size of storage required. The technology operates at a block level to find and eliminate redundant data. Deduplication creates hashes of each data block or file. If the calculated hash matches another block or file already stored, the system notes the duplication and does not store the new block or file.

"Single-instance" storage is another technology for eliminating duplicate ESI. Single-instance storage is limited to identifying only duplicate files, not specific content. Therefore, single instance storage is not as powerful as full deduplication technology, which works at the block (content) level.

Being able to access ESI that has gone through deduplication prior to storage can reduce e-discovery time and cost significantly.

## § 10.07 STORAGE VIRTUALIZATION

In simple terms, storage virtualization makes many separate hard drives appear as one large storage pool, with less time managing storage devices, since some tasks can be centralized. Virtualization also increases the efficiency of storage, by storing files wherever there is room, rather than allow some drives to be underutilized. Also, virtualization software enables drives to be added or replaced without requiring downtime to reconfigure the network and affected servers.

Backup and mirroring are also much faster because only changed information needs to be copied, thus eliminating the need for scheduled storage management downtime. In addition, most storage management software enables combining drives from multiple vendors as if they were one virtual drive, which is often less expensive than array-based proprietary systems.

Strategically, storage virtualization brings the most value to resource-intensive storage management tasks that protect information and keep it available in demanding environments, such as replication to keep distributed databases synchronized; mirroring to keep a redundant copy of information available for use in case the primary copy becomes unavailable; backup to keep both current and historical information available in case it gets deleted but is needed later; and snapshots to copy the original portions of changed information and make it easier to go back to the original version. All these activities have become harder to accomplish using traditional storage management techniques as information volumes surge and time for backup tasks decreases.

In order to achieve efficiency, storage virtualization technology used for the purposes described above only copies the individual parts of changed data, not entire files or drive volumes as in traditional host-based storage architectures. The advantage is that storage virtualization enables continuous backup and replication, and quick moves to new equipment in case of hardware failure. Another advantage is that storage virtualization enables the disaster recovery site and the production site to stay in synchronization. Storage virtualization also provides flexibility in terms of where information is stored, whether onsite or offsite.

Most storage virtualization technology can be combined with older technology and enable user drives to exceed their physical limit by storing the excess on another drive without user intervention. This reduces the burden on IT of dealing with individual configurations.

The most established form of storage virtualization is array-based, where a vendor provides an expandable array, to which that vendor's drives can be added. Management software virtualizes the drives so they appear as a common pool of data. These are typically proprietary systems restricted to that vendor's hardware.

The more recent implementation, network-based storage virtualization, uses software or a network appliance to manage a variety of disk drives and other storage media. The media can be supplied by multiple vendors, typically allowing for the purchase of lower-cost drives than the all-from-one-vendor options. This enables use of less expensive drives for non-mission-critical storage needs and allows reuse of older storage capacity.

## § 10.08 GRID COMPUTING

Grid computing refers to the use of multiple computers within a single dedicated network or within an open network such as the Internet to perform various independent parallel functions requiring intensive computer resources, such as mathematical calculations and data sharing.

In grid computing, the problem of storage requirement can be adequately parallelized, enabling conventional, standalone programs to run on multiple machines, which makes it possible to write and test programs on a single conventional machine, and eliminates complications due to multiple instances of the same program running in the same shared memory and storage space at the same time. Most grid implementations use a generic infrastructure that accommodates the use of disparate computers having different configurations and operating systems. Grids also offer the ability to scale up or down as requirements dictate.

Grid computing implementations usually employ security measures to prevent accidental or intentional misuse. For example, work may be assigned randomly to different nodes having different owners, with confirmation that at least two different nodes report the same results for a given work unit. Conversely, the participating nodes must have safeguards that the central administration system does not abuse access that is being granted—interfering with the operation of other programs, damaging stored information, transmitting private information, or creating new security holes.

The primary advantage of distributed computing is lower cost. Each node can be commodity hardware, as opposed to a supercomputer, which is a highly expensive custom made computer with multiple processors connected via a dedicated high-speed computer interface. The primary performance disadvantage of grid implementations is that the various processors and local storage areas in a grid network do not have high-speed connections. Grid computing is therefore better-suited to applications in which multiple parallel computations can take place independently, without the need to communicate intermediate results between processors.

## § 10.09 APPLICATION FABRICS

Application fabrics are used to create increased application processing and storage capacity at lower costs in comparison to more traditional "silos" of infrastructure.

An application fabric is a software-based computing environment that enables organizations to deploy extraordinarily scalable and dependable applications on commodity hardware, without recourse to expensive infrastructure, and without sacrificing dependability or manageability. With application fabrics, silos of physical infrastructure and layers of management infrastructure are replaced by an agile, self-managing fabric running fully virtualized applications.

An application fabric builds fault-tolerance into the applications that run within it, spreading responsibility for tasks across a self-organizing network of machines that automatically share state information. If a problem arises with any machine in the fabric, another machine assumes responsibility for the current operation immediately, with no loss of data and no interruption in service.

Application fabrics offer mainframe-level dependability for even the largest-scale applications, with fewer layers of infrastructure than traditional deployment approaches.

Because they can use commodity-grade hardware and industry-standard operating systems, application fabrics have much lower initial costs than traditionally deployed applications, and incremental costs for scaling are also dramatically lower.

Due to the inherent simplicity of the application fabric approach, developers can bring applications to market more rapidly than conventional applications and administrators can add more capacity simply by adding inexpensive computers.

## § 10.10 WEB-BASED STORAGE

Web-based storage typically includes the Internet in combination with open-source software, application fabrics, or grid or clustered architectures, and low-cost hardware to create solutions that reduce reliance on higher priced proprietary storage systems. Once only considered suitable for home and small businesses, Web-based storage is now mainstream as vendors such as Amazon have proven their reliability and sustainability.

Open-source software such as Amanda, Lustre, OpenAFS, and Samba provide some of the foundation for Web-based storage infrastructures. These software tools are complemented by applications fabrics, grid, or clustered architectures from vendors that provide a range of storage service options and features, including splitting files into combinable encrypted "slices" across hundreds or thousands of computers to achieve needed capacity, security, and high availability.

## § 10.11 TAPE-BASED STORAGE

The primary form of tape in use today is the tape cartridge—a tape reel housed in a plastic enclosure—used in tape libraries that are attached to a number of servers. Tape cartridges are produced in a large variety of configurations in terms of width, length, and compression, which combined determine capacity that can range from a few megabytes to several terabytes.

Data is usually recorded on and retrieved from tape sequentially, which presents several issues.

One issue is the synchronization between the rate at which the tape is moving and the rate at which information is being recorded. In a typical format, information is written to tape in blocks with gaps between them. Each block is written in a single operation with the tape running continuously during the write. However, since the rate at which information is written or read to the tape drive is not predetermined and may vary, a tape drive usually has to cope with a difference between the rate at which information goes on and off the tape and the rate at which information is supplied or demanded by its host.

Various methods have been used to cope with this difference. The tape drive can be stopped, backed up, and restarted—known as "shoe-shining" because of increased wear of the medium and the head. Some tape drives provide a speed matching feature, where drive can dynamically decrease physical tape speed to avoid shoe-shining. Also, a memory buffer can be used to queue the information. The host can assist this process by choosing appropriate block sizes to send to the tape drive.

Also, with sequential recording, information can only be added by appending a file at the end of previously recorded information, and information cannot be effectively accessed randomly. In addition, there is a long latency for actual information access since the tape must wind an average of one-third the tape length to move from one arbitrary data block to another. Most tape systems attempt to alleviate inherent latency, by using indexing, where a separate lookup table (tape directory) is maintained that provides the physical tape location for a given data block number, or by marking blocks with a tape mark that can be detected while winding the tape at high speed.

In tape systems, much of the enhancements attempting to achieve benefits comparable to disk-based systems are embedded in firmware (software on a chip) on the tape hardware device, or in software residing on a host computer. The various implementations of these enhancements are often proprietary and contribute to lack of interoperability.

### [A] Virtual Tape Library (VTL)

Virtual tape libraries are disk-based storage systems that emulate some of the characteristics of tape systems for one or a variety of the different tape systems in use. VTLs are offered in a variety of configurations that affect performance and interoperability. For example, some VTLs are offered as specially built appliances, while others are offered as software solutions, with various components supplied by different vendors. Some systems emulate tape and only write to disk, while other systems emulate tape, and write directly to disk and to tape. Some VTL systems can read tapes from a variety of systems, while others can only read tapes that the particular VTL created.

Use of VTLs helps organizations create additional and more flexible storage, while at the same time extending and enhancing the value of tape-based systems.

### [B] Conditions Affecting Tape Cartridge Reliability

The quality and integrity of tape cartridges, the primary technology used for archiving, has always been a significant issue in relation to discovery of ESI. The following information provides some insights that may be helpful to e-Discovery practitioners in understanding these issues when communicating with IT personnel.

Manufacturers typically build magnetic media cartridges under rigorous process controls to guarantee adherence to product specifications for durability and archival stability, and perform environmental and stress testing to assure that products will remain reliable over time. Magnetic media is manufactured to yield specific magnetic properties and remain reliable under repeated high speed motion, contact with tape path components and read/write heads, and various environmental conditions.

Results from testing organizations such as the National Media Laboratory (NML) and Carnegie-Mellon University have shown that the magnetic media itself has a reasonable life expectancy of 15 to 30 years under normal usage conditions. However, testing has also shown that overall life expectancy and performance of tape cartridges is affected by other factors such as usage frequency, handling and environmental conditions, such as debris, high temperature, or humidity, drastic temperature or humidity changes, and stray magnetic field sources. If not properly handled, cartridges are susceptible to damage due to the increased linear density, increased track density, and subsequent positioning of the data and servo tracks closer to the edges of the tape.

Conditions for proper handling, operation, and storage are usually specified by the hardware and the magnetic media manufacturers, with statements that non-compliance can affect tape cartridge performance. Typical topics covered include retentioning, head cleaning, magnetic field shielding, and transportation and storage requirements.

As indicated by the topics covered above, tape requires a significant amount of manual maintenance, a fact that increases its cost and makes it less attractive.

One of the most problematic issues is reduction in quality and reliability due to frequent, high-capacity overwriting. For example, if writing 10GB per week, durability lifetime ranges could be projected at 10 to 30 years, whereas writing 20GB twice per week could reduce that significantly.

Another major problem is dropping tape cartridges, which can cause misalignment of internal components, such as hubs and tape packs. Although it may not be immediately apparent, such damage may develop over time. Proper procedures call for immediately copying the contents of a dropped cartridge to another cartridge and discarding the dropped cartridge. Other problems occur because of:

- Inserting dirty or damaged tape cartridge in a drive
- Removing leader blocks and opening drive doors
- Touching tape surfaces—residue from fingerprints can create greater head-to-tape separation and result in loss of signal (data)
- Failing to clean cartridges when required, and using improper cleaning methods
- Failing to maintain and service tape drives according to the hardware manufacturer's specifications
- Transporting or shipping tape cartridges in containers that do not conform to manufacturer's specifications, and that subject the cartridges to damage or contamination
- Exposing cartridges to dust or a corrosive environment
- Failing to acclimate the cartridge for 24 hours to the same humidity and temperature as the operating environment

Aside from any problems with media reliability, tape hardware technology is advancing at a pace that causes the media itself to become obsolete in less than 10 years, which is shorter than its predicted useful life. This obsolescence often leads to lack of availability of qualified staff, which may in turn lead to lack of proper maintenance.

All of these factors contribute to creating difficulty in achieving effective and timely ESI discovery from tape.

### [C] Tape Restoration

Responsive information may be found on corporate backup tapes as well as on corporate servers or end-user computers. However, backup tapes are used more often for disaster recovery than information retention, and accessing backup information can be costly and difficult. Consequently, stored information on backup tapes often may be designated "not reasonably accessible" under the Federal Rules of Civil Procedure. However, newer technology is enabling more effective and efficient restoration of backup tapes, which makes the information on them more readily accessible.

It is helpful to determine which servers are actually backed up, whether incremental backups or full-system copies are performed, and whether there have been any system changes during the relevant time period—for example, changes in hardware or software or the adoption or removal of a third-party service. It is also important to establish whether individual hard drives are backed up, and whether the company uses any off-site or third-party systems for storage or backup.

Data restoration from backup tapes can be difficult and expensive, if not impossible, due to the unavailability of necessary hardware, software, or passwords. Accordingly, advance planning and the use of identifying information that may be physically labeled on the tapes or accessible through the use of tape reading technology can facilitate e-Discovery and shorten turnaround time. After the tape population of interest has been narrowed to the size necessary, a strategy can be developed for performing information restoration and transfer to a searchable archive or Web-based repository.

In addition, in discussing the handling of backup tapes for discovery planning purposes, it may be appropriate to negotiate the sampling of a smaller, representative set of tapes. Also, "pre-searching" other sources can help narrow the document population. For example, pre-search can include searching email servers, date-range searching, segregating by department, or segregating by key custodian. It is also necessary to establish which locations, such as hard drives or corporate servers, are likely to yield responsive documents. If there are no such locations, tape restoration and review may need to be a first step.

Simple backup systems commonly associate one tape drive per computer and are linear in nature, archiving selected information in sequential order and writing it directly to the tape. Enterprise backup systems employ a server backup system connected to a tape library, or tape array, in which information is stored as data packets, which makes extracting specific items of responsive information for discovery purposes relatively more difficult.

The objective of tape restoration systems is to either restore a complete system or a subset of files. In the first case, a complete system backup is required and incremental backup tapes or the last differential tape set may also be needed. During processing, a complete backup would be restored and then the differential set or the incremental backup tapes would be inserted chronologically.

A variety of methods can be used to restore a subset of files, based on the modification dates of the files in the restoration subset and the backup method used in archiving the information. If the modification and/or creation dates are within the same time period of a backup, they should be part of the same backup set, whether it is a full backup, differential, or incremental set. If the files reside outside the range of a particular backup, the backup sets for each necessary file will be needed. This could include a combination of tape sets much like the first method.

There are two methods for restoring information from a tape backup system—native environment restoration and non-native environment restoration. The first method is most commonly used by IT departments and requires the original software, including patches, passwords, hardware, and network configuration. This method is appropriate for handling a relatively small restoration that will not affect the current active information. However, the process can be costly and time-consuming and requires significant hardware and storage capabilities.

The non-native environment process refers to the restoration of information outside its native environment, and is the preferred method used by third-party vendors who specialize in backup tape processing. The non-native restoration process is fast and scalable, and can cull information from simple backup as well as complex backup tape types.

Once information has been restored, the next consideration is the relationships betweens the files or documents obtained—such as email messages and attachments containing linked or embedded data. Files can also be packed inside of other files. Messages and attachments are contained within archives (repositories), which can be nested within other archives. In addition, metadata must be extracted and preserved. The requirements of a case will determine the technologies that must be employed to extract and process this information as well as report the relationships within the information.

## § 10.12 ISSUES AND CONCERNS

Enterprise storage comprises a complex array of components, devices, and systems that are constantly changing within any given IT environment. And as mentioned earlier, storage is heavily dependent on other IT software and hardware technologies for success. This complexity and dependence within a dynamic IT environment creates a host of issues and concerns for the e-Discovery practitioner.

While each particular environment and storage technology has its unique issues, common and foremost among them are obsolescence, lack of interoperability, and gaps in knowledge of IT staff responsible for storage systems. These issues combine to make the task of ESI discovery challenging under tight time frames and constrained budgets.

## § 10.13 RECOMMENDATIONS

By far the most important requirement for understanding any storage environment is a complete inventory of all storage assets. The foundation for this inventory is a network diagram that identifies the location and purpose of each asset. The network diagram should be obtained as early as possible, even if a rough diagram has to be hand-sketched during the initial interview.

1. Identify each storage device, and the particular individuals, business units, functional groups, or applications served by a particular storage device or group of storage devices.
2. Obtain a detailed description of how each storage device stores information and how that information can be retrieved.
3. Gain access to disaster recovery plans, since these are often an excellent, but often overlooked, source for defining equipment ownership, configuration, and purpose.
4. Interview and/or depose the Network Administrator, Data Administrator, and Records Administrator to obtain the above information.
5. As with other information technology, storage technology is replete with buzzwords, acronyms, and arcane jargon that can confuse more than enlighten. Ensure that all terms are explained and mutually understood.

## CHAPTER 11

# DESKTOP AND PORTABLE COMPUTERS

## §11.01 INTRODUCTION AND BACKGROUND

As discussed earlier in Chapter 5, Overview of File and Storage Systems, ESI in computers can be found in computer memory, secondary storage, and removable storage media. In addition and as important, however, desktop and portable computers provide pointers to other locations of ESI via network connections, including the Internet.

Desktop and portable computers may be personally or company-owned, may be shared by more than one person, and can be found in many different locations, especially portable computers. Desktop and portable computers may be configured as thick or thin clients for general purpose or restricted to specific applications. (See Chapter 3, Overview of Information Technology Infrastructure, § 3.02[B], for discussion of thick and thin clients.)

In most commercial environments, desktop and portable computers are typically connected to networks as thick clients configured with the Microsoft or Apple (or other) operating system, standard office applications (email, spreadsheet, word processor, presentation, database), and specialized corporate applications. Desktop and portable computers may also have access to the Internet and company Intranet.

Any desktop or portable computer may be configured with restrictions by application software or via security measures imposed by the IT organization, including the following examples:

- Prevent opening and running certain software
- Prevent or restrict access to the Internet
- Control actions on files—open, save, delete, transmit
- Log, track, and impose rules on work process

Desktop computers can be built and configured in a wide range of power and capability, including multiple specialized processors, many gigabytes of memory, and terabytes of secondary storage.

Portable computers are typically laptops limited by necessity of mobility convenience to smaller size and weight. In addition to laptops, portable computers also include general purpose and dedicated handheld devices. Smaller size imposes certain limitations when compared to the capabilities of more powerfully configured desktops. However, because of a broad range of configuration and price options, there is overlap in capabilities among desktops, laptops, and handhelds.

There is also convergence in the capabilities of desktop and portable computers with other mobile devices. For example, computers can function as phones via landline or wireless connections, and mobile phones can contain powerful computing ability.

## §11.02 ISSUES AND CONCERNS

In an ideal situation, discovery of ESI on desktops and portable computers would simply be a matter of identifying owners and devices, defining capabilities of individual devices, accessing the individual devices, and retrieving/preserving relevant ESI. In an extremely adverse situation where many computers have been severely damaged or compromised, a team of forensics experts might have to be engaged to isolate the devices and conduct a thorough and lengthy forensic process of extracting the ESI. (See Chapter 19, Forensics Considerations, for discussion of forensics.)

In reality most discovery situations fall somewhere in between these two types of situations. While there may be some computers that have been damaged or compromised, most of the effort deals with identifying the owners and devices, and understanding the configuration and content of each. This is typically because most organizations do not have complete and accurate information covering these essential requirements.

## § 11.03 RECOMMENDATIONS

Chapter 3, Overview of the Information Technology Infrastructure, outlines recommended steps for gaining information and insight into who owns what ESI and why within the organization. With desktop computers, and especially portable computers, it is extremely important to accomplish those steps as soon as possible in the litigation hold process. In addition, e-Discovery practitioners must address the following.

1. Immediately identify those computers that have been damaged, compromised, or lost, and
   a. Interview the owners of those computers,
   b. Isolate the computers,
   c. Determine if any further legal issues apply, and
   d. Assign forensic experts to evaluate and address the situation.
2. Assess all network management systems for capabilities with respect to equipment configuration and security monitoring and management, and
   a. Ensure that all automatic and manual instructions of applicable network management systems support are not in conflict with the intent of the litigation hold and e-Discovery objectives.
   b. Obtain written confirmation of the above.
3. In concert with recommendations 1 and 2 above, conduct e-Discovery on all computers in accord with case requirements.
4. Gain access to corporate disaster recovery plans, which are often overlooked as a source for defining equipment ownership, configuration, and purpose.

CHAPTER 12

# MOBILE DEVICES

## § 12.01 INTRODUCTION

This chapter includes mobile phones/smart phones, personal digital assistants (PDAs), MP3 Players, Photo and Video Cameras/Players, Digital Audio Recorders, and GPS devices, all of which are being produced in smaller and smaller forms. (Laptop and handheld computers and some removable media, while also considered mobile devices, are discussed in other chapters.)

First and foremost, it should be noted that mobile devices and the infrastructure associated with them are comprised of a dazzling array of rapidly changing and incompatible technology. For example, mobile device manufacturers employ a number of different operating systems. Each operating system enables specific and sometimes different functionality and each requires different backend support systems.

Because of this, employees may use a mix of company-provided devices and personal devices in order to satisfy their needs—for example, a company smart phone that passes company email to a personal home computer that accesses personal Web-based email. All of these factors combined create a highly complex and difficult environment for discovery of ESI, especially metadata.

## § 12.02 CHARACTERISTICS OF MOBILE DEVICES

Mobile devices comprise highly sophisticated technology and, taken as a category, are capable of holding many forms of ESI, including voice messages, text messages, instant messages, calendars, client contact information, office applications and files, podcasts, conferencing, collaboration, audio files, emails, photos, videos, graphics, animation, maps, personal identification, transactions/logging, and location and route logging via GPS (Global Positioning System).[1]

Most mobile devices communicate via wireless technology to one or more hosting services. Accordingly, in addition to being stored on the mobile device itself, ESI is often stored on the telecommunications service providers' storage servers, the users' company servers, and/or the servers of third parties providing hosting services for the users' company.

## § 12.03 MOBILE DEVICE ESI

Mobile devices connected wirelessly to networks enable download of multiple forms of ESI. All mobile devices have in common the ability to hold ESI in memory—either in some form of RAM or in some form of removable storage media. In addition, as mentioned above, ESI may be stored on servers that communicate with the mobile device.

### [A] Voice Messages

Voice messages are probably the most ubiquitous form of ESI within the universe of mobile devices simply because mobile phones, while providing a variety of functionality, are primarily used for voice communication. Voice messages may be digitally stored on the device, and/or on the service providers' storage servers. Voice messages may also be automatically converted to text for storage. (See Chapter 15, Voice Mail, for further information.)

### [B] Email

Email, a close second to voice as a form of ESI on mobile devices, is easily one of the most critical forms of ESI in most litigation matters. Depending on how the mobile device is configured, emails may be received by the

---

[1] While music is not generally considered litigation-related ESI, MP3 devices are included because they are capable of holding other forms of content besides music.

device from within the user's company, private networks, or anywhere on the Internet. Emails can be plain text, rich text, or html, and can contain attachments of almost any form. Once on the mobile device, emails can be responded to and forwarded to any other recipient device. (Also see Chapter 7, Email and Collaboration Systems, for further information.)

### [C] Office Applications

Office applications typically include common documents such as spreadsheets, presentations, text documents, drawings, calendars, and contacts, developed via the desktop or laptop computers of individual users. Depending on the operating system of the mobile device, office applications can be generated, and modified as if on the original source device, and forwarded via email as attachments.

**Note:** The capability to modify and/or forward documents may be constrained by security features imposed by the sender or sending system of the office documents.

### [D] Multimedia

Multimedia, for purposes of this discussion, includes animations, graphics, photos, and videos. Depending on the operating system of the mobile device, multimedia can be generated and modified on the device, and sent directly to other recipient devices. The continuously improving technology of cameras and associated software on mobile devices is enabling capture and creation of higher resolution photos and video from longer range, making mobile devices an important source of multimedia ESI. Examples include a wide range of situations, including capture of crime scenes, capture of information on whiteboards and documents, videos of events, and recordings of conversations.

### [E] Instant Messaging

As discussed in Chapter 7, Email and Collaboration Systems, instant messaging offers real-time communication and collaboration between two or any number of participants, similar to holding a conversation. Instant messaging systems can have additional features, including video via Web cams, and voice communication over the Internet. In addition, it is possible to save a conversation for later reference. Instant messages are typically logged in a local message history.

### [F] Text Messaging

Text messaging (often referred to as "texting") is the common term for sending short (160 characters or less) text messages from mobile phones and PDAs that have on-board wireless telecommunications.

Short Message Service (SMS) gateways exist to connect mobile SMS services with the Internet, instant message services, desktop computers, and landline telephones through text-to-speech conversion. Devices that connect to mobile phones and PDAs through protocols such as Bluetooth can also send text messages over the wireless network.

The most common application of text messaging is person-to-person communication, but text messages are also used to interact with automated systems, such as ordering products and services. As with other mobile device ESI, text messages may be stored on the device and may be stored on the host service as well.

### [G] Location-Based ESI

The Global Positioning System (GPS) developed by the United States is the world's only fully functional global navigation satellite system. GPS uses a minimum of 24 satellites in medium Earth orbit transmitting continuous and precise microwave signals that enable GPS receivers to determine location, speed, direction, and time.

GPS receivers have been miniaturized to the point that they now fit within mobile devices such as mobile phones. With GPS and mobile phone tower relay information, embedded software from various vendors enables mobile phones to perform a wide variety of location-based functions, including:

- Defining routing information for any mode of transportation—pedestrians, bicycles, cars, buses, trains, and planes
- Defining points of interest in a database or along defined routes
- Alerting users about certain situations, such as points of interest, weather, and traffic
- Automatic notification and communication among mobile phone users in the same vicinity
- Automatic location identification during emergency calls

In addition to enabling these and other location-based functions, embedded software may provide temporary or permanent logging of itinerary, events, and actions performed, which are potentially discoverable.

It should also be noted that location-based ESI is unique to each GPS enabled mobile device, and that other GPS enabled mobile devices may provide functions not mentioned above.

## §12.04 ISSUES AND CONCERNS

Mobile devices, by virtue of their ubiquity (both personal and company-owned), wireless communication, functionality, and mobility, provide unique opportunities for creation, transmission, and storage of ESI. However, partly because of some of these characteristics, mobile devices pose a high risk of ESI breach—transmission interception, physical theft, or misplacement. Accordingly, pervasive discovery of ESI on mobile devices is extremely difficult.

## §12.05 RECOMMENDATIONS

In an ideal situation, all ESI generated, received, and transmitted via mobile devices would be stored on company servers. However, this is rarely the case. Accordingly, e-Discovery practitioners must ensure that the litigation hold process includes an inventory of all mobile devices and supporting infrastructure, along with detailed information about each regarding:

- Owners/users, their contact information and roles
- Device hardware/software functions and capabilities
- External and internal support infrastructure and capabilities, especially security tools that can authenticate users, transactions, and disable devices if necessary
- Third-party roles and responsibilities, especially with regard to record keeping and activity logging

Armed with this information, e-Discovery practitioners can filter out non-relevant personnel and devices, allowing focus on priority litigation hold and ESI discovery issues.

CHAPTER 13

# MULTIMEDIA AND VIDEO

## § 13.01 MULTIMEDIA

Multimedia includes animations, graphics, and photos as standalone content, mixed to create content, and as content embedded in Web pages, videos, and any form of office document, including spreadsheets, presentations, drawings, and word processing documents.

Multimedia content is important in its own right as discoverable ESI, but perhaps more important is the fact that multimedia, and the software that conveys it, can contain code that may spawn other actions within the host device or external to the host device. Clicking on a graphic element, for example, can spawn execution of code to perform other functions. Unfortunately, this particular capability is often used for illegal purposes as a vehicle for conveyance of viruses, spyware, and trojans.

Because of these characteristics, multimedia content and its associated metadata can be used to help trace the existence of other discoverable ESI.

## § 13.02 VIDEO

Video can be used to record for any purpose, and ranges from amateur personal video without sound, taken from standalone cameras or cameras embedded in mobile devices, to highly sophisticated video with sound and software that adds intelligence and other functionality, taken by professionals or via fixed surveillance cameras.

Videos are powerful ESI because they can provide rich visual recordings of actual events, often with significant metadata provided either within or external to the video.

For example, an amateur video can include a particular view, revealing location, and/or a clock, revealing time. In addition, metadata might reveal who took the video.

Even more powerful are the surveillance videos that contain software providing intelligence and other functionality. Examples of added intelligence include the ability to:

- Track the movement of an object of any distinct configuration, size, shape, color, etc.
- Parse video content into digital elements for insertion in SQL-type databases for data mining
- Identify selected objects and perform comparative recognition
- Perform automated lip-reading via software
- Perform in any light conditions, including infrared
- Provide data compression that enables low bandwidth transmission in real time of high quality video without frame dropping
- Create an alarm and notification for any defined event

## § 13.03 ISSUES AND CONCERNS

"Personal" multimedia and video can be created from desktop and portable computers and mobile devices and widely dispersed via networks and the Internet, directly through messaging systems, and as attachments to emails almost without restraints of any kind, influenced perhaps by the seemingly innocuous nature of the media. Multimedia and video created under the auspices of corporate systems are usually managed under a more controlled environment.

Both personal and corporate photos and video content can include an endless array of subject matter, including examples such as:

- Meeting whiteboards
- Meeting discussions
- Document pages
- Individuals and people in various situations

Much of this multimedia and video is transitory as new content is continuously exchanged among peers. However, when stored and annotated with notes and containing metadata, multimedia and video can comprise ESI with considerable potential impact.

## § 13.04 RECOMMENDATIONS

Because of the potentially transitory nature of multimedia and video, especially on personal mobile devices, it is very important to gather information as quickly as possible. Following are examples of questions for individuals that can help point to potential sources of ESI.

1. During the period _____ did you possess or use a personal or company central computer, desktop, personal or handheld computer, or mobile device that could take photos or videos? Please identify the device[s] and features.
2. Have you taken any photos or videos during the period _____ from any such device? Please describe the photos or videos: subject matter, dates, purpose.
3. Do you share photos or videos with others on a personal basis or through company channels? Please identify who received what photos/videos, when, and why.

CHAPTER 14

# REMOVABLE STORAGE DEVICES/MEDIA

## § 14.01 INTRODUCTION AND BACKGROUND

Removable storage devices/media are available in magnetic, optical, and solid state technologies, and are manufactured in a wide range of physical sizes, storage capacity, and capabilities. Removable storage devices/ media, as the name implies, were primarily developed for storage, but have evolved to include additional functionality as well. For example, it is now possible to boot and run a complete standalone operating system with a full suite of office applications from a single USB drive.

## § 14.02 TYPES OF REMOVABLE STORAGE DEVICES

### [A] Magnetic Drives

A magnetic drive consists of a rotating magnetic disk on which data is encoded and read by a device suspended above the disc. ESI can be recorded and erased any number of times. Common types of magnetic drives include:

#### [1] Floppy Drives

Floppy drives were originally manufactured in a standard size of 3.5 inches for permanent installation in computers. Standard capacity of the portable disk was 1.44MB. Due to their small capacity, floppy disks were primarily used for transferring or backing up small files. The 1.44MB floppy has now been replaced by portable devices capable of storing 750MB. The larger capacity drives retain backward compatibility with the 1.44 MB floppy, since many of these still exist in use today.

#### [2] Hard Drives

Permanently installed hard drives are the primary storage device on computers. However, both Internal and portable hard drives are continuously being manufactured in smaller forms, higher capacities, with lower costs, resulting in the increased use of portable hard drives to supplement internal storage. Portable hard drives typically connect via the USB port, range in capacity from several gigabytes to over a terabyte, and range in size from small devices about the size of a deck of cards to larger desktop models.[1]

#### [3] Tape Cartridges

Tape used for storage of ESI is typically in the form of cartridges, which come in a wide range of sizes and capacities. Depending on size and compression used, cartridge capacity can be from a few megabytes to several terabytes. Information is recorded on tape in a sequential mode, which makes them more suited to backup and archiving than general purpose access in routine operations. (See Chapter 10, Enterprise Storage Systems, for more information about tape media.)

### [B] Optical Drives

Optical disks record information by burning microscopic holes in the surface of the disk with a laser. To read the disk, another laser beam shines on the disk and detects the holes by changes in the reflection pattern. Prior to recording, optical media has a lifespan of between five and 10 years. For that reason, optical drives are not generally considered for long term storage. In addition, optical drives have suffered from incompatibility between older disks and newer readers. However, optical drives have replaced floppy drives as standard equipment on desktop and laptop computers. Forms of optical drives include:

---

[1] At the time of publication, a major discount chain was selling at $269 an external hard drive with 1 terabyte of storage and a triple interface that included USB, Fire Wire 400, and eSATA.

### [1] Compact Discs (CDs)

CDs are manufactured in three forms—CD-ROM (read only), CD-R (record/write once and read), and CD-RW (record/write multiple times and read). CDs have a typical capacity in the range of 750MB and are used primarily for general purpose secondary storage on desktop and laptop computers.

### [2] Digital Video Disks (DVDs)

DVDs are similar to CD-ROMs, but with enhanced technology that enables a minimum capacity of 4.7GB, which is sufficient to hold a full-length movie. DVDs are commonly used as a medium for digital representation of movies and other multimedia presentations that combine sound with graphics. As with CDs, DVDs are read only, record once, and record multiple times. DVD readers (players) are typically standalone devices.

### [3] Magneto-Optical Drives (MOs)

MO drives write magnetically and read optically, can have capacities of tens of gigabytes, and access data faster than magnetic devices and CDs. MO discs are reliable and resilient against normal wear and environmental damage, are highly portable, and can be read only or re-writable. Accordingly, MO drives are often used in backup and archiving where large image files are involved.

## [C] Solid State Disk (SSD)

SSD (often called Flash Memory) is a light and fast plug-and-play storage device that contains no moving parts (solid state memory similar to RAM in a computer). SSDs are manufactured in various sizes and capacities, usually for specific mobile devices (phones, cameras, audio players, PDAs, etc.), game consoles, and desktop, laptop, and handheld computers.

### [1] Mini Secure Digital (SD) Cards

SD cards are small and thin (about the size of a matchbook), removable flash memory mainly used in mobile electronic devices that require high performance and depend on small size for portability. SD cards can hold up to 128MB of data and have a high-transfer rate for copying and downloading files.

### [2] USB Flash Memory Sticks (USB Drives)

A USB drive is a small (⅛ × ¾ × 1 ½ inch), portable memory device that plugs into a computer's USB port and functions as a portable hard drive with up to 4GB of storage capacity. USB drives are easy-to-use, small enough to carry in a pocket or on a key chain, and can plug into any computer with a USB port. Their ease of use and portability make them popular for file sharing. In addition, as mentioned in the Introduction above, USB drives are beginning to incorporate additional standalone functionality.

### [3] High Capacity SSD (hSSD)

High capacity SSDs are similar to standard SSDs except that they are designed for storage capacities ranging from a few gigabytes to hundreds of gigabytes and usually for use in harsh environmental situations.

## [D] Hybrid Devices

Hybrid devices have special characteristics or employ more than one technology, usually for specialized functions.

### [1] Write Once Read Many (WORM) Drives

WORM disks are portable, non-erasable, and require specific software or hardware to be read, making them highly suitable for archival purposes. First developed using optical technology for long-term storage of medical images and patents, the proliferation of regulatory requirements has expanded use of WORM drives to archival of corporate documents as well. Accordingly, other technology such as hard disk cartridges, magnetic tape, magneto-optical disks, and ultra density optical disks are now supported by WORM drives.

### [2] Hard Disk Drive (HDD) Cartridge

HDD cartridge is a small (½ × ⅗ inch) removable device that contains a Serial Advanced Technology Attachment (SATA)[2] hard disk. The HDD cartridge fits into a docking station connected via USB port to a computer. HDD cartridges back up like tape drives but offer the performance of hard disk systems. Capacity ranges from 40 to 250GB. HDD cartridges are used where priority is placed on maintaining the integrity of very large individual files, such as medical images, architectural or engineering drawings, and animation renderings. HDD cartridges are also used for small and medium-scale backup and archiving.

## § 14.03 ISSUES AND CONCERNS

Personal and corporate-owned removable storage devices/media are truly ubiquitous. Organizations are faced with situations where employees have a wide range of personal and corporate applications requiring myriads of devices and media from tens if not hundreds of vendors.

Although companies attempt to implement state-of-the-art security measures to protect ESI, the sheer magnitude of the devices and the changing nature of the technology make effective controls extremely difficult. Even more problematic, companies may not even be aware of all the devices/media in use for storage of critical ESI.

## § 14.04 RECOMMENDATIONS

Recommendations for removable storage devices/media are similar to those outlined in Chapter 12, Mobile Devices, with emphasis on the imperative to determine who owns what and why as quickly as possible. First, e-Discovery practitioners must ensure that the litigation hold process has considered all removable storage devices. This involves obtaining an inventory, including information from and about owners/users, their contact information and roles, and the removable devices/media under their control.

---

[2] SATA is a computer connection for transfer of data between a computer and storage devices. SATA is designed for faster transfers, better cooling, improved reliability and data integrity, and hot swapping—enabling users to add or remove devices while still operating.

CHAPTER 15

# VOICE MAIL

## § 15.01 DESCRIPTION

Voice mail messages share similarities with email messages in that both are spontaneous, unfiltered sources of ESI and are increasing in use and volume. Contemporary voice mail systems are built on computer-based phone systems that store voice messages as digital "WAV" sound files. More sophisticated systems include digital metadata such as date, time, length of message, incoming phone number, and flags such as priority and follow-up. In some organizations, voice mail systems are integrated with email and collaboration systems (sometimes called "unified messaging" systems). Most systems encrypt the sound and metadata files for security.

Voice mail messages can be collected and processed in a number of ways. Sound files can be retrieved from the applicable storage device, decrypted, and preserved on a separate recording device for playback and transcription, and/or processed for conversion from sound to text via special speech-to-text software.

In addition, mobile phones provide the emerging capability to enable speech-to-text conversion. On a mobile phone configured with this optional capability, a message received by a subscriber is sent through the voice recognition process and a text version of the message is generated. That message is then sent to the subscriber as a standard email, or standard text message, with the audio file attached. As email and text files, messages can be sorted, cut, pasted, forwarded, and printed, or searched for specific content using common search tools. Voice to text technology provides users with a "virtual secretary," enabling users to dictate emails, leave messages, copy phone numbers into address books, and create memos that can be filed or forwarded.

This emerging speech-to-text capability of mobile phones is enabling business enterprises and other entities to capture and store mobile phone messages in much the same way as emails.

## § 15.02 ISSUES AND CONCERNS

Many voice mail systems use proprietary software, and extracting voice messages may require decryption using the same equipment.

Voice mail messages, unlike digital text, can be difficult to understand and interpret accurately and efficiently, due to a number of factors, including origin of language, accents, emotion, slang, context, and sound quality. Because of these factors, the integrity of transcriptions can be questionable. In addition, the skill of the interpreter/transcriber in listening, interpreting, and transcribing impacts the quality, time, and expense related to manual processes.

Converting voice mail to text using speech recognition software is a considerably less expensive process than transcription, and enables creation of digital files that can be searched. However, for many of the reasons described above, speech recognition software is not 100 percent accurate.

Voice mail backup and archival systems are usually tape-based and tightly coupled with the active voice mail system server, and are not designed with ease of data extraction in mind. Therefore, retrieval of voice mail from such systems requires considerable effort and expertise.

## § 15.03 RECOMMENDATIONS

Due to the nature of voice mail, the risk/reward scenario in producing and processing voice mail messages to find relevant information needs to be carefully considered by both parties. The following steps help in making voice mail discovery decisions.

1. Determine and interview the key technical persons (voice mail administrator) responsible for company voice systems.
2. Determine and examine all policies and procedures related to voice mail usage.
3. Determine the sources of voice mail, if the sources are standalone or integrated with other systems, how voice mail is stored, and how voice mail can be effectively retrieved.
4. Determine who the key players are in the particular discovery case, how they use voice mail, where their voice mail is stored, and what volume is involved.

5. Determine the potential effort required in the discovery processing cycle to reduce a large universe of voice mail to the few that meet specific criteria. In doing so, consider more targeted searching techniques, such as by role or by person, as alternatives to key word searching.
6. Determine the cost of retrieval from backup and archival systems.
7. Develop a strategy for agreement among the parties on how to contain voice mail discovery scope and cost.

Part III

# PERFORMING ELECTRONIC DISCOVERY

# CHAPTER 16

# INTRODUCTION

## §16.01 e-DISCOVERY LIFECYCLE

Chapter 2, Overview of the Electronic Discovery Process, summarized the six phases of e-Discovery and provided some context for understanding the role of technology in the e-Discovery process. This part of the book expands on that overview by providing additional information about the e-Discovery process, illuminating application of e-Discovery technology tools and techniques and typical issues encountered.

Figure (1) Electronic Discovery Process Lifecycle, from Chapter 2, is presented below for reference throughout this part of the book.

**FIGURE (1) ELECTRONIC DISCOVERY PROCESS LIFECYCLE**

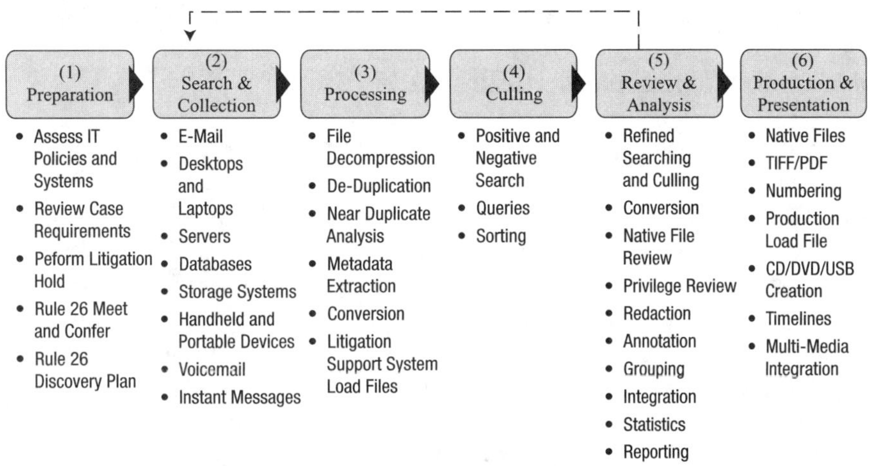


## §16.02 FRCP 2006 AMENDMENTS

Also presented for reference in this section is a brief overview of some of the more relevant provisions of the amended Federal Rules of Civil Procedure relating to electronic discovery that became effective on December 1, 2006. These rules govern the discovery process in federal courts and have been enacted in various modified forms by several states. The applicable parts to Rules 16, 26, 33, 34, 35, 37, and 45 of the FRCP are summarized below.

### [A] Early Attention to Electronic Discovery: Rules 16(b), 26(a)(1) & 26(f)

The new rules require early attention to electronic discovery issues in a manner that emphasizes the need for advance preparation by client and counsel. Rule 26(a)(1) was amended to require explicitly that initial disclosures must include a description of electronically stored information by "category and location" to the extent the information is "in the possession, custody or control of the party," and the information will be used to support claims or defenses.

For the discovery planning conference under Rule 26(f), parties are now required to discuss "any issues" pertaining to electronic discovery, including without limitation preservation and form of production. Judges are encouraged to take electronic discovery issues into account and provide for them in the Rule 16(b) scheduling order.

This is a significant change from prior practice in that it frontloads the discussion of electronic discovery to a very early point in the case. As a practical matter, this means that the attorney or outside counsel responsible for a matter will need to be fully prepared to address the spectrum of electronic discovery issues, including potentially all of the issues discussed below in connection with other rules amendments, within a very short time frame after a complaint is filed.

### [B] Two-Tier Procedure for Discovery of Electronic Information: Rule 26(b)(2)(B)

The amendments codify what was previously common practice in providing that parties may object to requests for production of information from sources the responding party designates as "not reasonably accessible" for reasons of undue burden or cost. Upon a showing by the designating party supporting the designation, the onus is then on the requesting party to show good cause why the information should be produced. If the court deems a sufficient showing of good cause to have been made, the court may then order production of the electronic information. The rule explicitly authorizes the court to impose conditions on the production, an example of which might be shifting certain associated costs to the requesting party. The notes to this rule contain an important cautionary message: this rule does not mean that information designated as "not reasonably accessible" need not be preserved; instead it is a procedure for assessing and resolving discoverability, as opposed to preservation, issues.

### [C] Privilege Waiver and Inadvertent Disclosure: Rule 26(b)(5)

The problem of inadvertent disclosure of privileged information is not unique to electronic discovery, but it is of particular concern and frequency of occurrence in this area because of the sheer volume and nature of electronic information. Recognizing this fact, the amended Rule 26 encourages parties to enter into agreements that inadvertent disclosures will not be treated as broad privilege waivers. In addition, the rule establishes a procedure that is commonly found in protective orders whereby a party notified of an inadvertent disclosure is required to return, sequester, or destroy the information, and refrain from using or disclosing it, pending adjudication of the propriety of the privilege claim (including any dispute as to whether a waiver occurred).

However, caution is in order because such agreements, even if ordered by the court, are not necessarily binding or effective as to third parties (such as plaintiffs in other lawsuits). While amendments to the Federal Rules of Evidence are under consideration to deal with this problem, they may not be implemented, if at all, until some time in the future.

It is common practice to include in the protective orders negotiated in litigation matters a provision providing that inadvertent disclosures of privileged documents do not constitute a waiver of privilege either as to the documents themselves or the subject matter of those documents.

### [D] Production Format for Electronic Information: Rule 34(b)

The amendments establish a procedure whereby a requesting party can request production of electronic information in a particular format. The responding party can object, but, absent an agreement to the contrary, is required to produce electronic information either in the form in which it is "ordinarily maintained" or in a form that is "reasonably usable." The phrase "ordinarily maintained" as it relates to electronic format will usually mean native file format—in other words, the format in which the file in question was originally created.

### [E] Avoidance of Spoliation Sanctions: Rule 37(g)

The new rules include a "safe harbor" from sanctions for spoliation of electronic information, but one should not make any assumptions that any given behavior falls within the safe harbor (particularly given the dearth of case law development interpreting the rule). New Rule 37(g) provides that "absent exceptional circumstances" a party will not be sanctioned for spoliation "under these rules" for the loss of information as a result of the "routine, good faith operation" of a computer system. Analysis of these conditions reveals several ambiguities in the "safe harbor."

First, it is unclear how broadly courts will interpret "exceptional circumstances." Judging from the committee notes, this appears to contemplate situations where a party has been so severely prejudiced by the loss of information that remedial sanctions are necessary to fairly allocate the harm from the loss. The limiting phrase "under these rules" is problematic because courts have sources of authority other than the Federal Rules under which they can sanction parties for spoliation, such as their "inherent powers," and typically do cite to these powers when issuing sanctions.

Moreover, the behavior qualifying as "routine" and "good faith" cannot be precisely delineated. The notes indicate that routine operation means operation for the business and technical purposes for which the system in question was designed. Good faith is much harder to pin down with clear boundaries, as the notes indicate that good faith may well require suspension of routine operation in response to a preservation duty, but that the extent of this obligation will vary depending on the circumstances.

Accordingly, the important point to recognize about the so-called "safe harbor" is that it may be a useful resource in defending against a spoliation charge, but it is not a safe harbor in the traditional sense of articulating clear steps, compliance with which will preclude sanctions with certainty.

### [F] Inspection or Sampling: Rule 34(a)

The amendments expressly permit requesting parties to "inspect," "test," or "sample" electronic information. This codifies the use of techniques that appear in electronic discovery case law as useful tools under certain circumstances. For example, there is already an entire jurisprudence of case law regarding when inspection of computer hard disks will be permitted and the protocols for conducting such inspections. (Such inspections are generally conducted for the purpose of locating data on the disk that was deleted by the user or is otherwise not accessible through ordinary means, or where there is reason to suspect spoliation or incomplete production on the part of the computer's custodian.)

Sampling has been used to determine the likelihood of finding responsive information on particular sources of electronic information, such as backup tapes, to aid determinations as to whether discovery from those sources is warranted and, if so, which party should bear the cost.

### [G] Interrogatories: Rule 33(d)

The amended Rule 33(d) makes it clear that interrogatories can be answered by providing access to electronic information, just as by identifying documents produced. However, the rule also indicates that the party referencing electronic information in response to an interrogatory will have to provide the requesting party with the means to extract the requested information, which could include, for example, proprietary software. For this reason, care must be exercised before choosing to use this mechanism in response to an interrogatory.

### [H] Electronic Discovery from Non-Parties: Rule 45

The amendments essentially transpose all of the foregoing procedures and standards to the world of discovery from non-parties under Rule 45. Generally, non-parties are subject to a heightened degree of protection from invasive discovery by virtue of their standing as non-parties. However, the fact that the amendments to Rule 45 incorporate the electronic discovery provisions applicable to parties suggests that non-parties will not be able to avoid electronic discovery completely in response to a subpoena. The case law regarding how far non-parties can be pressured in terms of burdensome electronic discovery is still in its infancy.

## § 16.03 CHAPTERS IN PART 3

e-Discovery, for the most part, is an iterative process of preserving and reducing a large universe of ESI to a smaller, relevant universe of ESI for timely presentation in a form acceptable to the parties and the court.

All e-Discovery projects are unique, and there is no single "right" way to conduct e-Discovery. In addition to the FRCP and/or other procedural rules that may be applicable in any given venue, however, there are certain general requirements that need to be considered because of their influence throughout the e-Discovery process. These requirements are covered in the following chapters:

- Management and Administration
- Standards and Best Practices

- Forensic Considerations
- Search and Retrieval Considerations
- Preparation and Preservation

In addition, Chapter 22, Quick Walkthrough of the e-Discovery Process, provides a brief overview of the typical steps taken, issues considered, and benefits derived as the e-Discovery process moves through the various phases. This chapter also provides a sense of the flow of e-Discovery activity.

Chapter 23, General Issues and Recommendations, provides a summary for consideration in relation to potential current and future requirements.

CHAPTER 17

# MANAGEMENT AND ADMINISTRATION

There are a number of management and administration requirements and responsibilities that should be addressed as early as possible in order to ensure effective performance and compliance with objectives throughout the e-Discovery process.

In order to address these requirements and carry out responsibilities, executive management and key players must first become educated regarding key aspects of the e-Discovery process. This includes at minimum:

1. Understanding generally the legal requirements relating to ESI
2. Understanding at a high level how ESI moves through the e-Discovery lifecycle
3. Understanding the concepts of how e-Discovery technology works in support of the different phases and functions within the e-Discovery lifecycle
4. Understanding how the IT Infrastructure impacts the storage and retrieval of ESI
5. Understanding that individual custodians of ESI must take responsibility for compliance

In addition, management must ensure that the enterprise has a litigation response plan and either an e-Discovery project management capability in house or access to such capability from a trusted advisor.

## §17.01 LITIGATION RESPONSE PLAN (LRP)

A litigation response plan is having documented policies, procedures, practices, and systems governing and guiding the e-Discovery process in response to potential or pending litigation matters.

The LRP provides a roadmap for litigation response teams to help ensure that the company meets its legal obligations while minimizing electronic discovery expense and burden. Following are overviews of some of the important areas addressed in the LRP.

### [A] Resources

Almost all e-Discovery projects require a combination of in-house legal, business, and technical staff and third parties such as outside counsel, e-Discovery experts and consultants, and service or technology vendors.

Resources required are dependent on a number of factors, including e-Discovery scope and timelines, capabilities and limitations of the IT Infrastructure, including e-Discovery technology and in-house staff, and the availability and capability of third-party service providers.

For most enterprises facing a significant discovery event, outside help is often required. Typically this outside help involves both expertise and technology. Professional services firms may be able to supplement in-house teams, providing skilled professionals who can work hand in hand with internal IT and legal staff. The same or different firms may also provide technical solutions for the various phases of the e-Discovery process, e.g., searching for, collecting, and hosting ESI for attorney review.

Taking all of the above into consideration, management must determine the initial resource requirements for each phase of the e-Discovery lifecycle and develop an appropriate project management plan that supports those requirements.

### [B] IT Infrastructure

Chapter 3, Overview of the Information Technology Infrastructure, and Part 2, Sources of Electronically Stored Information, provide background and insights that can help all parties understand and address how to effectively identify and access potentially responsive ESI.

As part of the litigation response plan, it is important to translate the information gained from those chapters, including results of the interviews recommended, into a systems overview that provides a clear roadmap of where **all** ESI resides and how to access it—active, backups, archived, legacy, online, offline, fixed, and portable—including all backup, archive, and restoration technology, procedures, and schedules.

This is not a trivial task, and one that is critical as a foundation to the execution of e-Discovery compliance. All subsequent e-Discovery efforts will be based upon the information assembled about the sources. Accordingly, if this information is incomplete or inaccurate, the omissions or mistakes may impact the rest of the process.

## [C] ESI Hold and Preservation

This section of the litigation response plan needs to define the legal requirements of litigation hold and preservation, the responsibilities of individual custodians and others, the timing of holds, and the communication and reaffirmation throughout the litigation process. These requirements are defined in Chapter 18, Standards and Best Practices, and in Chapter 21, Preparation and Preservation.

## [D] Control and Oversight

The best way to achieve control and oversight of litigation matters will differ to varying degrees among different organizations. Many business enterprises may find that these needs are best achieved through a governance body that includes senior stakeholders capable of resource fulfillment, problem resolution, and decision-making. A governance vehicle well-suited for this purpose is the Steering Committee structure.

A litigation Steering Committee may be chaired by an in-house attorney and should include members of IT, Records Management, and, depending on the organizational structure and the nature of the litigation the enterprise typically faces, stakeholders from business units and auditing. See Chapter 25, Guidance and Governance, for details on the formation of a steering committee.

The Litigation Steering Committee may authorize an e-Discovery Project Manager who initiates a formal project management process for the e-Discovery matter. See § 17.02, e-Discovery Project Management.

In addition, the Steering Committee may authorize creation of an e-Discovery audit process that verifies ESI preservation, integrity, security, and chain-of-custody. See Chapter 18, Standards and Best Practices.

The reality is that many organizations may not be able to spare internal resources to carry out these processes, and they may not have internal resources with the required expertise in any event. Accordingly, many organizations use outside experts in various ways to accomplish the necessary e-Discovery readiness objectives. The configuration of this division of responsibility as between internal resources and outside experts will vary depending upon timing, budgetary, and other constraints unique to any organization.

## [E] Reporting

Reporting is an important component of communication among stakeholders that facilitates understanding, control, and project management, including performance measurement. Many e-Discovery technology platforms and service vendors offer their own reports, but at minimum, the following should be considered.

1. **Deliverables**—Reports that track the progress of specified deliverables throughout the e-Discovery lifecycle.
2. **Chain-of-Custody**—These reports track possession and are critical to ensuring evidentiary integrity. Physical chain-of-custody reporting begins when physical information is collected. File-level reporting begins when information on the media is uploaded to a repository, and each file is then tracked.
3. **Culling**—Detail reports track and validate culling techniques used—deduplication, search, and filtering—providing information regarding why a file was segregated and to which search term or metadata the file was responsive, number of files responsive to each search, and number of times the terms were contained within the files. Culling Summary Reports track the culling process—name and location path of the file, and information regarding other instances of the same file—to help ensure that all information is properly processed.

4. **Custodian**—Reports that track information by individual or groups of custodians, including information-volume, percentage and/or volume of information culled by deduplication, searching, or other technique. This information helps ensure that all information for an individual or group of custodians has been delivered in preparation for depositions.
5. **Custom**—Reports that provide different views of information unique to the particular case requirements, in order to provide insights that facilitate analysis and decision-making.
6. **Exception**—Reports that track problems or issues such as files unable to be rendered to an image, unable to be viewed as a native file, or files where encryption or passwords were not cracked. Reports provide file name, location, and reason the files could not be delivered to the client.
7. **Media Analysis**—Reports are used to determine how much information requires processing to guide resource, cost, and delivery schedule estimates. Reports catalog within individual media, the number of files, the type of files, size of the files, and directory of file names.
8. **Resource Measurement**—Reports that track human and machine performance to measure utilization for load balancing, costing, and scheduling. Reports track by custodian, document category, media, function, and other discernable process categories.
9. **Status**—Reports that summarize the overall condition and progress of the project.
10. **Time and Billing**—Accounting type reports that track time and expenses for all assigned personnel.

## §17.02 e-Discovery PROJECT MANAGEMENT

Project management is a relatively simple construct, but is often made overly complex by application of technology not suited to the particular purpose. There is no argument that e-Discovery projects can benefit from project management techniques, but there are different opinions regarding the best project management approach.

In essence, project management is comprised of four essential components.

- Resources—Project Manager, Team, equipment, and facilities
- Task-Resource Schedule—Who does what and when
- Deliverables Schedule—Completion of work product
- Open Issues—Unresolved problems in escalation mode

The approach outlined below provides a simple and easy method that practitioners can use to manage any size e-Discovery project.[1]

1. Assign a Project Manager
2. Identify Team Members (full time and part time, either in-house personnel or outside counsel/vendors/contractors):
   a. Working Team Leaders (Managers) for each phase or major processing function
   b. e-Discovery Task Specialists
   c. Staff from IT, Records Management, In-house Counsel
   d. Staff from Outside Counsel, Consultants, Vendors

[1] The approach defined has been used to manage multi-million dollar projects with hundreds of people spanning several years.

3. Define Deliverables and initial Milestones in accord with e-Discovery phases/functions and requirements[2]
4. Develop scoping estimates for each Deliverable (see § 18.06, Metrics and Measurements)
5. Determine resources required to complete each Deliverable[3]
6. Develop a schedule for completion of the Deliverables
7. Identify the tasks required to complete the Deliverables
8. Assign resources to complete the tasks
9. Produce the Deliverables Schedule and the Task Resource Schedule from steps 4 to 8
10. Define any open issues and produce the Open Issues List

Project management software is a helpful tool in translating scoping estimates into task resource schedules, but is no substitute for the "hands on" involvement required to effectively manage projects.

It is extremely useful to include key players in initial project planning and estimating in order to gain input and support that helps ensure project success. Some of the considerations to take into account during the planning process include:

- Agreements made during the meet-and-confer process, e.g., under FRCP 26(f)
- Discovery deadlines
- Resource limitations
- e-Discovery technology available
- Volume and complexity of ESI
- Third-party capabilities

Also, it is important to keep in mind that tasks represent the work performed that results in Deliverables. Accordingly, tasks should be defined in such a way as to enable measurement of performance and progress so there are no surprises when Deliverables and Milestones are due.

[2] A Deliverable is a tangible product, such as "All collected emails." A milestone is a marker, such as "The end of the Collection Phase."

[3] Production of Deliverables may be constrained either by limited resources or by tight schedules, or both. As an example, twice as many resources would typically be required to complete a fixed amount of work in six months as it would take to complete the same amount of work in a year.

# CHAPTER 18

# STANDARDS AND BEST PRACTICES

Preservation of ESI and execution of e-Discovery are guided and facilitated by standards and best practices from a variety of sources, including rules and regulations, case law, and legal and other industry organizations with interests in litigation and e-Discovery. e-Discovery practitioners are encouraged to become knowledgeable regarding these sources, especially those imposing legal requirements.

Following are important standards and best practices that apply within the e-Discovery lifecycle:

- Auditability
- Chain-of-Custody
- Copying and Fingerprinting Original ESI
- Custodian and Key Person Interviews
- Data Sampling
- Metrics and Measurement
- Preservation Notices and Letters
- Quality Control
- Security

All of these may be necessary to demonstrate the reasonableness or defensibility of an e-Discovery process, or to lay the required foundation for the admission of ESI as evidence.

## § 18.01 AUDITABILITY

Auditability refers to the transparency, openness, or receptiveness of a system or process to being examined, and usually includes inherent features such as logs that facilitate the examination process.

For e-Discovery, this means embedding fields within records, whether by manual or automated processes, that enable auditors to track the details of who did what, where, when, and how for every piece of ESI handled throughout the e-Discovery lifecycle. Most of these auditability requirements are expressed in the chain-of-custody tracking.

## § 18.02 CHAIN-OF-CUSTODY

Chain-of-custody procedures and records must be maintained to establish the integrity of evidence, proving it has been properly preserved from the original hold through to final production.

All participants, whether internal, external, or third parties, must adhere to procedures that define strict protocols for collecting, transporting, accepting, storing, retrieving, and processing documents, and ensuring that documents have not been altered. In addition, chain-of-custody records must document every instance of contact with ESI and the action performed. To accomplish this, the following items should be considered and consistently applied throughout the e-Discovery lifecycle.

Use of a "Primary Custodian" is recommended as the single point of responsibility and contact for chain-of-custody assurance and reporting.

Because of the volume of physical media and embedded ESI required, and the need to maintain integrity throughout the process, it is essential to use a database to capture information, preferably through automation embedded within the e-Discovery tools. Use of a barcode labeling system is ideal for providing certain identification requirements.

Data element headings should include at least the following as applicable to any particular evidence item or task within the e-Discovery lifecycle, such as transporting, receiving, collecting, searching, filtering, converting, reviewing, and producing.

- e-Discovery Case Identification: matter, client, primary custodian, inventory ID
- Actions Taken: dates, reasons, custodian ID, specific action taken, ID and involvement of second party if any

- Custodian and Participant: name, role, action taken, and description of any problems, including refusal to release ESI, breaches of security, or chain-of-custody
- Evidence: items, type of media and manufacturer name and model, unique identifier/serial number, media label, content description, volume of ESI, media access/write protection methods, collection method, problems if any, and digital fingerprint whenever possible
- Transport: shipper and receiver ID, evidence ID, method of transport, dates
- Search: custodian ID, user ID, date, project, keyword, phrase, concept
- Collection: evidence ID, custodian ID, user ID, collection method, actions taken

Effective chain-of-custody requires written procedures applied to the entire discovery process, addressing best practices such as:

- Using automation to improve process integrity and to reduce user involvement,
- Ensuring that software used has appropriate reporting and audit capabilities,
- Restricting the number of users touching evidence to minimize handling errors and mistakes,
- Considering three teams: a group of forensic investigators to collect evidence and document the process; a team to log, inventory, and safeguard the evidence; and a team in charge of copying, fingerprinting, and analyzing the original data,
- Using only trusted or bonded point-to-point transportation carriers/couriers for evidence transport
- Using forms for consistency of chain-of-custody data recording and to validate data entry into databases
- Ensuring that the e-Discovery provider takes physical custody of evidence as soon as possible after collection
- Restricting access to original evidence to the team in charge of logging and securing it
- Logging any activities involving original evidence, and providing confirmation of receipt to the evidence owner

## § 18.03 COPYING AND FINGERPRINTING ORIGINAL ESI

Ideally, immediately after logging and safeguarding, original evidence should be forensically copied using a tool certified for non-intrusive duplication by someone trained to operate the tool correctly.

Forensic copies are made using a hardware device that prevents information being written to the target drive. Specialized software is used to copy the drive, including temporary workspace and deleted file space, from the target drive to the evidence drive. Reproducibility is key to forensic copies, so that any number of new forensic copies can be made at any time of the original target drive that exactly match the original and all copies.

Despite the fact that in many cases forensic imaging may be the only practical way to make sure that relevant evidence is preserved, parties are often reluctant to perform such imaging due to the perceived added expenses and burdens of doing so. Often, the imaging of computer hard drives triggers the retention of an expert by the adverse party for the same purpose. In addition, imaging a hard drive may result in the retention, analysis, and even production of large amounts of potentially irrelevant, and/or privileged information.

Accordingly, imaging hard drives is most often performed in cases where it is essential to preservation of demonstrably relevant evidence, where evidence only accessible by forensic imaging goes to the heart of the case, where a judgment is made that the potential exposure or liability involved in the case demands it, or of course where it is ordered by the court or demanded by a prosecutor or government agency.

While forensic copying may not be necessary in all cases, the decision on what copying methods and tools to use is one that should be explicitly considered and rationalized.

After a forensic duplicate is made, the original should be tagged with a summary of the logged information, and/or with an identifier that ties it back to the evidence log, using a combination of written tagging on the evidence bag and a bar code. The evidence should be placed in a sealed bag and placed in an environment with limited access and with protection from damage.

A unique electronic fingerprint of the evidence should be made using a non-destructive tool that creates a hash or hash value, which enables verification that the original evidence was not altered from that point forward and that duplicates of the media are truly identical.

The hash of the original media should be compared to the MD5 hash of the duplicate media, a step documented by most media copying hardware. The receipt document generated by the hardware should be kept with the original evidence and a copy kept with the duplicate media.

In addition, as part of the forensic duplication process, it is a best practice to create a hash of every file and .pst. When .pst or other compilation-type files are separated into messages or smaller segments, a hash should be created for every message or segment. This process confirms that future duplicates have not been altered and enables native-file productions to be tracked.

If files are put into a new tool or environment, a sample of the files should be re-hashed or re-fingerprinted to confirm that they remain identical.

In native-format productions where an exchange of information is being provided instead of an exchange of paper or .tiff images, it is important to perform one final MD5 hash of all files produced and received. The indices of these hashes can determine the source of the file. See Chapter 19, Forensic Considerations, for additional information regarding hashing.

## § 18.04 CUSTODIAN AND KEY PERSON INTERVIEWS

Interviews are conducted with potential and known custodians who may be fact witnesses, and other key persons, such as IT personnel who may or may not be fact witnesses, as part of the process to identify ESI potentially responsive to impending or actual litigation. When conducting such interviews it is often important to cover the following topics in relation to the specific time period of interest in an effort to gain a comprehensive view of potential ESI sources.

In this list, "person" refers to a custodian or key person as may be appropriate for the specific situation.

- Administrator-level access privileges
- Backups of the person's mailboxes and file systems
- Databases to which the person had access and all database entries created, modified, or deleted by the person
- Email distribution lists of which the person was a member
- Employees who worked with or in proximity to the person
- ESI within categories of ESI associated with the person, such as certain customers, sales reps, financial information, legal information, for example, and any changes to that ESI
- Fixed and mobile computing and storage devices used or accessed by the person—cell phones, PDAs, PCs, laptops, flash drives, with configuration and software installed
- Identities, including alias for all access to all systems—email, mailboxes, collaboration systems, applications, and the Internet
- Individuals with access to the person's mailboxes
- Listings of any custom software used by the company/person
- Listings of changes or moves related to passwords, aliases, mailbox moves, and/or migrations
- Listings of commercial off-the-shelf applications used by the company/person
- Messaging backups and logs for the person
- Network file shares accessible to the person and all files created, modified, backed up, or deleted by the person

- Printers accessed and/or shared by the person
- Public folders or collaborative objects to which the person had access
- Security groups in which the person was involved
- Third parties that worked with or in proximity to the person
- Tools and procedures used during database or system maintenance to accomplish changes or moves
- Voice mail system backups and logs for the person

## § 18.05 DATA SAMPLING

Data sampling is a technique whereby a statistically representative portion of ESI is examined to determine if and how much responsive information a body of ESI may contain. Data sampling is often used to avoid objections by either party, especially when discovery involves a large number of backup tapes, which are more expensive and time-consuming to analyze than other media such as hard drives, and the process can become extremely burdensome and costly.

In addition, data sampling can help narrow the discovery focus, for example, by determining whether there are time periods in which relevant documents do not exist. This makes it unnecessary to process or review that particular document set. Both parties should agree to use a court-approved statistical sampling protocol.

## § 18.06 METRICS AND MEASUREMENT

Because of the complexity and dynamic nature of the e-Discovery process, it is extremely difficult to reliably determine volumes, hours, and schedules required for any given project. However, estimates are required for a variety of reasons, not the least of which is the requirement of proposing a schedule to the court. Accordingly, a typical approach is to attempt to derive estimates by parsing ESI in various dimensions within the lifecycle process—for example:

1. Determine the volume of responsive ESI to be collected by specific source—disk, tapes, etc.
2. Determine the volume within each category by type of ESI—email, application, non-printable, database, etc.
3. Determine the number of documents within each type of ESI.
4. Estimate the amount of hours and schedule for **collection** for each document set within each type within each source category.
5. Estimate the amount of hours and schedule for **processing** for each document set within each type within each source category.
6. Apply a rough estimate of the percentage reduction due to deduplication and culling during the processing phase.
7. Estimate the amount of hours and schedule for **reviewing** for each document set within each type category. (Source category no longer applies.)
8. Apply a rough estimate of the percentage reduction due to deduplication and culling during the review phase.
9. Estimate the amount of hours and schedule for **production** for each document set within each type category.
10. Using the estimated raw hours within each e-Discovery phase and the available headcount hours for that phase calculate the calendar time required to complete each phase. Place the time frames derived in

sequence to derive the total calendar time. Adjust this initial estimate in accord with experience and other judgments.

11. Revise the estimates as necessary during and after each e-Discovery phase.

Estimating e-Discovery costs is rarely achievable with accuracy merely through application of mathematical algorithms or formulae. Instead, there inevitably will be elements of human judgment entering the cost estimate equation that are likely to be more or less accurate based on the expertise and experience of the individual(s) making those judgments. Estimates posited in ranges rather than as absolute numbers are more realistic.

In most cases, the ideal approach in terms of developing a discovery schedule is for the parties to agree early on regarding the estimating method to be employed, although in many situations estimating is done without enough knowledge about the ESI sources to be precisely accurate. It is important in those situations for the client to understand what variables or factors will most heavily influence changes in the actual timing and cost.

## § 18.07 QUALITY CONTROL

Discovered ESI is potential evidence and must be processed with a high degree of quality control to ensure that tasks are being performed in accord with standards, are producing expected results, and are not causing spoliation or other problems. For example, a quality control process might include identifying:

- password protected or encrypted files that could not be searched;
- containers that could not be expanded (for example, Zip/rar files, PSTs, etc.), which may have a large number of documents within them that were not processed;
- documents that encountered indexing errors, which is common with PDFs or protected Excel workbooks (these items cannot be keyword searched (or require a separate OCR process);
- documents with long file path errors (documents with path lengths longer than 255 characters that Windows cannot access during a review);
- containers that require manual conversion prior to processing (certain file types cannot be processed by certain tools);
- documents where the file header does not match the extension, which indicates documents that have been renamed; most review tools base processing on the header, but some still filter based on extension only.

In addition, quality control reporting keeps stakeholders informed by confirming that processes are producing expected results, and is indicating exceptions, such as those identified above, that might produce unexpected results.

Quality control involves a combination of automated and manual controls. For example, automation tools can flag files as containing a disproportionately high number of binary characters or size thresholds. Once the files are flagged, they can then be subject to visual inspection as the rest of the collection is processing, then integrated back into the collection. Another example of automated quality control includes file count checks at each stage of the process to account for all information.

## § 18.08 CODING MANUAL

A Coding Manual can greatly assist the review process by defining its objectives, delineating its scope, and establishing rules for the review team. Coding Manuals typically include rules that cover topics such as the following examples:

- Adding annotations to documents in the form of attorney notes and work product
- Coding and tagging emails, their attachments, and email threads

- Handling of documents requiring redaction
- Handling unreadable, password-protected, or other faulty documents
- Identification and subjective coding and tagging of responsive and producible documents
- Identification and tagging of non-responsive documents, spam, and junk email
- Identifying and coding or tagging privileged documents
- Identifying and handling confidentiality issues
- Providing additional bibliographic information to the database

In addition, Coding Manuals provide lookup tables such as those used to aid in identification of key players and known entities.

## § 18.09 SECURITY

Security is the process of protecting ESI from accidental or intended alteration or destruction, restricting access to ESI, or segregating one body of ESI from another. Security is achieved automatically through embedded IT infrastructure or e-Discovery software security systems and/or manually through the efforts of custodians. Security measures must be communicated to practitioners to be effective, and audited daily via automated logs to ensure compliance.

Preservation, chain-of-custody, and protection of privileged work product dictate that management develop policies and procedures and apply technology that achieves these security related objectives. These security measures include:

- Auditable access and usage session tracking by users, applications, databases, and files
- Auditable identity and authentication log-in and access controls at the network, workstation, application, database, and file level
- Data and file encryption
- Role-based limitations on users

CHAPTER 19

# FORENSIC CONSIDERATIONS

## § 19.01 INTRODUCTION AND BACKGROUND

For e-Discovery, computer forensics relates to the science and art of examining and retrieving ESI from technology devices and their associated storage devices, and the Internet, using methods validated by legal authorities and designed to facilitate the admissibility of evidence.

Discovery and extraction of ESI often requires working with computers and other information technology, and related storage devices that require special handling where there is risk of ESI being inadvertently or purposefully altered or destroyed, or because certain ESI can only be extracted using special forensics techniques.

Contents of storage media may be compromised because the media has degraded, has been damaged, or some or all of the content has been deleted accidentally or on purpose by reformatting, repartitioning, reimaging, or using specialized software to perform thorough overwrites. Metadata may be altered by merely moving a file to a new location, as is done using common copying utilities. Refer to Chapter 6, Native Files and Metadata, for more information on spoliation of metadata.

However, most computers do not remove the contents of a file when it is deleted, either when deleted manually by users or automatically by the system. In most operating systems, the contents of the file remain on the storage medium, while information about the file is removed from the file system directory. In some systems, even much of the metadata remains. ESI will remain on the storage medium until the operating system reuses (overwrites) the space for new data. Even when extreme attempts have been made to delete content, or the storage media has been severely damaged, forensics experts have been able to recover substantial evidence.

An exact copy of a system and all its ESI might be considered an ideal situation for e-Discovery practitioners, but is impossible in conditions that most companies must operate under. Consequently most ESI resides in systems undergoing automatic operations that can potentially disturb relevant information. In addition, normal user operations such as opening files, copying files, sending and receiving files, or turning a computer on or off can compromise metadata ESI.

As discussed in Chapter 18, Standards and Best Practices, litigation holds and preservation requirements address a portion of this issue by requiring that potentially relevant ESI be safely stored, preferably so that it is not accessible for alteration.

Where forensics intervention is required, a system or device may have to be powered off, and a mirror image created that can be analyzed "offline" from a system that must continue operating. In those cases where ESI can only be captured from live systems, it may be necessary to only capture partial content from operating servers.

Forensic experts and e-Discovery practitioners are guided in any particular ESI acquisition situation by the circumstances and requirements of that particular situation, such as agreements reached among the parties, relevance and importance of ESI, cost and time constraints, potential business interruption issues, and claims of privilege.

Aside from these circumstances and requirements, forensic experts and e-Discovery practitioners need to be able to represent that they have taken all reasonable steps to ensure that all captured content has been preserved unaltered.

Computer forensics is conducted in four phases—Identification of Sources, Acquisition and Preservation, Analysis, and Presentation of Findings. In addition, documentation is a function that spans all phases, as complete documentation is essential to substantiation of proper procedure. Forensics is an inherent part of the overall e-Discovery process as discussed in the following chapters of this Part 3.

## § 19.02 ISSUES AND CONCERNS

It is possible that some potential sources of ESI are disregarded simply because employees believe that potential relevant content has been deleted or that the storage medium has been damaged, is degraded, or is otherwise not accessible due to issues such as equipment incompatibility.

However, because of the demonstrated success of forensics experts, **all media** (including via the Internet) must be considered as potential sources of ESI until mutually determined otherwise by the parties or the court.

Because of budget or other constraints, some companies may attempt to perform computer forensics using internal IT staff familiar with information or network security. There are some important issues to consider before doing so. IT staff do not usually have the in-depth knowledge, experience, or tools to properly perform computer forensics. Handling ESI for purposes of legal proceedings is a specialized field with specialized technology. IT staff may also not have the time to conduct e-Discovery given their other commitments to ensure the IT operations of the business. In addition, they are not independent, and accordingly the original evidence is being handled by a party with an interest in its contents.

## § 19.03 RECOMMENDATIONS

Organizations seeking to handle collections internally will need to devote significant resources to training and dedicating personnel to perform computer forensics. A significant investment will also be required in the software and hardware tools necessary to handle ESI properly from an evidentiary standpoint. However, in many litigations, less expensive methods of collection may be acceptable. The enterprise needs to assess its appetite for risk based on the adversary, the nature of the threat, and the potential exposure to the business in terms of reputation and monetary liability.

## Chapter 20

# SEARCH AND RETRIEVAL CONSIDERATIONS

## § 20.01 INTRODUCTION[1]

Search is an iterative process inherent in the effective execution of the identification, collection, processing, culling, and review phases. It is the key process for reducing the initial universe of ESI down to a smaller set of relevant and producible documents.

Because of the complexity of most IT infrastructures and the volume of potential ESI, the only effective way to perform search is through application of automated tools. Search software tools provide techniques that enable reduction of ESI based on selected criteria.

The effective acquisition of ESI requires diligent planning for maximum effectiveness. As indicated in Part 2, Sources of Electronically Stored Information, there are a large number of complex considerations related to storage of ESI. In addition, as indicated in Standards and Best Practices, in Chapter 18, there are many requirements imposed on processes involving search and filtering. Accordingly, search and filtering is one of the major planning components within e-Discovery project management.

## § 20.02 SEARCH TECHNIQUES

There are a number of considerations related to conducting searches, including the scope of the search, the objectives of the person performing the search, the search criteria used, the capabilities of the software, and the interpretations of the results of the search. The legal team should work with someone thoroughly knowledgeable about the search protocols and tools and their application to the sources under consideration. It may be necessary later in the legal process to provide affidavits certifying the accuracy and comprehensiveness of the search methods employed.

The most common approach to searching is through use of keywords. This is a simple method in which a person enters selected words into a text field of the search program, the search program searches through a list of documents, and returns a list of those documents containing the search terms that were entered. Keyword searching can be effective in minimizing the amount of producible records, which can in turn reduce the cost of generating a reviewing database. Keyword searching identifies documents in which a search term appears, but cannot determine the relevance of the document to the subject being researched. In addition, keyword searches must rely solely on the specificity of the terms used in the search, and cannot "learn" through use. Because of inherent limitations, keyword searching tends to return more documents than necessary in some situations and fewer in other situations, and consequently, should be used in conjunction with other search techniques.

There are a variety of search techniques that expand on simple key word searches to provide more robust and useful search results. Some of these techniques are used during the collection phase, and some are more appropriate during the processing phase and the review and analysis phase. An overview of common search techniques is presented below. Also see Chapter 29, e-Discovery Technology and Tools, for more information on search tools.

- Boolean searches include limiting operators ("AND," "OR," "NOT") and proximity operators ("NEAR," "WITHIN," "PRE") that provide the ability to achieve considerable refinement of searches.
- Clustering uses techniques to reconcile disparate documents so they can be intelligently analyzed to gain content insight and context that enables grouping according to a coherent relevance among all documents. Clustering often uses visual techniques to aid in various functions of the search process.
- Conceptual searches accept content such as a sentence, paragraph, body of an email, or page of text, for example, and return references to conceptually related documents ranked by relevance or contextual distance, which are then used to generate automatic hyperlinks between pieces of content. Conceptual searches use a variety of methods, such as contextual usages, algebraic modeling, and probabilistic categories.

---

[1] Although this chapter is focused on and uses the term "Search," it is recognized that "Filtering" is a subset or form of search that is also used in the identification, collection, processing, culling, and review phases.

- Contextual searches associate terms with other information in which the terms are used, such as "social security number" only within the context of "insurance application."
- Correlation searches find relationships among various criteria. For example, finding those emails authored by Joe on a computer other than the one assigned to him, but sent to Jane and Mary between two dates.
- Filtering is an approach that limits search to specific parameters, such as a date and time range, or a specific term such as a key Custodian, for example.
- Fuzzy searches create a list of results based on likely relevance, enabling users to find matching keywords even if the word being searched is misspelled.
- Noise words are common words, such as such as "the," "and," "of," "is," and "are," that are optionally ignored by indexing or search engines as a way of simplifying search and making it more efficient.
- Privilege searching locates information from custodians such as in-house counsel, who are likely to maintain privileged information.
- Stemming is a linguistic analysis process that compares the root forms of a search word and returns documents that contain words that derive from a common stem, such as "help," "helping," and "helps."

## § 20.03 ISSUES AND CONCERNS

Although electronic search techniques and search technology can be highly effective and in any event are necessary given the staggering volume of ESI, human error in implementing searches is always possible, and search results should be evaluated in terms of completeness, accuracy, and relevance. Flawed searches can create issues potentially harmful to the producing party, including providing a basis for motions to compel production and motions for evidence spoliation.

The most common causes of search problems include:

- Acceptance of search results or collected documents without validating the search criteria or document collection methods. For example, document creation dates could be in error because of an improperly set system clock, or improper document retrieval methods.
- Erroneous structuring of queries, filters, and search criteria. For example, specifying a "creation date" when "revision date" is the criteria most relevant to the search purpose.
- Excluding potential sources of ESI in the search. This could include any number of storage devices overlooked for one reason or another, for example, because the search tool is not able to search certain types of files. It could also include improper configuration of search engines to exclude metadata or certain classes of ESI.
- Failure to understand the language of the creators of documents—their abbreviations, acronyms, short hand, slang, and other usage particular to the creator's job context.
- Inability of the search software or tool to scale in response to large volumes of ESI or to perform federated searching.
- Inability to recognize changes in case requirements, and therefore failure to revise search criteria to meet new requirements.
- Structuring searches that are too broad, inadvertently over burdening downstream processes, and potentially compromising case results.

## § 20.04 RECOMMENDATIONS

Search of ESI can only be performed with software, and there are hundreds of software vendors offering search tools, ranging from using the "Find" function in Microsoft Word, to sophisticated enterprise data mining software suites that probe terabytes of ESI for hidden meaning and relationships.

Within e-Discovery, search is typically not a standalone function. Instead, search is more effectively applied in conjunction with other processes that allow users to interact with results of the search to achieve complementary objectives. For example, a search for the emails of a particular custodian might be followed by placing those emails in a secure e-Discovery repository, or channeling them through workflow software to a function that could extract attachments and metadata.

Because of this need for integration of processes, it is prudent to consider e-Discovery software suites that address other needs in addition to search.

The bottom line is that, like many other aspects of the e-Discovery process, search is a complex function requiring considerable expertise to perform effectively.

CHAPTER 21

# PREPARATION AND PRESERVATION

Subsequent to known pending or actual litigation, an identification process is conducted that enables company principals and counsel to identify ESI custodians and locations of all ESI potentially relevant to the matter that may be disclosed during litigation. During identification, key company personnel are identified, relevant documents and information are cataloged, the sources and locations of this information are established, and a litigation hold is drafted and distributed.

## § 21.01 IDENTIFICATION

The scope of the identification process generally encompasses time frames, custodians, and responsive information by category, type, or subject matter.

Where possible, reviewing relevant pleadings and discovery requests can establish the relevant time period for the litigation, and these dates can assist in finding, cataloging, and culling relevant information. Often, where identification is required in advance of such documents, other methods must be employed. Factual investigation including interviews of key witnesses may be indicated.

Identifying the key corporate personnel early in the process is essential to effective discovery. In most cases, these players are identified by opposing parties, although requesting parties may be reluctant to limit a search, for fear that responsive information may be missed.

When identifying key witnesses and custodians, it is important to decide if the process should be based on department, geography, job function, or other criteria. In addition to specific individuals, entire departments or divisions may be deemed responsible for subject matters, such as contracts or specific projects, identified in a document request.

The types of information relevant to the litigation must be identified, and a decision made as to whether all other types may be excluded from a search. The type of document may also be established and can be negotiated during the meet-and-confer process.

## § 21.02 LITIGATION HOLD

### [A] Determination to Trigger Litigation Hold

In general, the legal duty to preserve relevant information (ESI and paper) arises when a party anticipates or knows that the information is or may be relevant to anticipated or pending litigation or regulatory or government investigation. Accordingly, the actual filing of a lawsuit or issuance of a subpoena is the latest point that the preservation obligation is triggered. This means that, in connection with the early attention to electronic discovery required under the revised FRCP, the "meet and confer" under Rule 26(f) is likely to be an opportunity for an adversary to assess compliance with preservation duties. Accordingly, while negotiation with an adversary may resolve preservation protocols going forward, in terms of historical responses to preservation duties the 26(f) conference occurs too late to be of any help.

The first step for a party faced with facts that may give rise to a legal preservation obligation is to assess whether a litigation hold should be initiated. This is essentially a legal judgment made based on available facts and circumstances. Procedurally, entities need to do what they can to make sure that such facts and circumstances are reported to people in the organization (or outside advisors) who have been designated to handle the assessment of whether a preservation obligation has been triggered, and if so what steps are necessary to implement a litigation hold. In contemplation of the possible subsequent need to justify these decisions, they should be documented along with their supporting rationale in a manner that preserves applicable legal privileges.

### [B] Implementation and Compliance of the Hold

Once a litigation hold has been decreed by the appropriate decision makers, all custodians of potentially relevant information are identified, along with other pertinent information defining the parameters of the hold, such as, for example, types of documents, subject matters, and date ranges. Once custodians are identified, the litigation hold notice is issued, usually by the legal or compliance staff, to the applicable custodians to instruct them regarding the nature and scope of information under their control. In addition, the IT organization must be provided with a list of custodians who are subject to the hold in order to ensure that any routine deletion of ESI from electronic information systems is suspended for the applicable custodians. Note that in certain cases, primarily where a large number of custodians are involved, an entity may choose to issue hold notices to managers or supervisors of custodians for further "down the chain" implementation rather than sending a notice to each and every potential custodian.

The litigation hold is designed to preserve all documents and information that may be relevant to the legal proceeding or investigation. It may require a company to immediately freeze its usual document management and disposal efforts. Handling a hold effectively and in conformity with the dictates of the case law in this area requires regular monitoring, updating, and reissuance of the litigation hold notice. This process can be complicated by custodians and information uncovered subsequent to the issuance of the original hold notice, as well as by changes in the litigation scenario such as the addition of claims or defenses. Accordingly, developing a process for managing this ongoing hold activity is essential.

Technical solutions are beginning to emerge that facilitate management of the hold process. For enterprises with multiple ongoing holds involving a variety of custodians and systems, automating the parts of the process that can be automated (such as recording confirmations of receipt of hold notices) or at least using the best available means of managing the hold process is prudent. Using the old method of having a paralegal manually update a table or spreadsheet can be risky. Going forward, adversaries are likely to point to the availability of technical aids to the hold process as a reason why "human error" claims of inadvertent spoliation should be viewed with skepticism by the courts.

### [C] Technology Issues

Typical technology issues involved in legal hold implementation include:

- The importance of timing because of routine operation of information systems that deletes information;
- The viability of sending out and following up on hold notices by email;
- Requiring of confirmation of receipt from recipients and tracking the progress of steps to carry out the hold;
- The impact of removing backup tapes from the routine recycling, overwriting, or destruction process;
- The automated implementation of holds across various systems, whether unstructured or semi-structured content repositories, application databases, or database archive environments;
- Whether collection is the best or most appropriate method of hold implementation under the facts and circumstances presented;
- Stopping "auto-delete" functions; and
- Ensuring that all ESI sources are properly identified and addressed, including online, near-line, and offline servers and storage devices.

## § 21.03 PRESERVATION NOTICES AND LETTERS

Companies entering a contested matter, such as litigation or investigation, have a clearly established duty to preserve evidence regardless of whether it is supportive or detrimental to the company's legal position. Typically, witnesses, non-parties, and adverse parties in such cases are notified of duties to preserve through the Preservation Notice and the Preservation Letter.

### [A] Preservation Notices

Witnesses or non-parties to litigation may be in possession of relevant materials and may be subject to preservation obligations. One of the key elements of a sound litigation hold procedure involves the distribution of hold notices to those custodians. These hold notices should require suspension of the normal disposition or processing of potentially relevant information.

Preservation notices often precede the issuance of a formal legal demand for the production of the needed items. While the content of preservation notices will vary from case to case, they should be consistent where there is no reason for revision. The key to effective preservation notices is simplicity and clarity, because notices that are difficult to understand or take too long for employees to read hinder compliance. Elements of successful hold notices include without limitation a brief description of the subject matter and date range of the target information, an indication that any location or medium of storage is included, instructions for the custodian to ensure compliance, and a resource to contact with questions.

### [B] Preservation Letters

The preservation letter is basically the same as the preservation notice, except that the preservation letter is issued to an adverse party from which a litigant expects to seek information.

The fundamental purpose of the preservation letter is to educate the recipient about the varieties of relevant electronic evidence which may exist and the importance of taking prompt, affirmative steps to discontinue routine document destruction practices, to place a hold on all relevant materials, and to ensure that evidence remains accessible.

Enough specificity should be used to prevent ignorance from being used as a defense. However, it is important that the request not be overbroad. Accordingly, the request should address only those documents important or relevant to the case. Preservation letters are often viewed as an invitation to negotiate, and an overly broad letter can be seen as a bad faith litigation tactic.

## § 21.04 PRESERVATION

The objectives of preservation are to preserve and prevent spoliation of potentially relevant ESI. Accordingly, timely affirmative action is required by individuals throughout the organization, and by third parties that may be in possession of ESI, to not only identify potential sources of ESI, but to also prevent loss or alteration of potential ESI.

Actions to prevent loss or alteration of potential ESI include preventing any manual or automated system operations such as:

- Using any software, hardware, or other means that might cause the overwriting, erasing, alteration, concealment, discarding, or destruction of any online, offline, removable, or hosted storage media and its content (including metadata and native files), or that might make the media content inaccessible;
- Disabling any process that might prevent the normal logging of any form of transaction related to any form of ESI, including, but not limited to, emails, messaging, file activity, database activity, and Web activity;
- Reassigning, altering, or disabling passwords, user authentication, document certificates, or any other form of custodian, user, and ESI identification and access capability; and
- Altering or preventing access to any desktop or portable computing or communication device that might contain potential ESI.

In addition, preservation of ESI requires affirmative action that includes:

- Establishment of a secure repository for housing collected ESI;
- Preservation of archival and backup media, including differential and incremental backups;
- Preservation of the content for specified individuals that may be stored on email and file servers, desktop and laptop computers, portable devices, removable media, and in online accounts;

- Forensic imaging and/or removal from service and securely impounding selected computing and storage devices and media related to designated individuals; and
- Preservation of tangible items that may be required to access, interpret, or search potentially relevant ESI, including logs, control documents, specifications, indices, naming protocols, file lists, network diagrams, flow charts, instructions, data entry forms, abbreviations, user IDs, passwords, authentication keys, encryption keys, license keys, installation disks, user manuals, software drivers, network components, and other legacy or proprietary media or devices required to access potential ESI.

## § 21.05 MEET-AND-CONFER

Once a legal hold is issued, opposing counsel must meet in accord with Amended Rules 26 (f) and 16 in order to make best efforts to reach agreement on a mutually acceptable Discovery Plan. This requires parties to discuss any issues relating to disclosure or discovery of ESI, including:

- What information each party has in electronic form and where that information resides, including archival or backup tapes and legacy systems;
- Whether any potentially relevant information has been deleted;
- Any anticipated problems in retrieving or producing information;
- The format, media, and schedule for production;
- The cost and reallocation of costs of producing the information;
- The responsibilities of each party to preserve ESI; and
- Discussion of issues related to claims of privilege or work product protection as trial-preparation material.

A successful meet-and-confer process depends heavily on how knowledgeable the attorneys are regarding their client's IT infrastructure. It is especially important for attorneys to know what information is available, how it might be changed by routine operations, and how it can be retrieved and produced in a timely, cost effective manner. Accordingly, attorneys are well advised to gain this knowledge well in advance of the Rule 26 conference.

The conference and order under Rule 16 provide early opportunity for the court to discuss, memorialize, and resolve any disputes related to the agreements or shared understandings the parties may have reached in their Rule 26 conference. In addition, Amended Rule 16(b) provides that scheduling orders may include provisions for disclosure or discovery of ESI and any agreements the parties reach for asserting claims of privilege or of protection as trial-preparation material after production.

Rule 26(a)(1) requires disclosure of the identities of individuals likely to have discoverable information, as well as a copy of, or a description by category and location, of all ESI that the disclosing party may use to support its claims or defenses. These disclosures must be made within 21 days after the Rule 26 conference unless a different time is set by stipulation or court order.

Determining the scope of disclosure and discovery is one of the most important aspects related to discovery of ESI, and potentially one of the most contentious for resolution among the parties, especially when an attempt is made by one party to use "scope" as a weapon against the other party. Accordingly, it is important for both parties to understand the intent of the court under Rules 26(b)(1) and 26(b)(2), especially the "principles of proportionality" and the tools available to the court in making a determination as to whether or not ESI is "reasonably accessible."

The meet-and-confer process is, by intent of the courts and the economic necessity of the parties, evolving into a collaborative, rather than combative, approach to discovery, with both sides working together to limit the costs and burdens of electronic discovery. A thorough understanding of client systems can help facilitate this, as can an understanding of the challenges that production of electronic documents imposes.

Attorneys have different philosophies about when to have experts present or absent for conferences with opposing counsel or the court. However, it would be hard to contradict the notion that it is prudent to have an e-Discovery expert available for consultation to determine that agreements are both feasible and appropriate. For example, specifying that "all deleted files" must be recovered for discovery may seem a straightforward order, but this sort of overly broad directive can lead to escalating costs. It is better to have an expert available to guide the process and offer appropriate, cost-effective strategies and solutions.

Last, the collaborative communication between opposing parties can be a persuasive demonstration of the intent to fulfill the duty to preserve electronic evidence.

## §21.06 DISCOVERY STRATEGY AND PROJECT PLAN

Following a tentative agreement or understanding reached and communicated in the Discovery Plan developed under the Rule 26 conference, the parties should finalize their respective "Discovery Strategy and Project Plan" for execution under Phases 2 through 5. As stated before and as illustrated in Figure (1), these phases are iterative and highly dynamic. These phases also typically involve high volumes of information acted upon within constrained time frames using limited resources. Accordingly, these phases require experts and use of a variety of ESI discovery software tools designed to automate certain tasks. Therefore, a discovery strategy should include provision for these special resources.

## §21.07 ISSUES AND CONCERNS

The initial response to a litigation matter is the single most critical issue facing both parties; simply because the initial response may have the potential to inordinately impact the e-Discovery and litigation process throughout the remaining phases.

As implied in this chapter, the initial response includes a number of important components.

- Knowledge and understanding of the case itself
- Effectiveness of the litigation hold
- Knowledge and understanding of the IT infrastructure
- Ability to negotiate and develop e-Discovery strategies
- Ability to leverage the appropriate resources

## §21.08 RECOMMENDATIONS

Readers of this book have the opportunity to begin implementing the recommendations outlined in the next Part, Discovery Readiness Planning. However, in the interim, the following recommendations should be considered:

1. Perform a quick, initial assessment of how much documented information and staff expertise exists within the organization regarding the IT infrastructure, the e-Discovery process, and compliance requirements and capabilities.
2. Assemble a multi-disciplinary e-Discovery Response Team that includes individuals knowledgeable as to legal issues, as well as those knowledgeable about technical issues.
3. Develop an Information Asset Inventory.
4. Ensure that the litigation hold is effectively implemented.
5. Develop an initial e-Discovery strategy in advance of the "meet-and-confer" conference.
6. Refine the e-Discovery Strategy and Project Plan following the conference.

## CHAPTER 22

# QUICK WALKTHROUGH OF THE e-DISCOVERY PROCESS

The e-Discovery process begins with some degree of preparation in anticipation of an investigation or litigation matter and ends with production of relevant material and presentation to the investigating entity or before the court at trial. Accordingly, the overarching goal of e-Discovery is to satisfy legal requirements. However, effective discovery of ESI is largely dependent on information technology, which places a high degree of reliance on technical resources, both human and system.

In most organizations, the IT infrastructure is designed and optimized to satisfy business objectives, not e-Discovery. This divergence creates a number of gaps that make the e-Discovery process difficult for all concerned, starting with the need to identify potentially responsive ESI. Therefore, the first priority in the e-Discovery process is to gain an understanding of IT and the sources of ESI.

When an impending or actual investigation or litigation matter is first known, the company typically brings together an existing Litigation Response Team or appoints an e-Discovery Project Manager who forms a team of stakeholders to plan and execute their response.

Usually, there are no system or information maps with sufficient detail to discern how ESI is generated and stored, and so the team must conduct rigorous interviews with IT staff and likely custodians in order to uncover the information required. This interview process requires interviewers with both IT and e-Discovery expertise and experience in order to anticipate questions required, understand and interpret answers, and advise regarding the potential issues related to each unique situation. Interviews usually focus on moving from gaining *general* insights to gaining *detailed* insights as the process unfolds. Examples of typical interview topics covered include:

- Applications: What do they do, where is their ESI, who uses them, what are the workflows
- Auditing: What is audited, what are the audit requirements, exceptions
- Compliance: What are the compliance requirements, internal, regulatory, how are they enforced
- Computing and Mobile Devices: Where are they, what is the ESI on them, who uses them, what is their configuration
- Controls: What are the controls, how are they enforced, monitored
- Custodians: Who are they, what are their roles, what are their account privileges, passwords
- Databases: Where, specifications, ESI as report, dataset or extracted tables with redacted records
- Electronic Messaging and Telephony: What are the systems used, how are they archived, how can they be collected, what are the storage sizes
- ESI: What are the file types, how is ESI classified, what are the "big bucket" categories, what are the storage sizes
- Preservation: What safeguards are in place/required
- Records Retention: What are the policies and procedures, are they enforced
- Servers: Where are they, what is ESI on them, what are the file sizes, who are the users, what is the profile of each user account

- Storage Devices: Where are they, what is the ESI on them, what is the storage size, what are the protocols, what are the retrieval methods
- Time Frames: Relevant to the current matter, for backups, for archives

Once the interviews are conducted and assessed, the team conducts a high-level automated search to confirm locations and scope of ESI, initiates a litigation hold, and develops a preliminary e-Discovery Plan in preparation for the meet-and-confer with opposing counsel.

The litigation hold is communicated verbally and in writing throughout the organization, and is monitored and reinforced throughout the lifecycle of the litigation matter. Litigation holds are case specific, and accommodate the unique requirements of individual cases that may be active concurrently.

Following the meet-and-confer, the organization develops a detailed e-Discovery Strategy and Project Plan that defines resources, schedules, deliverables, and constraints applicable throughout the e-Discovery lifecycle. The e-Discovery Project Plan is typically structured to accommodate a strategy, such as addressing higher priorities first, or "big bucket" items such as email first.

Once the Strategy and e-Discovery Project Plan is in place, the organization conducts a more refined search and filtering process to further identify and collect responsive ESI.

The conduct and documentation of the collection process should be guided by applicable rules of evidence. The observance of rigorous "Chain-of-Custody" procedures will support the admissibility requirements necessary to use the ESI effectively at trial or hearing. Adherence to these protocols throughout the e-Discovery lifecycle requires expertise in the form of the knowledge and skills required to safely collect ESI from specific devices without risk of spoliation.

In a typical situation for example, a third-party expert might image all mobile devices and selected computers, while a service bureau specialist might index and restore tapes in accord with defined time frames. The internal team would continue to collect files, email, and database ESI from the remaining sources.

The collection phase and the remainder of e-Discovery phases are facilitated through automation by software packages that range in scope from single-purpose tools to software suites that integrate almost all of the e-Discovery functions under one platform. These software tools help ensure that chain-of-custody is maintained, that all documents are properly marked with unique identifiers, that audit logging is maintained, and that performance reports are generated.

As collection continues, the collected ESI is processed through further refinements intended to eliminate non-relevant documents, reduce the volume of documents, and improve the efficiency of physical review. This processing and culling includes:

- Deduplication and near-deduplication
- Enhanced search and filtering
- Extraction of emails/attachments and Zip files from container files
- Extraction of metadata from native files and creation of indices and file links
- OCR processing to capture text from images
- PDF and TIFF processing to convert documents to images
- Creation of files for loading into a review platform

As documents are collected and culled, some are converted to image formats, such as TIFF or PDF since these formats are considered less susceptible to alteration and can be used for both review and production. Because these files generally do not themselves contain metadata, for organization into a database and enhanced ability to search, they are often accompanied by files containing the text of the document and/or metadata (load files) and may in some instances be connected to copies of the files themselves.

An alternative to converting electronic documents to images prior to review is to perform an initial review of documents in their native format after the metadata has been preserved and linked via a read-only format to the document. If a converted format is preferred for production, this approach enables the review team to only convert what is relevant, non-privileged, or otherwise to be produced.

Many search programs and e-Discovery review programs provide generic viewers that convert native documents to plain HTML format so they may be viewed within any browser. Keeping documents in native format can save money by avoiding image conversion costs. Native formats also allow reviewers to see information that may not appear in some types of images, such as tracked changes, formulas, and hidden rows or columns.

As the processing and culling process continues, high priority or big-bucket document sets, identified earlier in strategic planning sessions, are made ready and staged for the review and analysis process. Some of the considerations related to priorities include:

- Key legal issues and deadlines with internal and opposing counsel, and the court
- Data considered most critical to the case
- Important key positions, departments, and custodians
- The level of accessibility of ESI
- Team limitations such as availability, domain knowledge, foreign language skills, and legal or technical expertise
- Availability of e-Discovery technology or third-party services

At the most basic level, the review and analysis process is designed to determine what documents to produce, what documents not to produce, and the reasons for each. It also involves determining which documents will be designated as privileged and why, as well as identifying documents to be used for specific purposes, such as certain witness examinations or motion papers.

The review and analysis process may involve a higher degree of sophisticated search and filtering refinements—visualization, clustering, navigation, topic mapping, social network mapping, contextual mapping—as well as coding and sampling techniques to gain insights into relevancy and case assessment. In addition, requirements such as annotations and redaction are accomplished in preparation for final production.

Completion of the review and analysis phase results in document sets that are ready for production, a technical process that typically involves storing the documents on portable media and creating a load file for the requesting party's document review platform.

Following production, the trial preparation and presentation functions are accomplished using systems to seamlessly integrate documents, transcripts, photographs, animations, deposition videos, and demonstrative graphics into a trial preparation and presentation tool.

CHAPTER 23

# GENERAL ISSUES AND RECOMMENDATIONS

As discussed in the previous chapters, there are issues and concerns unique to each function within the e-Discovery process. The issues and recommendations presented in this chapter, however, are more general in nature, are interrelated, and have broad potential impact. These general issues include:

- Management Commitment and Support
- Cultural Issues
- Education and Training
- Planning
- Methodologies
- Standardization
- e-Discovery Technology

## §23.01 MANAGEMENT COMMITMENT AND SUPPORT

Management commitment and support is paramount for any major initiative within the enterprise. It is especially important for e-Discovery because of the potentially severe consequences of failing to comply with regulatory, statutory, or common law legal duties. In addition, e-Discovery involves everyone in the organization, and so everyone must be on the same page and committed to fulfilling their respective responsibilities.

Regardless of how sophisticated the IT infrastructure or other capabilities within the enterprise, satisfaction of e-Discovery requirements most likely will have some disruptive impact on people and systems. In addition, although proper execution of e-Discovery can significantly reduce overall litigation costs, implementation will incur expenses.

Every organization has internal competition for resources and priority objectives, and e-Discovery will most likely be considered by many as a burden.

Consequently, because of these and other factors unique to each organization, executive management must establish the mandate for e-Discovery, ensure that resources are available, gain support of key stakeholders, and continuously support the process and the people involved.

## §23.02 CULTURAL ISSUES

At best, e-Discovery is a nuisance. At worst, e-Discovery can be an imminent threat of criminal liability to individuals, to organizational units, and even to the company. Combine this range of impact with the propensity for people to retain the status quo, and it is not surprising that e-Discovery often meets with considerable resistance. Such resistance must be overcome or it will impede implementation of best practices and technology solutions critical to success in meeting e-Discovery objectives.

Recognizing these potential cultural issues is difficult. Effectively addressing them is even more difficult. But management must make best efforts, through the internal human resources organization, or through external resources, to ensure that the culture of the organization facilitates e-Discovery compliance.

## §23.03 EDUCATION AND TRAINING

Education and training is one of the best tools for addressing cultural issues. Education and training is also required to address a number of other issues critical to effective e-Discovery. At minimum, management and key personnel should receive education and training in the following areas. Not only will the investment in education and training benefit individuals in these specific areas, it will facilitate better understanding and communication among teams.

- Understanding of Legal Obligations Relating to e-Discovery
- IT Retention Issues Impacting on e-Discovery Obligations (e.g., regular purges of email from live servers)

- Basic Understanding of e-Discovery Lifecycle and Key Functions
- Overview of e-Discovery Technology

## § 23.04 PLANNING

Many e-Discovery projects fall short of requirements or expectations because of inadequate planning. The next Part, e-Discovery Readiness Planning, addresses a number of initiatives for ensuring that the organization is properly prepared to address e-Discovery. But even in the absence of these initiatives, the e-Discovery team must ensure that they understand, and are prepared for, all options related to the particular matter, especially with respect to identification, preservation, and chain-of-custody.

## § 23.05 METHODOLOGIES

Among the most significant recurring problems with respect to methods is the lack of accommodation for iteration in the e-Discovery process. The iterative process enables continued evolution of projects by providing for ways to continually test, analyze, and refine as the project progresses. In e-Discovery, the original parameters set during the preparation phase will undoubtedly change, often in unanticipated ways. For example, this could include expanding the number of custodians of interest, changing date ranges, and challenging assumptions about keywords. For this reason, concluding search and collection efforts early in the process in a manner that does not allow for revisiting could ultimately prove insufficient, overlooking key evidence.

While many e-Discovery technology solutions already accommodate iteration, their ability to do so in practice requires that the e-Discovery team plan for, and be open to, adjusting and balancing their work and workloads in line with the iterative process. To be effective, this requires continuous communication among team leaders and project management.

## § 23.06 STANDARDIZATION

Acceptance of standards by all parties minimizes problems later in projects. Within e-Discovery, standards can cover many functions across the lifecycle, ranging from definition of relevant metadata and search terms to production media formats.

Defining a complete set of standards acceptable to both parties requires patience and negotiation, a process that is unfortunately often compromised by resource and time constraints. For example, not all search software treats "noise" words (prepositions, articles, pronouns, and commonly used adjectives and verbs) the same. This may create problems if both sides do not agree about the final inclusion or exclusion of noise words in the term list, since it may be difficult to renegotiate keywords at a later stage of litigation based on a perceived technological deficiency that could have been addressed earlier. Therefore, it should be recognized that effort devoted to mutually acceptable standards will pay dividends later, which is the policy expressed in the Federal Rules of Civil Procedure, specifically Rule 26(f).

## § 23.07 e-DISCOVERY TECHNOLOGY

Two of the most important concerns related to e-Discovery technology include the assurance that proper technology is in place, and that users understand the technology.

Ensuring that proper e-Discovery technology is available requires a complete assessment and evaluation process, which is covered in the next Part, e-Discovery Readiness Planning.

Addressing the second issue, user understanding of technology, requires an assessment of the skill sets of individual team members. e-Discovery software vendors devote considerable resources to ensuring that their technology is easy to use. However, all technology requires some degree of learning, especially where user independent judgment and discretion are involved.

One way to achieve user training is to enlist the help of the respective technology vendors. Testing user competency can be achieved by executing a mock e-Discovery walkthrough using the applicable technology and a repository of ESI designed for training purposes.

# Part IV

# e-DISCOVERY READINESS PLANNING

CHAPTER 24

# INTRODUCTION

## §24.01 OVERVIEW

Business enterprises and other entities with significant volumes of ESI should strive to remain current and prepared in all respects as electronic discovery requirements evolve through application of emerging technology and continuing interpretation by the courts. While there will always be unforeseen circumstances associated with individual situations, there are certain strategies and programs that can be initiated to ensure that organizations are in the best reasonable position to cost-effectively deal with e-Discovery requirements and simultaneously fulfill their legal and business obligations.

As stated in the Introduction to this book, the authors recognize that most organizations face budgetary and other resource constraints that impose limitations on whether they practically can implement some of the recommendations set forth in this book. This does not mean that the recommendations should not be considered where resource constraints exist. On the contrary, in all situations, the recommendations should be viewed as incremental objectives that can move the organization forward in terms of achieving effective e-Discovery capabilities. Accordingly, each organization should consider the recommendations, set priorities, and establish plans for selective implementation that optimize that organization's respective capabilities.

The strategies and programs discussed in the chapters within this Part cover four foundational components to being well prepared.

- **Guidance and Governance**—Litigation and e-Discovery are cross-functional initiatives that have impact throughout the organization. Preparation for litigation and e-Discovery is a long-term process that must be continuously supported, guided, and governed by senior stakeholders that have ownership in the results.
- **Information Lifecycle Management (ILM)**—The term *Records Management* has traditionally been associated with the formal requirements set forth by regulations and company business policies that dictate what records must be maintained and for how long. Information lifecycle management, within the context of this book, takes a broader interpretation and includes considerations related to all processes affecting information from an e-Discovery perspective—content creation, transformation, communication, storage, retrieval, and effective, efficient e-Discovery.
- **e-Discovery Process Methodology**—The e-Discovery process methodology, as briefly discussed earlier in Chapter 2 and discussed in detail in Part 3, is a formal framework for structuring the objectives, tasks, deliverables and schedules necessary for achieving effective e-Discovery. An e-Discovery process methodology is essential to establishing a repeatable, quality-controlled process.
- **e-Discovery Technology**—ESI discovery is inherently impossible without use of technology. ESI discovery technology includes software and appliances that address aspects of each phase of the e-Discovery lifecycle. In today's environment, e-Discovery technology is an inherent component of information lifecycle management.

## §24.02 "STATE OF READINESS OF CORPORATE IT INFRASTRUCTURE"

FTI Consulting, Inc. sponsored research by IDC titled the "State of Readiness of Corporate IT Infrastructure."[1]

The purpose of the research was to:

- Evaluate IT's knowledge about their firms' current efforts regarding electronic discovery (e-Discovery) and regulatory audits
- Assess the current state of litigation response and readiness initiatives among U.S. businesses
- Identify current and planned technology investment priorities in support of litigation response and readiness initiatives

[1] A summary of the research survey may be accessed online from the FTI Consulting Web site at www.fticonsulting.com/idcsurvey.

Results of the survey revealed that while most IT executives were confident in their ability to respond to litigation events, the state of the corporate IT environment was lacking in many respects. Some of the areas requiring greater attention included:

- Definition of retention policies and legal hold procedures
- Automation of legal hold in unstructured or semi-structured content repositories
- Automation of legal hold in application database and database archive environments
- Use of case management and review applications in the corporate IT infrastructure
- Search and content analytics in the corporate IT infrastructure

Companies that had reached what IDC refers to as "Stage 3—Maturity Level" had demonstrated several characteristics, including a formal interaction between legal and IT; governance through Steering Committees and formal policies and best practices; a high level of automation in enforcing records management, information retention, and acceptable use practice and "Life Cycle Management" for litigation communication, legal holds, and discovery.

In summary, ample evidence exists to support the imperative to invest in the effort to be prepared for litigation and e-Discovery. Nonetheless, quantifying the return on investment can be difficult due to the nature of the risk—e.g., losing cases and incurring reputational damage in the form of punitive sanctions. However, parties that ignore lessons learned by others will most likely pay a significant price for their inaction.

CHAPTER 25

# GUIDANCE AND GOVERNANCE

## §25.01 INTRODUCTION

As mentioned earlier, litigation and e-Discovery are cross-functional initiatives having impact throughout the organization. Therefore, senior stakeholders must set in motion a framework for guidance and governance that embraces a holistic view of the organization. In addition, this framework must take into account that litigation and e-Discovery readiness is a continuous long-term process, and a critical component of information lifecycle management.

The guidance and governance recommendations set forth below address this and other major issues related to implementing a litigation and e-Discovery readiness program. Because of its overarching role, information lifecycle management is at the core of the recommended guidance and governance framework.

## §25.02 ILM STEERING COMMITTEE

Steering Committees are traditional structures for providing guidance and governance oversight to long-term initiatives that require commitment and active support of senior stakeholders.

An ILM Steering Committee typically is comprised of key management and technical staff chartered with the authority and accountability for setting strategies, policies, budgets, implementing procedures, dispute resolution, and oversight of the information lifecycle management program.

Key members of the committee should include a mix of senior staff representing legal, human resources, business units, and IT. Ideally, the committee might comprise:

- **Chairperson**—A senior member of the legal staff who brings strong knowledge and experience of regulatory compliance and electronic discovery requirements in regulatory and litigation matters
- **Chief Financial Officer, Chief Operations Officer, or Senior Business Unit Head**—Or equivalent senior member of financial or business operations who provides an overarching business perspective of information management issues and requirements within the enterprise
- **Senior Human Resource Officer**—Who provides knowledge and guidance regarding HR compliance requirements and issues
- **Chief Information Officer**—With a strong focus on the issues and requirements related to application of information technology in satisfying business objectives
- **Chief Technology Officer**—Or equivalent who has in-depth technical knowledge of how the information technology infrastructure functions, especially its limitations regarding electronic discovery
- **Records Retention Expert**—Who has in-depth knowledge of capabilities, requirements, and issues related to information creation, flow, access, storage, and retrieval across the enterprise
- **e-Discovery Expert**—Who has in-depth knowledge of the capabilities, requirements, and issues related to the e-Discovery process, technology, and tools.
- **ILM Program Director**—Who combines the capabilities associated with large-scale program management, information technology management, and business functions and management

The ILM Steering Committee is chartered to address the following matters, and authorized with the attendant authority to cause implementation of, and compliance with, their recommendations.

1. Confirm corporate mission and goals
2. Establish information management policies, procedures, and standards that support the corporate mission and goals, including e-Discovery requirements such as legal, process, technology and tools, and third-party involvement
3. Establish an ILM Program Office, with required project management resources

4. Define an e-Discovery Process Methodology
5. Create an e-Discovery Response Team
6. Define and ensure proper allocation of resources throughout the organization
7. Ensure compliance
8. Resolve issues
9. Report to Executive Management

## § 25.03 ILM PROGRAM OFFICE

Where resources permit, an ILM Steering Committee would authorize and create the ILM Program Office, thus initiating the first phase of an ILM methodology that starts with a Situational Assessment and ends with Implementation of ILM as shown in Figure (7) below.

The ILM Program Office is an independent, full-time administrative function that manages the day-to-day requirements for projects associated with implementing ILM. This includes obtaining and allocating resources, budgeting, time and expense accounting, scheduling, project planning and execution, and progress reporting.

The Program Office functions in collaboration with business units, drawing on their resources as required to execute individual projects.

## § 25.04 ILM GOVERNANCE AND IMPLEMENTATION METHODOLOGY

The ILM Methodology recommended adheres to a traditional implementation methodology for initiating large-scale programs. The methodology includes five phases. Phase 1—Situational Assessment—and Phase 2—Gap, Impact, and Risk Analysis—answer the questions, *Where are we now*? and *Where do we need to be*?, Phase 3—Requirements and Priority Setting—and Phase 4—Project Plans—answer the question, *How do we get there*?, and Phase 5—Implementation—addresses the actual implementation of Information Lifecycle Management over time through execution of the Project Plans.

**FIGURE (7) ILM GOVERNANCE AND IMPLEMENTATION METHODOLOGY**

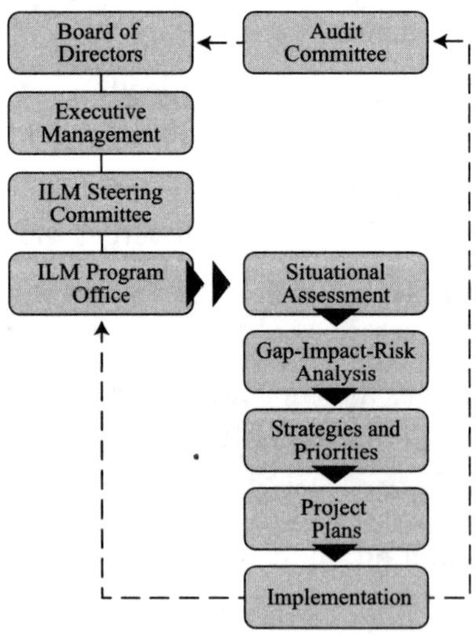


It is also important to note that implementation includes oversight by the Audit Committee in addition to normal reporting channels—from Program Office to the Steering Committee to Executive Management and to the Board.

ILM components and implementation methodology are discussed more fully in Chapter 26, Information Lifecycle Management.

## §25.05 THIRD-PARTY INVOLVEMENT

In most situations, the major platform components of an ILM program will likely require use of third parties to provide technology and additional resources to help with assessment and implementation. In addition, third parties are likely to be involved in ESI storage and management services when scale exceeds a certain volume. Where that line is drawn will vary depending on the resources available and business strategy chosen with respect to outsourcing of technology and technical expertise in general.

The essential governance requirement with respect to third parties is the creation, execution, and monitoring of contractual obligations between the parties.

As an example, it is especially important to understand the obligations of third-party hosting services with respect to discovery of ESI. A third-party hosting service may, for example, use yet another third party for a portion of its services such as storing tapes. Accordingly, contracts should define and allow for the testing and certification of the ability to effectively preserve and provide ESI when legal obligations to do so arise, for all third parties, not just the primary ones.

Also, third-party involvement is one of the major issues to be addressed within ILM implementation, starting with the Situational Assessment phase. The legal department, working with the Steering Committee and ILM Program Office, should be responsible for this initiative—creating and maintaining the required contracts and assuring that contract performance is properly monitored and adhered to. Shifting ESI to a third party does not shift e-Discovery legal burdens, and must be treated accordingly.

## §25.06 ISSUES AND CONCERNS

Guidance and governance for large-scale programs primarily centers on the leadership qualities of executive management to demonstrate commitment and sustain support over the long term, to ensure that financial, technological, and human resources are available, and to resolve critical issues among constituents.

In most organizations there is considerable internal competition in terms of priorities and resources, especially as stakeholders attempt to overcome challenges and achieve their individual objectives.

These pressures can cause conflicts and result in diminished ability for the organization to meet common objectives.

## §25.07 RECOMMENDATIONS

To address these issues, it is important for organizations to develop a framework that supports a disciplined approach to large-scale programs. Such a framework requires the following essential elements:

1. Clear articulation of goals and expectations
2. Transparency in all processes and decisions
3. Sustainable processes
4. Workable policies and procedures
5. Supporting technology
6. Education and training
7. Continuous communication
8. Accountability
9. Incentives to excel
10. Recognition

Accounting for these elements should provide organizations with a high probability for success in developing and implementing the four major programs covered in this Part:

- Guidance and Governance
- Information Lifecycle Management
- e-Discovery Methodology
- e-Discovery Readiness Program

# CHAPTER 26

# INFORMATION LIFECYCLE MANAGEMENT

## § 26.01 INTRODUCTION

Access to the Internet and use of mobile devices and removable storage media create immense opportunity for access, creation, communication, and storage of content—much of which may be valuable, but also some of which may be potentially detrimental to company interests.

While it is impossible to prevent all potentially harmful content exposure, companies should make reasonable efforts to achieve the modicum of control appropriate to their activities and standing.

This includes technology enabling selective access blocking, filtering, and restrictions on copying, saving, and transmission capabilities for individuals, groups and classes of computers, and ESI. It also typically includes written confirmation from employees regarding understanding and adherence to company policies and procedures with respect to information content, both personal and business.

Such an initiative goes beyond traditional compliance monitoring, and requires greater coordination among separate disciplines within the organization in order to be effective. All organizational units are directly involved with information lifecycle management—how to classify, policy manage, store, effectively search, retrieve and produce, and defensively destroy ESI in accordance with legal requirements and business imperatives.

In addition to the human resources necessary, in today's typical enterprise environment, with hundreds of terabytes to many petabytes of ESI, some degree of software automation is the only viable approach to effectively manage information lifecycles of this magnitude. This chapter discusses ILM and its components, which individually and together help satisfy the imperatives for managing information assets, and ESI content, compliance, storage, and discovery.

We have expressed all of these considerations in a conceptual model illustrating the economics for implementing ILM, as depicted below in Figure (8), Conceptual Model of ILM Economics.

Without ILM, the aggregate volume and associated costs and risks arising from e-Discovery related incidents, including preservation requirements as well as discovery and evidentiary admissibility issues, would increase significantly. With ILM, significant increases in volume and associated costs and risks of handling e-Discovery can be kept under control.

**FIGURE (8) CONCEPTUAL MODEL OF ILM ECONOMICS**

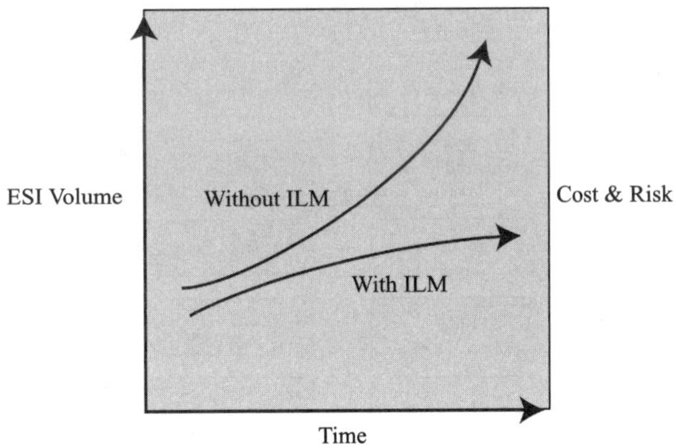


## § 26.02 BACKGROUND

Managing information started as a paper-based function consisting primarily of official corporate documents (*records*) and has transitioned over time to consist predominantly of electronic information. Guidance with respect to records management is available from the International Standards Organization (ISO) and other organizations.

ISO-15489, for example, provides definitions and an international best-practices framework for records management, with the goal of improving efficiency, reducing risk, and facilitating international trade. ISO, 15489 standards comprise two sections:

- Section 1 provides a general overview of records and information management and examines the principles and methodology behind its adoption.
- Section 2 is more involved with the practicalities of moving towards records management compliance. It provides an in-depth approach to implementing electronic records and information management.

For the most part, traditional records management has primarily focused on the classification of records and their corresponding legal storage requirements and retention periods.

However, the combination of unprecedented growth in information technology, the explosion of information content, and the expansion of regulatory requirements has resulted in an accelerating transition from records management to information lifecycle management.

## § 26.03 DOCUMENT LIFECYCLE MODEL

ESI lifecycles comprise six phases in which various user actions are performed, as illustrated in Figure (9) below. In this example, User "A" performs each one of the functions once. All the other users perform one or more functions once.

In the real world, any number of users can perform any of the functions (four of them any number of times) against any number of documents. Extrapolating this model to an organization of 1,000 users, for example, demonstrates a potential to create a staggering number of instances of potentially discoverable ESI.

Because of this ability for large numbers of users to generate extraordinary volumes of ESI, combined with the complexity of user requirements, ILM lifecycle management can only be effectively achieved using centrally managed automated systems.

**FIGURE (9) DOCUMENT LIFECYCLE MODEL**

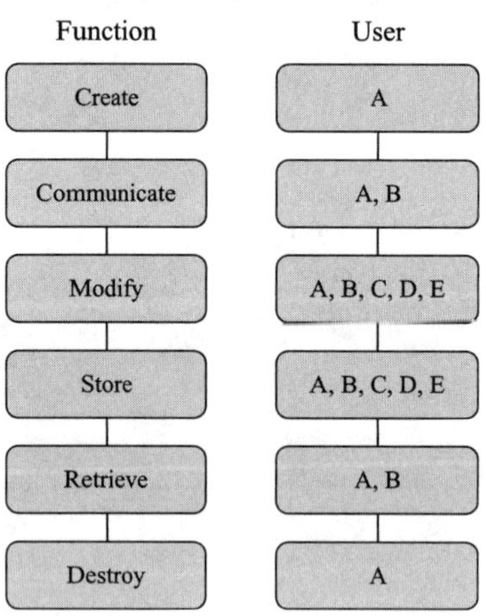


## § 26.04 COMPONENTS OF ILM

In an ideal enterprise model, the information needs of all constituent stakeholders would be met through integrated, automated systems that intelligently managed information throughout its lifecycle—from creation to destruction. Today those needs are met through disparate "point" solutions that independently address the specific needs of individual stakeholders. These disparate point solutions generally fit within five requirement categories:

- Information Asset Management
- Content Management
- Compliance Management
- e-Discovery
- Enterprise Storage Management

As illustrated in Figure (10) below, in an information lifecycle management framework, these requirements are bound together through functions that include deduplication, search, retrieval, and defensible destruction. Following are descriptions of these components.

**FIGURE (10) INFORMATION LIFECYCLE MANAGEMENT**

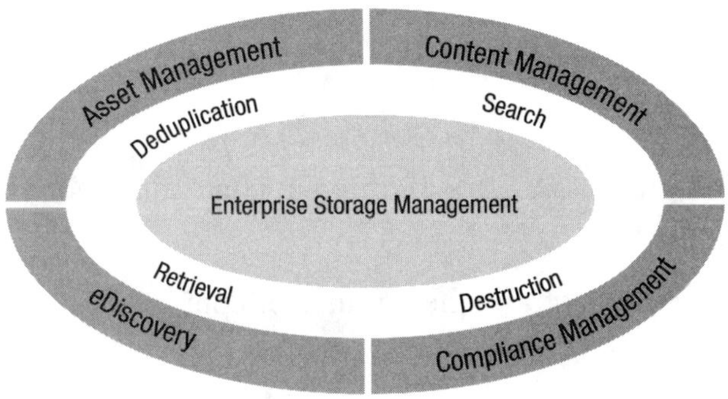


## [A] Information Asset Management

Recommendations at the end of chapters in this book have stressed the need to inventory information assets as a starting point for further e-Discovery actions. Information asset management is a critical component of an ILM program. However, organizational units will have to implement bridging solutions if that component is not yet implemented.

One way to help bridge any gaps is to populate a database with an inventory of information assets by gathering information from available sources, including taking physical inventory if necessary. The database would be kept current through use of an "ESI Asset Impact Notice" that identifies the user/owner of the asset and the impact of the particular change.

An example would be a notification that certain records stored on archive tape system XYC have passed their retention date. As a result, those records would have been scheduled to be destroyed on a certain date and the particular tape system, which was considered obsolete, would be scheduled for destruction as well. Recipients that may be impacted by the particular action conveyed by the ESI Asset Impact Notice would be required to respond with their confirmation or objection to the intended action.

All ESI Asset Impact Notices would be communicated by means of a work flow process that would include automatic review by certain organizational units such as human resources and the ILM Program Office for example, which would evaluate each ESI Asset Impact Notice on certain criteria.

The creation of an interim information asset database and use of the ESI Asset Impact Notice provides a number of benefits.

- Helps keep the Program Office, the Steering Committee, and other stakeholders fully apprised of relevant changes in information assets and the impact of those changes.

- Addresses one of the foundational requirements for effective e-Discovery
- Helps facilitate the transition to an automated information asset component within the ILM platform

### [B] Content Management

Content management systems (CMS) are collaboration systems designed to help manage the creation, organization, maintenance, and storage of content by any number of contributors. Content management systems are often used for publishing large volumes of material and for Web site content, and can include computer files, image media, audio files, electronic documents, and Web content.

CMS are server-based and enable easy file sharing, email, and automated workflow processes that facilitate document lifecycle management—storing, controlling, versioning, auditing, publishing, and destruction—of a wide range of corporate documentation such as proposals, contracts, policies, procedures, news articles, operating manuals, technical manuals, sales guides, and marketing brochures.

A Web content management system is a specialized content management system with additional features to ease the tasks required to publish Web content, manage Web site user activity, and retrieve information from Web sites.

Most content management systems include some of the following functions and features:

- Identification of users and roles
- The ability to assign roles and responsibilities to different content categories or types
- Definition of work flow tasks and event messaging
- Track and manage multiple versions of a single instance of content
- Automated templates over format and content
- Establish default controls over specific content format
- Publish content directly to a repository
- Enable enterprise search and retrieval

### [C] Compliance Management

Compliance management generally fits in two primary categories—*regulatory/legal*, which is externally driven, and *corporate*, which is internally driven. Both of these categories contain many sub-categories, depending on the industry served. A publicly traded insurance company doing business internationally, for example, must comply with regulations and standards such as Sarbanes-Oxley, the SEC, the Foreign Corrupt Practices Act, U.S. and international financial and accounting regulations and standards, individual U.S. state insurance regulations, and various international insurance regulations, as well as internal policies and standards for developing and delivering insurance and paying claims.

Complying with this web of requirements is a daunting task under any circumstance, and so many companies have installed software tools to help facilitate the compliance process. These tools vary considerably in their functions and features, but generally offer some of the following capabilities:

- Identify specific regulations and standards
- Map corporate policies and procedures to the regulations and standards
- Implement some work process control and compliance tracking
- Identify and report deviations and compliance statistics
- Facilitate audits and investigations
- Include training and certification modules

Granularity of compliance software also varies considerably, but many tools attempt to track, at the level of individuals, specific documents and processes.

For example, one of the major compliance issues for U.S. companies doing business internationally is complying with the Foreign Corrupt Practices Act. Accordingly, vendor contracts, and all activity by individuals related to those contracts, are tightly controlled throughout their lifecycle. Continuing the example, if there is a mismatch between an invoice and a payment, an alert is generated and an investigation started promptly. As illustrated by this example, the ESI related to this matter would be placed under a litigation hold.

In addition, many governments are requiring greater privacy and security, especially for customer and employee financial and medical information, all of which can be considered compliance issues.

### [D] e-Discovery Platform

An ideal e-Discovery platform would integrate within an ILM framework, leveraging other ILM components to deliver essential e-Discovery functionality in a seamless, highly efficient process. For example, deduplicated ESI residing in a managed storage repository would be more efficiently discovered than unmanaged ESI.

Today, however, much of the universe of e-Discovery products comprises individual solutions designed only for one or a few standalone functions. These standalone solutions are used throughout the e-Discovery lifecycle in different ways depending on the particular litigation matter and the information environment encountered.

e-Discovery tools include a variety of common functionality, some of which overlap with other ILM component functionality, for example:

- Bates Numbering
- Case Management
- Conversion
- Deduplication
- Imaging
- Load File Creation
- Metadata Extraction
- Redaction and Annotation
- Review Management
- Search
- Statistics and Reporting
- Trial Presentations

## §26.05 MIGRATION TO ILM

Figure (7), ILM Governance and Implementation Methodology, also depicted in the last chapter, is presented again on the next page as a reference for discussing the migration to ILM.

The essence of ILM is the creation of repeatable, cross-functional policies, processes, and systems that recognize the changing value of information over time and enable that information to be managed in accordance with its specific purpose.

Formation of the ILM Steering Committee and the ILM Program Office would establish a governing and operating staff comprised of senior stakeholders that can bring disparate business "silos" into a consensus necessary to understand and define requirements and effect universal change. The changes required are actualized through actions carried out within the phases of the implementation methodology.

FIGURE (7) ILM GOVERNANCE AND IMPLEMENTATION METHODOLOGY

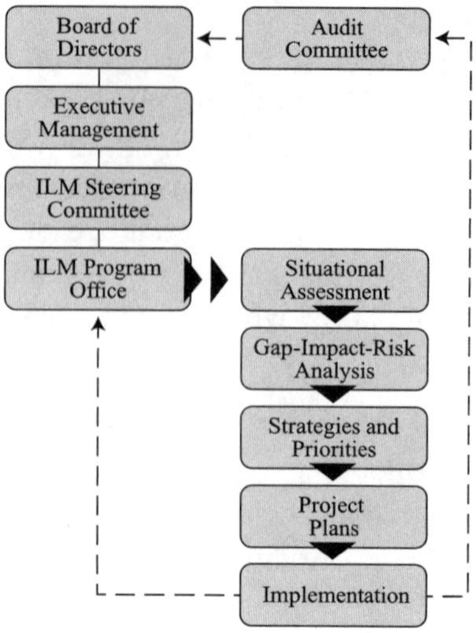


## [A] Ground Rules

In moving forward along the methodology on a path to ILM, there are certain ground rules worth considering.

1. View comprehensive ILM as a marathon, not a sprint, and move forward at an orderly pace that meets objectives but that can be absorbed by the organization without severe business disruption.
2. Create a vision of the ideal solution and think holistically, taking into account the requirement for integration of information across the enterprise, but accept compromises and incremental wins to sustain momentum.
3. Create overarching goals, objectives, and performance measures that enable everyone to understand and play by the same rules.
4. Create strategies and priorities to achieve the most benefit as early as possible.
5. Leverage existing infrastructure when it makes sense, but investigate new technology aggressively.
6. Put substance over form to reach milestones and completion of deliverables.
7. Leverage specialized expertise and experience to supplement internal resources and transfer knowledge.
8. Proactively demonstrate senior executive commitment and support continuously.
9. Consider ILM as a closed loop, iterative process of continuous assessment and improvement.
10. Train, educate, and communicate rigorously to maintain competency and sustain transparency.

## [B] Moving Through the Process

There are a number of ways to execute the ILM Implementation Methodology. Each one has its advantages and disadvantages depending on a number of factors, including the size of the enterprise, the current state of information management, and various priorities within the organization.

One approach is to conduct each phase of the methodology in linear fashion for the entire enterprise. This approach provides the most complete view of issues and requirements, but postpones achieving any benefits until the end of the process, which could take many months depending on the resources available.

Another approach is to select one or more business units, for example, finance or human resources, and conduct each phase of the methodology in linear fashion for those business units. This approach enables implementation of ILM for those selected units on a priority and phased basis, while putting other organizational units in a priority-based queue. It also provides valuable information about application of the methodology to these other units.

A third approach is to select an information category that spans all organization units, and that offers the most benefit from ILM. A good example would be email, which typically comprises the largest volume of ESI, is of greatest concern to compliance and legal personnel from a risk perspective, and presents multiple problems for effective e-Discovery. This approach helps solve an immediate and significant problem and provides early benefits.

A fourth approach is to implement ILM starting with an individual component that might best address one or more priority issues. For example, if litigation is a high priority, implementation of e-Discovery procedures and tools might return the most immediate benefit.

Before choosing any given approach, however, it is prudent to first conduct an initial high-level, top down assessment across the enterprise. A major component of this assessment is an inventory of all information sources, as described above. This provides a baseline of information that enables early decisions regarding initial objectives and priorities, helping make the case for one of the four approaches discussed. No matter which approach is chosen, more granular assessments can be conducted on a selected basis as the ILM program moves forward.

Once the initial assessment is complete, an analysis is conducted to determine any *gaps*, their *impact* and their *risk* (GIR Analysis), priorities are set, and project plans developed.

## [C] Focusing on e-Discovery Readiness

Completion of an initial assessment and gap-impact-risk analysis should provide an understanding of the current information environment, including an information source inventory, and a strong indication of priorities that need attention. In most situations, this will result in creation of a number of concurrent projects, including one that addresses e-Discovery readiness. Accordingly, there are a number of important matters to address.

### [1] e-Discovery Response Team

Compliance with ESI preservation and discovery obligations often is a critical, time sensitive matter that requires immediate attention by experts, whether internal or external, that can act quickly and decisively to protect company interests. An e-Discovery Response Team, created by the ILM Steering Committee, and led by a senior member of the legal staff, would be comprised of experts "on call" for such situations. Relevant expertise would include legal, IT, human resources, e-Discovery (process, tools, and techniques), and forensics.

### [2] Adoption of Common Functions

Three major e-Discovery functions are shared across ILM components—search, deduplication, and storage.

As mentioned earlier, it is much more efficient to perform e-Discovery on ESI that has already been deduplicated. In the same way, enterprise search of ESI (also referred to as federated search) enables a holistic view of relevant content, typically resulting in significantly less material for review. Also, a separate e-Discovery repository under a managed storage environment can automatically enable controlled access, chain-of-custody, and required protection of discovered ESI.

Accordingly, implementing these functions across the enterprise will facilitate e-Discovery readiness.

### [3] Controlling Email

The most obvious and typically the most voluminous form of unstructured ESI is comprised primarily of email, which is generally recognized as a top priority e-Discovery issue. There can be no serious debate as to whether the effective management of email can reduce e-Discovery burden and cost considerably. It can and it does.

Managing email may be considered through the prism of three major aspects—effective classification, email management systems, and managed storage, all of which require automation to be effective in practice.

At the highest level, email can be classified in three categories—content required or desired for business purposes, content deemed required for legal or corporate compliance reasons, and junk email, defined as email with no perceptible business or legal value to the enterprise, with additional sub-classifications and rules enabling further segregation for managed storage.

Automated email management systems apply classifications and rules, along with deduplication and workflow software, to place emails within appropriate managed repositories for appropriate retention, access, and defensible destruction. Requiring human beings to manually sort their email according to an array of classifications can significantly increase the risk of non-compliance and reduce the efficiency of information availability and flow operationally. In fact, the realities of the current volume of email besieging users can raise these risks to unacceptable levels under many circumstances.

Establishment of a carefully selected and implemented automated email management system can provide one of the best "bangs for the buck" of any e-Discovery component. Payback results are particularly achievable within organizational units that are process oriented, such as financial, accounting, purchasing, and human resources, for example, where the process integrates easily with email management.

Except for explicit legal requirements that set forth mandated time periods for retention, the retention periods for emails are a matter of business and IT strategy, determined on an individual company basis. However, in determining retention schedules for email, attention must be directed to the impact of such retention periods on the ability to comply with legal preservation and discovery obligations. For example, a short period might have benefits in terms of reducing the volume of information to be searched and reviewed, but may raise the risk of delay in identifying the trigger of a legal preservation duty. Care must also be taken to articulate and document the business and technical rationales for the retention periods, in order to demonstrate that the retention policies were not implemented for "bad faith" reasons, like ensuring the unavailability of frequently requested electronic evidence.

### [4] Process and Tools

The remaining aspect of e-Discovery readiness revolves around effective process and tools applied to accomplish respective tasks. These two subjects are discussed in detail in the next two chapters.

CHAPTER 27

# ESTABLISHING THE e-DISCOVERY METHODOLOGY

## § 27.01 METHODOLOGY COMPONENTS

Figure (1), discussed in Chapter 2, Overview of the Electronic Discovery Process, is displayed here for reference as we discuss establishing the e-Discovery Process Methodology.

**FIGURE (1) ELECTRONIC DISCOVERY PROCESS LIFECYCLE**

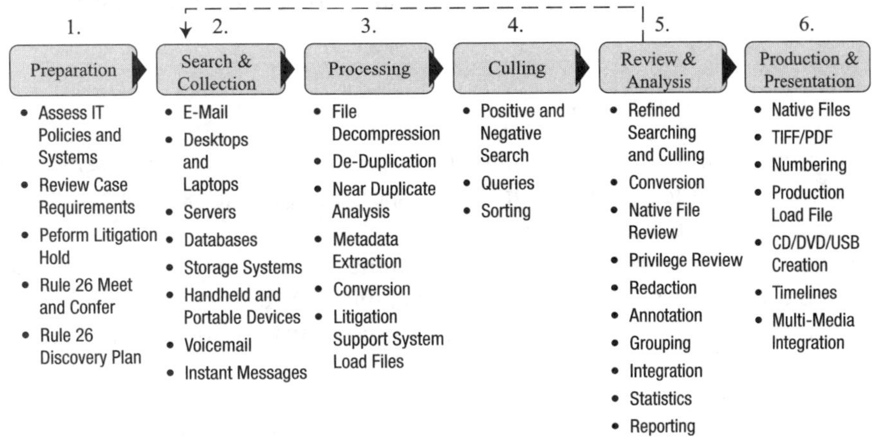


The e-Discovery methodology comprises standard project management disciplines—***allocating resources*** to ***execute tasks*** resulting in ***completion of deliverables*** within ***defined schedules***. These project management requirements map closely to the six phases of the e-Discovery lifecycle.

Establishment of the methodology can be assigned to the ILM Program Office as one of the projects under that office, or delegated by that office to the e-Discovery Response Team.

In any case, the methodology includes the following components, to be applied when conducting specific e-Discovery projects.

- **Senior Leadership**—Overall guidance for litigation and e-Discovery matters is typically provided through general counsel, with support from technical and administrative staff.
- **Project Managers**—There may be several projects underway throughout the phases of any particular e-Discovery matter. Accordingly, people with specific technical expertise may be assigned to head specific projects.
- **Human Resource Inventory**—This includes the external and internal human resource bios—education, skills, and work experience—applicable to each phase of the e-Discovery lifecycle.
- **Technology Inventory**—This includes a description of the IT infrastructure—including external hosting—and specific e-Discovery tools applicable to each phase of the e-Discovery lifecycle.
- **Information Asset Inventory**—This includes a listing of information assets as defined in Chapter 26 (§ 26.04[A]).
- **Policies and Guidelines**—These are required to frame company and individual responsibility, accountability, and requirements associated with the tasks and deliverables within each phase of the e-Discovery lifecycle. Some examples of topics addressed include, litigation holds and preservation of ESI, methods of collection, form of production, and hiring of outside technology consultants and vendors.
- **Education, Training, and Certification**—This should follow the same approach used when an individual acquires technical skills or when implementing a compliance assurance process. Individuals need to be formally educated and trained, with confirmation that they are qualified in their job and accept responsibility and accountability for the results of their work.

- **Project Management Software Program**—In many companies, this might consist of a simple, general-purpose project management software program, such as Microsoft Project, used to help plan an overall schedule and to track progress.
- **e-Discovery Workflow Program**—This is specialized software that addresses some or all of the individual phases of the e-Discovery lifecycle, providing specific capabilities to facilitate management of the respective process. (See Chapter 29, e-Discovery Technology and Tools, for more information on e-Discovery programs.)

## § 27.02 PROJECT PLANS

Development of project plans assumes completion of the Situational Assessment and GIR Analysis, formation of the Steering Committee, Project Office, Response Team, appointment of the Project Manager, and development of the components outlined above.

Project plans include descriptions of the tasks, deliverables, schedules, and performance measures applicable to each phase of the e-Discovery lifecycle for any specific e-Discovery project.

The next chapter outlines implementation of an e-Discovery Readiness Plan using components of the e-Discovery methodology.

CHAPTER 28

# IMPLEMENTING AN e-DISCOVERY READINESS PROGRAM

## § 28.01 INTRODUCTION

Development of project plans assumes completion of the Situational Assessment and GIR Analysis, formation of the Steering Committee, Project Office, Response Team, appointment of the Project Manager, and development of the components outlined in the last chapter.

Also, e-Discovery readiness takes place within the overall transition to an information lifecycle program. Accordingly, there are overlaps in some of the tasks and deliverables, including those flowing from the Situational Assessment and GIR Analysis.

In addition, e-Discovery readiness is best accomplished under the leadership of individuals that have the specialized knowledge and experience to deal with the technical and legal as well as the cultural and political issues inherent in this process.

## § 28.02 e-DISCOVERY READINESS PROGRAM

An e-Discovery Readiness Program essentially follows the methodology described in the previous chapters—Situational Assessment, GIR Analysis, Strategies and Priorities, Project Plans, and Implementation, along with appropriate and necessary documentation of the foregoing.

### [A] Situational Assessment and GIR Analysis

For the e-Discovery Readiness Project, the Situational Assessment and GIR Analysis ideally would be conducted concurrently in the following steps.

1. Determination of corporate goals, objectives, and constraints to establish the overall framework in which the project is conducted and to ensure that results are aligned with management needs.
2. Interviews of key staff within all the major organizational units to understand their perspectives, capabilities, and expectations regarding e-Discovery, especially how they generate, communicate, use, and store information. This includes heavy focus on the IT infrastructure and respective technologies for ESI—backup systems, schedules, and retention of information, network data shares, email, instant messaging, voice mail systems, Web services, and databases.
3. Determination of third-party roles and responsibilities, and review contracts—hosting services, technology vendors and consultants—with respect to their respective component of information lifecycle management.
4. Review of documentation—information technology and lifecycle management, business process, and governance—related to every major organizational unit.
5. Review of internal and outside counsel legal requirements and processes—regulatory, compliance, and litigation—related to the respective business functions.
6. Development of documentation that enables the process to move forward and is available for future reference, without jeopardizing protections applicable to work carried out for legal purposes under the direction of and in conjunction with legal counsel.

### [B] Strategies and Priorities

Each company and the individual organizational units within each company will express their preferred strategies and priorities depending on a number of factors, including their strengths and weaknesses and their goals and objectives.

For many companies, however, the e-Discovery Readiness Situational Assessment and GIR Analysis typically result in establishing ESI management and the e-Discovery process as the top priorities. This is because many companies have not implemented ILM programs as described earlier, and are struggling with managing the storage and discovery of ESI. Accordingly, the following discussion on project plans and implementation focuses on addressing ESI management and the e-Discovery process.

## [C] Project Plans and Implementation

As discussed and illustrated in Figure (9) in § 26.03, staggering volumes of potentially discoverable ESI are created through the interaction of many users creating and performing various functions on a wide variety of files and systems.

In the absence of an existing ILM Program, the best way to begin to understand and address this universe of ESI is to work from the top down, starting with large categories of ESI and working toward granularity as the process unfolds.

Figure (11), Storage Decision Process, below, illustrates a decision process that can be applied to selected categories of information to help in this process. Categories could be identified through, for example, IT architecture characteristics, operational uses, applicable regulations, standards, and interviews with key staff.

**FIGURE (11) STORAGE DECISION PROCESS**

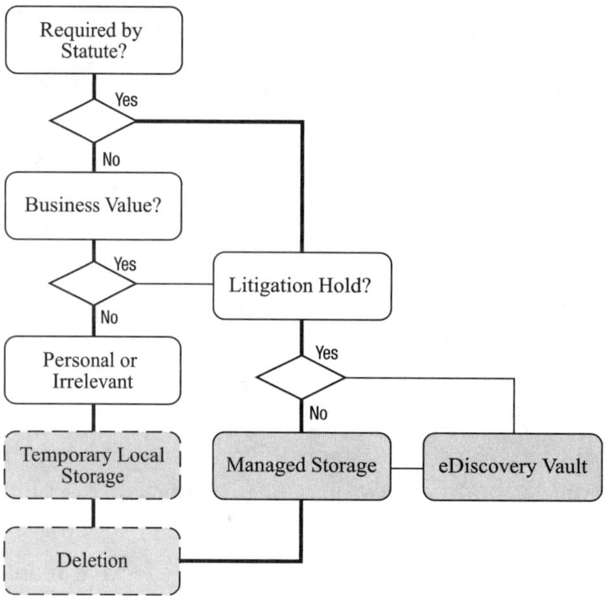


One category, for example, could be all Corporate Formation and Governance records—Articles of Incorporation, Bylaws, Licenses, Board Minutes, Contract and Agreements, etc. The retention of such documents may be legally mandated. As such, they may be permanently archived, and could be subject to litigation hold, which would require placement in the e-Discovery vault.

On the other extreme, personal emails, for example, that are determined to have no business relevance and are not subject to any pending litigation hold or regulatory retention requirement, could be maintained in temporary local storage until permanently deleted.

This top down process may be outlined in 10 steps, beginning with creation of the Information Asset Inventory.

1. Define the large categories to be used, and classify the records within these categories according to category, creator/owner, business application, legal/regulatory status, business value, retention period, and preservation/destruction requirement.

2. Starting with the largest category (or category determined by other priority criteria), develop an "ESI Map" that identifies the source (person, transaction, device) of ESI, the associated business process flow, and associated storage device(s) and disposition.
3. Continuing with the largest ESI category, determine potential legal hold requirements and establish the appropriate policies and procedures to ensure compliance with those requirements.
4. Continuing with the largest ESI category, determine the requirements for fulfilling the functions required during the phases of the e-Discovery lifecycle defined earlier—Search and Collection, Processing, Culling, Review and Analysis, and Production and Presentation. This includes human resources, technology, and processes.
5. Document the policies, standards, procedures, and performance measures associated with each of the e-Discovery lifecycle activity requirements defined in step 4 above.
6. Develop documentation of the above that is sensitive to the potential discoverability of such documentation.
7. Take necessary actions to implement the determined course of action regarding policies, procedures, standards, etc.
8. Develop education, training, and certification programs for applicable staff.
9. Repeat steps 2 through 8 for other categories in priority order.
10. Test the results of the e-Discovery Readiness Project by conducting a "walkthrough" of the complete process using a small subset of controllable ESI.

Note: The steps outlined suggest starting with the largest category and continuing with other categories in priority order, then testing the project as a last step. However, it may better suit some organizations to start with smaller categories, test, then continue with other priority categories.

CHAPTER 29

# e-DISCOVERY TECHNOLOGY AND TOOLS

## § 29.01 THE e-DISCOVERY MARKETPLACE

The e-Discovery marketplace comprises hundreds of vendors offering many hundreds of products and services to end users, and to each other as they bundle products and services of others into their own offerings. According to IDC, the market for legal discovery and litigation support infrastructure is estimated at $12.2 billion in 2007 and projected to reach $21.8 billion in 2011.

To gain a flavor of this marketplace, consider that Fulbright & Jaworski's 2006 Trends Survey reports that billion-dollar plus companies field 556 litigation cases on average, and almost half of those face 50 new litigation matters annually. Within that universe, insurance companies confront an astounding average of 1,696 lawsuits, followed by retailers and energy firms.[1]

This e-Discovery technology landscape includes players in several major categories, as indicated in Figure (12) below.

- Regional/Local Service Bureaus
- Point Solutions
- Integrated Platforms
- Enterprise Solutions
- Consulting Firms
- Law Firms
- End User Entities

### [A] Regional/Local Service Bureaus

Service Bureaus are small to medium-size vendors primarily providing services such as the scanning and imaging of paper documents and possibly simple processing of ESI for viewing in a searchable repository. These operations provide convenience to end users that may not have any internal capabilities, or that are faced with e-Discovery requirements that exceed their capacity or response time-frame capability.

As shown by the solid arrows in Figure (12), in addition to being vendors, Service Bureaus are, by virtue of the services they provide, end users of point solutions, and for some Service Bureaus, end users of integrated platforms. The dotted arrows in Figure (12) indicate the flow of acquisitions in the e-Discovery landscape.

**FIGURE (12) e-DISCOVERY TECHNOLOGY LANDSCAPE**

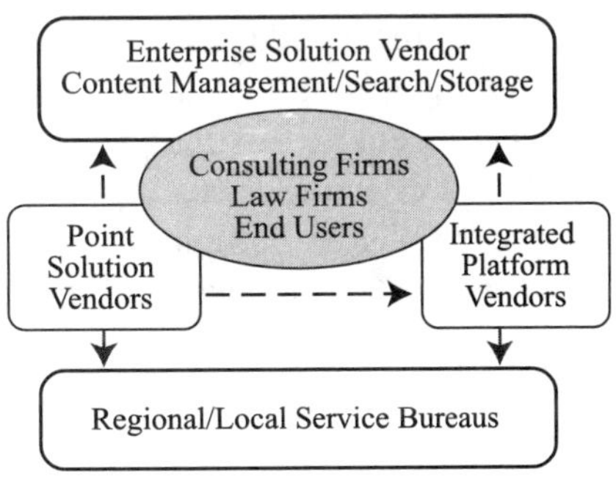


[1] Fulbright & Jaworski, "2006 Litigation Trends Survey."

### [B] Point Solution Vendors

Point Solution vendors comprise start-ups and established companies offering technology that addresses one or more specific solutions, usually as standalone products capable of working together with other products. Point Solution vendors often are started by and comprise individuals with significant domain expertise that provides added value to their specific technology solution. Point Solution vendors are usually the leading innovators within the e-Discovery marketplace. Accordingly, they are often acquisition targets by Integrated Platform vendors and Enterprise Solution vendors attempting to enrich their offerings with state-of-the-art capabilities.

Point Solutions products are primarily offered on an in-house per-seat license basis, but may be offered on a hosted basis via the Internet.

### [C] Integrated Platform Vendors

Integrated Platform vendors are large, established vendors that integrate their own products and certain products from point solutions vendors. Integrated Platform vendors may also be acquisition targets of Enterprise Solutions vendors.

Integrated Solution vendors are characterized by their collaboration review platforms that offer a rich suite of software capabilities addressing a wide range of functions within the e-Discovery lifecycle. Often these capabilities are offered as individual modules in order to accommodate clients that may have some existing solutions in place.

Integrated Platform vendors may offer their suites on an in-house per-seat license basis, or on a hosted basis via the Internet. Billing schemes can be based on per-file, per page/image, or per-megabyte charges or may be assessed according to number of users.

### [D] Enterprise Solution Vendors

Enterprise Solution vendors comprise the very large, well established major players within the information technology industry. When such vendors put forth an e-Discovery offering, it is in the context of their larger product offerings covering a broader range of requirements within the information lifecycle, from creation to long-term retention.

These firms may be interested in acquiring e-Discovery point solutions that fit within their overall information lifecycle solution strategies, complementing or adding capabilities to their existing technology portfolio.

### [E] Consulting Firms

Consulting firms play a major role in delivering a wide range of critical services to the e-Discovery industry. Some consulting firms can address requirements throughout the complete e-Discovery lifecycle, while others specialize in one aspect of e-Discovery, such as forensics. A small number of consulting firms provide technology solutions in addition to services, either licensed or under a hosting arrangement.

Consulting firms that deliver e-Discovery services include firms ranging in size from sole practitioners to multi-national public companies with thousands of employees, and include firms dedicated to e-Discovery and those in which e-Discovery is a small portion of their service portfolio.

### [F] Law Firms

Law firms, for the most part, primarily focus on the legal issues related to e-Discovery in response to urgent litigation matters before their clients, leaving the e-Discovery technology to consulting firms and vendors that may be part of their particular engagement team.

Law firms are, however, beginning to bring e-Discovery technology in-house, so they can deliver more services directly in an effort to capture additional revenue and suggest a competitive advantage vis-à-vis law firms that do not offer such services. However, law firms have been cautious to enter the realm of directly providing e-Discovery technology to clients for a number of significant reasons. These include liability risks associated with potential mishandling of complex technology, but also because participating too closely in the handling of sensitive electronic evidence can put a law firm in a difficult posture as a fact witness when testimony is later required to authenticate such evidence.

### [G] End User Entities

Notwithstanding the inclusion of consulting firms and law firms, end users of e-Discovery technology and services cover the complete spectrum of size and industry, from small companies with a few employees to government entities and large multi-national public companies that must contend with hundreds of litigation matters on a simultaneous and continuous basis.

End user entities have typically responded to litigation in a reactive manner, based largely on their lack of e-Discovery readiness and the urgency and scope of the litigation matter. However, with the advent of the December 2006 Amendments to the FRCP, combined with the increase in volume of ESI in general, end users are considering more proactive measures to ensure effective e-Discovery responses.

## §29.02 MARKET CONSOLIDATION AND IMPLICATIONS

Even though some e-Discovery firms have delivered e-Discovery technology and/or services for several years, the e-Discovery market as a whole is considered immature, fragmented, and in the early stages of consolidation, driven by several factors.

Foremost among these factors in the short term is the need to comply with the FRCP and corresponding changes in state law as well as rising expectations on the part of government regulators. This means addressing priority issues such as collection and storage—being able to collect ESI across the enterprise and understanding and managing storage, especially backup and archival tapes, which to this day present some of the most significant e-Discovery challenges. In addition, end users are aggressively seeking improvements in efficiency of processing, production, and review to reduce overall litigation cost.

In the long term, it seems likely that e-Discovery solutions will become more embedded within the overall technology solutions comprising information lifecycle management, as discussed in Chapter 26. Within the information lifecycle management arena, much of the early focus will be on retention management, especially storage solutions.

Accordingly, larger players will seek acquisitions that complement their technology and services and increase their customer base and market share. This cycle of acquisitions has important implications for those considering a choice of vendors.

It is not always possible to predict which vendor will be acquired in advance of any choice of vendors. But it is possible to set a strategic direction, on a path toward information lifecycle management for example, and choose a vendor that fits that strategy. Once a vendor is acquired, it is very likely that their technology will be integrated within the acquiring company's existing solution. If the acquiring company's solution strategy is in line with your strategy, then you are likely to receive additional benefit from your choice of vendors.

There is no "one size fits all" e-Discovery solution. The situation is different for every provider and every user of e-Discovery technology and services, and so all options must be considered. Service Bureaus offer convenience, but usually do not offer a full range of services. Point Solution vendors typically offer the most innovative solutions and domain expertise, but are usually limited to one or a few specific capabilities, with the potential for issues when attempting to integrate disparate products. Integrated Platform vendors offer the efficiencies of multiple functions in one platform, but require higher financial commitments, and may not be completely compatible with existing technology or practices. Enterprise Solution vendors offer large-scale storage management and a migration path toward information lifecycle management, but may not fit within current budgets, existing technology, or future direction of the company.

## § 29.03 SOLUTION CATEGORIES

e-Discovery solutions tend to fit within certain categories according to their primary functions. These categories include products available as software suites and with some vendors as "plug-and-play" appliances:

- Case Management
- Collection and Preservation
- Search
- Integrated (Processing, Review and Analysis, and Production)

### [A] Case Management Suites

Case management suites are not typically considered e-Discovery platforms since they are primarily designed to focus on the collaboration requirements of attorneys dealing with the legal and project management aspects of litigation matters, as opposed to other e-Discovery lifecycle functions. However, we have included them here since case management suite vendors are attempting to bridge the gap between case management systems and e-Discovery collaboration systems by enabling the load and review of documents within their systems.

### [B] Collection and Preservation

A wide range of solutions have been designed to meet the needs of large entities in their collection and preservation efforts. These products specialize in collecting ESI from desktops, hard drives, shared network drives, and tape systems. They are able to create forensically sound data and metadata captures, and to manage, sort, and archive email. The more robust collection products provide for "pre-search," which enables users to refine ESI identification, and for deduplication, which further reduces the amount of ESI requiring processing.

Some products can perform direct Indexing, search and extraction of offline tape content from proprietary formats, with reconstruction of files to allow full search and review of content—without needing to restore the original files. Also see § 29.03[C][4], Offline Tape Search.

### [C] Search

Search and retrieval can be as simple in scope and function as using *Find* to locate a keyword within an MS-Word document; and as complex as using sophisticated enterprise data mining engines to discover meaning and relationships among varieties of documents within terabytes of ESI across multiple domains. The class of search products referred to as *Enterprise Search* provide the more robust functions and features needed to satisfy the complex needs of most organizations. Some of the typical search capabilities are described in Part 3 in Chapter 20, Search and Retrieval Considerations. Various additional capabilities of enterprise search products are described below.

#### [1] Federated Search

Federated search enables users to search multiple information sources with a single query from a single user interface, usually a browser portal. Search queries are sent to every individual database within the portal or the federated search list. Results of the search are merged and presented in a unified format with minimal duplication, and sorted automatically or manually by the user.

An example of a federated search is searching various business information stores such as financial, legal, marketing, and sales for information bearing on specific vendors in relation to a specific sales person.

### [2] Multimedia Search

These are specialized "non-text" search engines. Search is usually based on certain metadata, such as subject, format, or length, for example. Some multimedia search engines include speech recognition and visual analysis, enabling highly sophisticated searches.

Video search, for example, is typically conducted on surveillance videos, and corporate videos of meetings, conferences, and other business functions. Video search can also be used to search for video on desktop computers and servers.

### [3] Hybrid Search

This new breed of enterprise search is a hybrid of business intelligence, database, and federated search, focused on finding ESI across an organization without breaking up the relationships among information, or having to move one type of information into a different format to be searched. Hybrid search is a virtual repository with an analytics layer and search capabilities, enabling users to search structured information, such as database fields, as well as unstructured information, such as email.

### [4] Offline Tape Search

The capabilities represented by emerging indexing and search engines include the ability to perform direct Indexing, search, and extraction of offline tape content from proprietary formats, with reconstruction of files to allow full search and review of content—without needing to restore the original files, unless warranted on a selective basis. These appliances also enable the automatic sorting and cataloging of all tapes in the library.

## [D] Integrated (Processing, Review and Analysis, and Production)

These categories are combined in this overview because the advanced vendors combine much of the functionality into a single platform. These platforms provide for a variety of automated and manual capabilities that increase the effectiveness of resources. Capabilities to look for in integrated platforms from advanced vendors include:

- Advanced Search: Application of unlimited user constructs using iterations of search functionality—Boolean, clusters, concept, context, fuzzy, proximity, wildcard—in single or nested arrangements
- Classification: Organization of ESI into defined logical categories that segment and facilitate processing
- Communication Mapping: Relationships among individuals and groups
- Conversion: PDF, TIFF
- Culling: Deduplication and Near-Deduplication
- Custodian Identification: Alias, email addresses, domains
- Database: Relational, fields user definable
- Data Import/Export: From multiple sources and languages
- Discussion Threads/Maps: Chronological, key custodian
- Export: To any litigation support platform—native, image, folders
- Filtering: Automatic and manual, predefined and custom terms and parameters
- Import: From any source
- Indexing: Organization of all information
- Installation: In-house or hosted

- Integration: Leading e-Discovery and litigation support products
- Intelligent Coding/Ranking: Relevance, responsiveness, privilege
- Metadata Preservation
- Metrics: Case analytics, performance measurement
- Format/File Support: Multiple documents, emails, attachments, files
- Native Files: Processing, review, export
- Nested Search
- OCR: Creation and search
- OLAP (Online Analytical Processing): Auto creation of data and metadata fact tables for subsequent OLAP Queries (1,000 percent faster than SQL queries)
- Organizational Discovery: End user email aliases and domain information, automatic filters by domain, geography, department, and end user
- Quick Search: Initial search across entire case
- Pre-processing: Enable identification, collection, and processing in one tool and one step
- Redaction and Annotation: Logging
- Reports: Pre-configured, templates, custom
- Review Configuration: User defined modes
- Scalability: Hundreds of users, locations, Terabytes
- Secure Access: Role-based at platform, function, file, data levels
- Tagging: Individual, groups, result sets, pre-defined auto-tags
- Three Dimensional Review: Simultaneous multiple queries with results mapped to interactive 3-D dashboard interface
- Topic Mapping: Relationships among entities using defined terms and linguistic analysis
- Unicode Compliance: Support for multiple languages
- Web Interface
- Workflow: Templates and user definable flows

# CHAPTER 30
# CHOOSING VENDORS[1]



[1] This topic, "Choosing Vendors," is useful to both parties subject to potential litigation, and to law firms and companies providing e-Discovery services to such parties. Also, the steps outlined under this topic may also be applied in the selection of experts.

As noted earlier, performing effective e-Discovery often demands assistance from experts and vendors providing expertise, technology, and services that facilitate processes and enhance the credibility of results. However, such reliance creates a dependence that can introduce risks as well as rewards, both of which are primarily owned by the party making not only the purchase, but the representations to the court or regulator about the integrity, completeness, or accuracy of preservation or discovery efforts.

Accordingly, it is prudent to perform a responsible degree of due diligence prior to any purchase. Not only can due diligence help in the selection and purchase process, it can also help shield the purchaser from liability if, for example, an individual or vendor on a project subsequently has difficulty meeting requirements.

## § 30.01 NEEDS ANALYSIS

Before performing due diligence, conduct a "Needs Analysis" to determine the requirements for fixing any existing e-Discovery-related deficiencies. The Needs Analysis itself requires education regarding solutions available so that solutions can be matched to requirements. The Needs Analysis should result in identification of those vendors capable of addressing the requirements defined in the analysis.

Some factors worth considering when identifying vendors include:

- Products that comply with industry standards, and that can scale to handle large volumes of information, whether paper based or electronic[2]
- An integrated system that addresses all phases of the e-Discovery lifecycle, versus solutions that address only one aspect of e-Discovery, such as deduplication, scanning, etc.
- Products that can be tailored to the needs of individual buyers
- Customer service—education, training, and installation services, including project management, workflow development, and problem solving, versus no or few after-purchase services
- Competitive value[3] and depth of technology offerings
- Performance assurance—consistently meeting commitments on deliverables, schedules, and budgets
- Reputation and standing in the marketplace
- Project management skills and specific expertise regarding the requirements defined in the Needs Analysis
- Clear identification and definition of processing efficiency gains in relation to costs

Perform a function and feature comparison of competing vendors to determine the strengths and weaknesses for each item being compared. Rank each item in terms of priority or importance. Develop a qualitative rating for each vendor on their overall comparative performance. Eliminate those vendors that do not meet a minimum threshold on the qualitative rating so that only one or more vendors remain.

## § 30.02 REQUEST FOR PROPOSAL (RFP)

Once the applicable vendors have been narrowed to a few that best meet defined criteria, develop an RFP that enables the vendors to formally respond to your stated requirements. The RFP should include a statement that a contract award will be based on consideration of all factors, not just price. The RFP should address, at minimum, details covering the following items.

1. Description of your environment and the products and services needed
2. Description of products and services to be provided by vendor

[2] The term "products" refers to individual software, software suites, and/or combinations of software and hardware (appliances).

[3] Price should be competitive, but should not be the primary determinant. Viewing the eDiscovery process in a vacuum apart from the issues of risk and cost of the overall litigation process is a critical mistake. Value, a combination of cost and derived benefits, is a better measure for selecting vendors.

3. Description and timing of deliverables
4. How the vendor intends to deliver the product or service within your environment
5. How the product or service interfaces with other products or services
6. Definition of problem identification and dispute resolution process
7. Pricing and billing options
8. Definition of applicable agreements, warranties, and certifications
9. Confirmation of financial stability
10. Bios of applicable personnel
11. Identification of vendor contact with decision-making authority

## § 30.03 DUE DILIGENCE

Once the RFPs have been evaluated and the leading vendor has been identified, perform the following tasks to accomplish basic due diligence. Some of the items in the due diligence process may be covered in the RFP. Basically, due diligence seeks to understand issues related to Stability and Risk, Architecture, Fit for Purpose, Performance, Ease of Implementation, and Support.

1. Determine how long the vendor has been in business and how successful the business has been. Ask for references that can be checked and follow through by calling them to confirm the vendor's work product and how the vendor treats customers.
2. Determine how long the vendor has been providing ESI services. Many vendors have only recently migrated into e-Discovery products or services from other related disciplines. Accordingly, relevant experience may be short, even though the vendor has been in business for a good number of years.
3. Determine the experience of the vendor staff, especially with the applicable e-Discovery technology. Some vendors have experience limited to a particular e-Discovery technology or IT infrastructure. Some vendors may claim broad staff experience, but have only one person with applicable experience. Confirm the certifications of vendors and individuals.
4. Ask for representations of work performed and/or technology demonstrations that enable evaluation with respect to your particular situation and infrastructure.
5. Confirm how the vendor responds to stress and problem situations. Focus on quality and process controls that demonstrate competency and reliability.
6. Determine if the vendor needs to contract with other third parties to supplement the vendor's capabilities, and if so, perform the same due diligence with the other third parties.
7. Consider both the quantitative rating and the qualitative factors within the RFP and due diligence findings to make a final selection.

Most vendors will have their own contracts. Following selection of a vendor, work with the vendor to ensure that whatever agreement is executed is clear and that both parties understand with specificity their respective obligations. Quality vendors will have internal counsel capable of facilitating the contract process so that both sides feel that they have a fair deal.

Part V

# APPENDICES

# APPENDIX

TABLE OF CONTENTS

# APPENDIX 1

# INTRODUCTION

The Appendix contains sample material that helps make the content of the book more meaningful by illustrating how selected components of the eDiscovery process have been implemented, or might be implemented and supported in actual practice.

- **Systems Overview Provisions**, extracted from an actual operating environment, are representative of findings that might result from an assessment of the information technology infrastructure during Phase 1 of the eDiscovery process. As with the sample policies and procedures, this Systems Overview is intended to educate the reader. Creation of a systems overview in any given situation will depend on the actual information technology infrastructure in place, the accuracy and completeness of information available, and the skills and expertise of the eDiscovery practitioners.
- **Guidelines: Developing a Records Management Program** is a high-level summary of essential steps required for developing a formal records management program, which is an essential component for sustaining an effective eDiscovery program. Please note that records management is considered by the authors as a subset of Information Lifecycle Management, which is addressed in Chapter 26 of the book.
- **Sample Records Management Policies and Litigation Hold Procedure Provisions** included herein are a limited representation of actual policies and procedures in use within various firms of all sizes and operating requirements. While any particular policy or procedure may apply in any given situation, each policy or procedure may not represent a "best practice" in any given situation. Accordingly, these samples are presented to educate readers regarding what they might expect to find within various organizations. Determination of suitability of a particular sample, or combination of samples for any particular application, rests solely with the individual decision-maker, after taking into account the unique legal, regulatory, and operating requirements of the organization in which the samples are to be applied.
- **High-Level Litigation Hold Checklist** is a summary of respective material in the book, and is designed to help practitioners facilitate their preservation obligations. The checklist is especially useful in helping eliminate problems associated with overlooking and failing to address sources of ESI. This "open-ended" checklist provides a reference that can help practitioners avoid those kinds of errors of omission. As with any checklist, users must expand beyond the items contained therein to address the details of their particular environment.
- **Depositions of Corporate Representatives: Selected Topics Regarding Facts Impacting ESI Availability to an Examining Party** contains high-level suggestions as to topics that might be covered by the attorney charged with conducting an examination before trial. As a generic outline, the topics presented are more general than would be the case in a real deposition and are not intended to be comprehensive. Also, there are many more topics that could be explored and questions asked depending on the particular situation in which the deposition occurs. Likewise, there are many different ways to ask these questions. Accordingly, these topics and questions are intended to assist in planning for the deposition by providing some directional guidance, and to assist those preparing for these types of depositions with some insight into what might be covered.

# Appendix 2

# SYSTEMS OVERVIEW PROVISIONS

## STATEMENT OF PURPOSE

The Overview should describe its intended use and limitations and cautionary language supporting confidentiality. For example:

> This document describes, at a high level, certain relevant characteristics of IT governance and architecture at the Company and the sources of electronically stored information ("ESI") that may be available. This document was drafted at the request and direction of counsel for the Company. Although necessarily technical in nature, it is intended exclusively to serve as a resource for lawyers and legal counsel rather than any other technological or business purpose. This document is a guidebook—subject to adaptation as required by the circumstances of particular cases—to ensure that inside and outside counsel are able to understand the nature and scope of the Company's computer systems and to use that information as necessary in a variety of legal contexts including litigation. The Company's information systems are necessarily dynamic and are always evolving.
>
> THIS DOCUMENT IS INTENDED TO BE PRIVILEGED AND CONFIDENTIAL AND IT CONTAINS HIGHLY CONFIDENTIAL AND PROPRIETARY INFORMATION. THE DOCUMENT IS NOT INTENDED TO BE DISCLOSED OUTSIDE OF THE COMPANY OR COMPANY COUNSEL.
>
> Before any particular information below is used in the context of a legal proceeding, the information in question should be checked with appropriate Company IT personnel to ensure that it has not been subsequently updated or otherwise modified. This document is meant to be reviewed and updated periodically by IT and/or legal counsel, or at any time when material changes to the Company's IT infrastructure or systems occur.

## DESCRIPTION OF IT PERSONNEL AND THE IT DEPARTMENT STRUCTURE

In this section of the Overview, the key players and positions in the IT organization would be identified and their roles described. An organizational chart of the IT Department is useful to allow the eDiscovery team to discern a path toward obtaining necessary information about relevant systems. For example:

> The Company's systems are operated, maintained and supported by the Information Technology ("IT") team. The corporate Chief Technology Officer ("CTO") is ____ and his direct reports are depicted in the IT organizational chart shown below.

## GRAPHICAL REPRESENTATION OF THE IT ENVIRONMENT

Sometimes it is helpful to see a graphical representation of the information systems handling ESI. Care must be taken, however, to convey to those using the graphical depiction as an aid to understanding that any simple graphical depiction of a complex IT environment cannot be taken "literally" and does not tell the whole story. An example of such a graphic appears below:

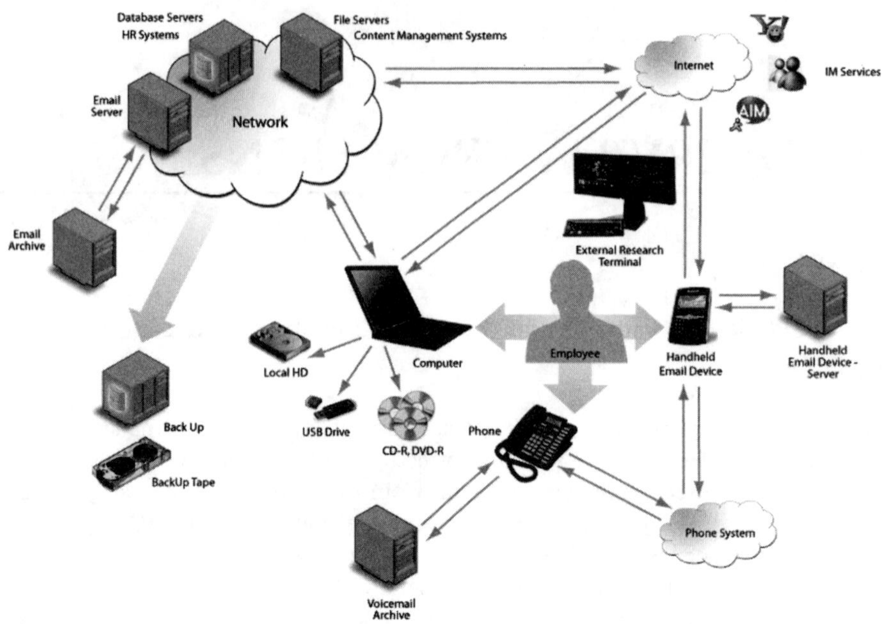


## ELECTRONIC COMMUNICATIONS

### Email

#### General

A general description of the email environment, along with the usage, backup, and retention policies applicable to that environment as well as any other characteristics of the environment impacting on available information content, should be provided. For example:

> The Company uses a Microsoft Exchange 2003 email system. All Company employees receive an Exchange email account. Under normal circumstances and in the absence of a legal retention obligation, email messages are managed by users individually and users can delete messages from their mailbox (and therefore from the Exchange servers) at any time. Users also have discretion over the creation and use of custom folders and subfolders for the efficient organization of their messages. All email messages reside on the Exchange servers themselves, and users have the ability to send, receive, or view email only while they are connected to the Company network . . .
>
> The Company's policy forbids users to "archive" or save email on their individual computers, whether in the form of a PST file or otherwise . . .
>
> Company policy prohibits automatic forwarding of Company email to an external or third-party email account (e.g., Google's "Gmail" or Yahoo! Mail), which is not permitted. Users are strongly discouraged from accessing third-party email systems from within the Company network, and the use of Company email services for personal correspondence is expected to be kept to a minimum. Users are also discouraged from using non-Company email accounts for business correspondence . . .
>
> The Company has implemented mailbox quota limits . . .
>
> User email can also be accessed using Outlook Web Access (OWA) via a Web browser or by using a Virtual Private Network (VPN) connection, which allows users to access the Company network securely over an Internet connection.

## ELECTRONIC COMMUNICATIONS

### Email

#### Servers—Routine Purging or "Auto-Delete"

It is common for companies with large volumes of email traffic to implement routine purging of email from their servers. Any such policies and their manner of implementation should be described in the Overview. For example:

The email servers purge email not subject to legal preservation obligations on a routine schedule (i.e., "auto-delete") as follows:

| Email Message Location | Retention Period (from date of receipt) |
|---|---|
| Email in Inbox | 21 days |
| Email in Sent Items Folder | 5 days |
| Email in Deleted Items Folder | 2 days |
| Email in Drafts Folder | 21 days |
| Email moved to User Created Folders | indefinite |
| Outlook Calendar Items | 21 days |

## ELECTRONIC COMMUNICATIONS

### Email

#### Servers—Backup

The Overview should describe the way the email servers are backed up. For example:

The Company uses SuperDuper Backup to perform nightly backups of the email servers onto tape.

The following table shows the backup schedule for the Company mail servers, as well as the backup tape recycling schedule for each:

| Location | Email Server | Backup Schedule | Backup Retention |
|---|---|---|---|
| Location A | Mail1 | Daily – Full | 5-day rotation; Tapes offsite daily |
| Location B | Mail2 | Daily – Full | 5-day rotation; Tapes offsite daily |
| Location C | Mail3 | Daily – Full | 5-day rotation; Tapes offsite daily |
| Location D | Mail4 | Daily – Full | 5-day rotation; Tapes offsite daily |

## ELECTRONIC COMMUNICATIONS

### Instant Messaging

The Overview should describe the parameters of any Instant Messaging use at the Company. For example:

Instant Messaging (IM) is an application that allows for real-time communication between users via an Internet connection. IM is used at the Company by certain employees to communicate both internally and with users outside the Company. Company employees are able to use a variety of IM services that they can access via the Internet. The Company permits the use of AOL Messenger, Microsoft Messenger, and Yahoo Messenger. All IM clients are configured by the IT Department with the required "proxy settings" prior to their use. The Company blocks users from downloading and installing IM clients that are not configured by IT; this is accomplished by denying administrator access to users on their desktops and laptops . . .

## FILE SHARES

Most companies provide shared server space for users to store files like word processing documents, spreadsheets, slide presentations, etc. These may be configured and organized in a variety of ways. The way a company maintains these types of business documents, which are often critical information assets operationally as well as for legal compliance purpose, should be described in the Systems Overview. For example:

The Company's network includes locations that store data created by employees (such as Word documents, spreadsheets, etc.) and by applications (such as server logs, database transactions, etc.). Depending on the nature and source of this data, the location where it is stored can vary. The Company's local area network (LAN) is used to securely connect employee desktops, printers, file servers, Exchange servers, and database servers that are geographically proximate to each other. A wide area network (WAN) is then used to connect multiple LANs together. For additional storage space, the Company uses a storage area network (SAN), network attached storage (NAS), and content addressed storage (CAS).

A SAN is a separate network apart from the LAN that is specifically configured to allow servers to communicate with large storage arrays. As more storage is needed, additional disks are simply added to the SAN and access to this storage space is given to the required server(s) on a particular LAN. NAS devices are also used for additional storage space but are connected directly to the LAN and can be accessed and used by servers that are provided with access. CAS is used to store data that is "fixed", i.e., data that is written once and never changed.

The Company provides each employee with his or her own private home share, as well as the ability to access group-shared folders which may be accessed by multiple employees.

Private home shares are used by individuals to store documents that may not necessarily need to be shared with other employees. Examples might include drafts of documents, internal reports, or financial models for testing. Access to these home shares is restricted to the particular employee for whom the home share was created.

Group shares are used by employees to store documents to be shared between teams or groups of employees. The folder structure within each group share is generally organized by a business unit and then further broken down into subfolders that are classified into working groups. Access to the group's share is granted only to members of the group. Employees also have the ability to rename and create folders and subfolders within the group share at their discretion, which can be used as shared storage space by multiple employees . . .

The Company makes use of file servers for personal/group shares. The backup procedures for each server vary depending on the folders that are being backed up. It is important to note that the size of the data on these servers varies from time to time depending on the amount of data being used . . .

## BACKUP SYSTEMS AND MEDIA

Whether undertaken for disaster recovery or other reasons, systems and media that backup live data are often a critical source of information sought after for legal and compliance purposes. Accordingly, it is critical to accurately and comprehensively describe the backup policies, procedures, and systems environment. For example:

The Company uses SuperDuper Backup to perform, track, and manage its backup procedures. SuperDuper Backup is an enterprise level backup and recovery suite that has the capability of communicating with various robotic libraries and tape drives. Backup tapes are sent offsite daily to a third-party storage facility, Safe Haven, which also maintains an inventory of all tapes in its possession. There are no backup tapes in Safe Haven's possession that pre-date the implementation of SuperDuper. The Company uses Linear Tape-Open (LTO) tapes for storing backup content . . .

> The Company's backup systems are controlled by the IT Department, but the data that is involved in the backup process is controlled by the respective business units that created and stored the data. These business units control the retention period for the data they wish to have backed up from their departments. A backup request form must be completed and sent to the IT Department for any new backup or changes to any existing backup procedures . . .

## USER ASSETS

In most situations, it will at least be possible that unique ESI resides on local machines or storage media in the custody of individual users. The Systems Overview should present a complete picture of these repositories of ESI that are "in the hands" of users. For example:

### Desktops/Laptops

Company employees typically are issued desktops (while some users are also issued laptops) to access the Company network in order to perform required business functions. These machines are also used by employees to create data, which can include but are not limited to, personal and work-related spreadsheets, Word documents, images, presentations, PDFs, and local databases.

### Local Hard Drives

Laptop users have discretion over where to store files on local hard drives. Users can store files and documents on their local laptop hard drives; there are no Company-required naming conventions followed by users when saving information to these local hard drives. Desktop users, however, are only able to store data locally in approved folders, which are generally used by Windows applications to store system-related information. Desktop users are not able to save documents to areas on their machines such as the Desktop or My Documents folder.

Laptops have limited space available for file storage and applications; therefore, employees generally delete unused or unneeded documents from their machines on a regular basis absent legal requirements to the contrary. In addition, the Company does not backup local laptop/desktops hard drives as a standard practice or policy. Individual users who want files/documents backed up from their local hard drives do so by saving files/documents to their personal home share or group shares to which they have access.

### Inventory Tracking

Inventory tracking of user machines is controlled through the Company's internal tracking system. When new hardware is required for an employee, a ticket is submitted to the help desk, which then distributes the requested hardware. The system is used to track the type of hardware that was issued, as well as its physical location. New computers are issued to users with a standard operating system image that varies slightly depending on the intended use of the machine. Additional software required by the user is then pushed to his/her machine over the network using the Company's software distribution system.

### Installing of New Software

Company users do not have administrative rights on their laptops or desktops; accordingly, users do not have the ability to install software or remove software on their machines without assistance from the IT Department.

### CDs/DVDs

Employees cannot burn CDs and/or DVDs using Company-issued computers without assistance from an administrator.

### Removable Media

The use of removable media storage (such as USB drives, memory sticks, and external hard drives) is prohibited; all mass storage USB devices (e.g., external hard drives, "thumb drives") are explicitly blocked on the desktop and the laptop. Users who wish to copy information to removable media must obtain approval from their manager.

### PDA/Mobile Devices

There currently are 655 Blueberry users at the Company. These devices allow users to send and receive email messages while not physically connected to the Company's network. These messages are then synchronized with the email server and appear in the respective user's Inbox, Sent Items, etc. All email messages that are sent and received by Company employees using a Blueberry will exist in the email server mailbox for that user . . .

## VOICEMAIL

The difficulty of searching voicemail with current technology continues to make it one of the thorniest challenges from a legal and compliance perspective. However, there can be no denying that voicemails could in a variety of scenarios constitute critical records and evidence. Moreover, the propagation of "unified messaging" systems that store voicemails in email or other formats has increased the incidence of stored voicemail persisting in the IT environment. The Systems Overview should spell out the details of how voicemail content is handled in the Company's environment. For example:

> Each Company employee is given access to a mailbox within the company's voicemail system, Voice Mail ("VM"). VM is a unified messaging system that has the ability to send users an email message containing their voicemails in the form of email attachments . . .
>
> VM works with a separate email server instance to store and access voicemail messages on the email server. All voicemail subscribers must have a mailbox set up on the email server, which stores only voicemail messages and it is not used for email storage. The messages are stored as audio (WAV) files in individual subscribers' email mailboxes. VM does not automatically associate an employee's name with his/her voicemail account. When a new mailbox is created, the help desk manually enters the associated employee name into the VM system for that account. There are no message quotas or retention limits for voicemail messages on any system.
>
> Backups of the VM servers occur weekly. However, only certain data (such as extensions, passwords, and greetings) are stored. The actual voicemail messages are not part of the backup routine . . .

## APPLICATIONS AND DATABASES

Companies utilize a wide array of applications and enterprise databases for an equally wide array of business purposes. These are important sources of ESI often overlooked in the haste to find smoking gun emails. As such, they should be identified and described carefully in the Systems Overview. For example:

> The Company utilizes and supports a number of databases and software applications which run on those databases. The main applications utilized by the Company include:
>
> **The Human Resources System:**
>
> The Human Resources System ("HR") is the Company's main HR system, which holds employee status, department information, and some basic benefits information. HR was implemented in 1992 and the data has never been purged. All entries to the system are entered as new line items in the database; i.e., if an

employee's status or department were to change, the modification is entered as a new record in the system with the appropriate effective date, rather than an update to an existing record . . .

**The Accounting System:**

The Accounting System ("Accounting") is used to maintain and manage the Company's Accounting function . . . Accounting consists of various components, including:

- General Ledger, for integrating and reporting on information from all modules;
- Accounts Payable for processing payments;
- Accounts Receivable for entering and maintaining customer information, processing invoices and receivables, and registering payments;
- Asset Management for maintaining capitalized assets as well as non-capitalized inventory items . . .
- Purchasing for creating, approving, editing, budget checking, dispatching, modifying, deleting, posting, and reconciling purchase orders for goods and services . . .

**Database Overview**

These databases are stored on an SQL Server 2000 cluster. The following is a list of database servers used by the above in-house applications as well as the applications that access those databases and brief backup descriptions:

| Location | Database Server | Applications | Backup Description |
|---|---|---|---|
| Location 1 | Server 1 | HR, Accounting | Backup to disk, then to tape. Daily full, retained for 3 weeks. Weekly full, retained for 4 months. |

## DEPARTING EMPLOYEES

Most companies follow certain procedures for addressing ESI and storage media left behind by former employees. Since very often this ESI may be critical for legal or compliance purposes, it is essential that these procedures be well understood and described in the Systems Overview. For example:

When a user's employment with the Company terminates, his/her employment status is updated within the HR system by the HR Department. This triggers an email notification to be sent to the help desk and the IT Department informing them of the employee's last day. The email account of the departing employee is disabled at 5pm on his/her last day of employment, and his/her home directory is reassigned to his/her manager for 15 days. At the end of this 15-day period, both the home directory and mailbox undergo a manual deletion process which, in the absence of any applicable legal preservation duty, is performed by members of the IT Department.

Desktops and laptops of departing employees are re-imaged with a base image and kept in stock until needed. If the machine is to be decommissioned and sold, the hard drive is wiped using the Mr. Clean Data Cleaner utility. This utility is used for the secure erasure of data from PCs, laptops, and servers. If the hard drive cannot be wiped for any reason (such as drive failure), the hard drive is shredded and discarded. If the departing employee was subject to particular legal preservation instructions or requirements, the hard drive from the machine is removed, stored, and recorded by the IT Department until further instructions from the Legal Department.

APPENDIX 3

# GUIDELINES: DEVELOPING A RECORDS MANAGEMENT PROGRAM

Records consist of paper-based and electronically stored information. Records management is the practice of identifying, classifying, archiving, preserving, and destroying records. Developing an effective records management program (also referred to as a "records retention program") requires addressing the above functions under guidelines and policies that enable proper governance and compliance. Within an eDiscovery context, this means being able to effectively and lawfully respond to potential or actual litigation or regulatory review without causing unintended negative consequences.

*Note: Records Management is a subset of Information Lifecycle Management, which is discussed in detail in Chapter 26.*

Developing a records management program typically involves moving through several phases, as outlined below.

1. **Develop a Records Classification Scheme**: Information classification is designed to place information into manageable buckets, making it easier to understand how to interpret business, legal, and regulatory requirements related to importance, priorities, confidentiality, privilege, privacy, retention, and destruction.
2. **Develop a Records Retention Schedule**: This is essentially a matrix that associates the record with its classification, its custodian or owner, its business, legal or regulatory requirement, and its retention period and destruction requirements.
3. **Develop an Information Map**: This is a visual representation of where and how information assets are created and reside, and how information flows through the organization, including destruction. An Information Map (also referred to as a "Data Map") identifies the information asset, the custodian (or "owner"), and the equipment on which the information resides.
4. **Reconcile the Schedule and the Map**: The reconciliation process ensures that the retention schedule requirements and the information flow process are in accord and do not conflict.
5. **Develop Policies**: This represents the overarching body of information that guides and enables effective execution of the records management program. Policies define Who, What, Where, Why, and When. Policies are supplemented by Procedures that define How.

   *Note: It is important that policies and procedures define the specific destruction methods applicable to the specific information asset and the media upon which it resides in order to ensure that complete destruction is actually accomplished.*
6. **Develop a Governance Program**: This consists of selected individuals that have the authority and responsibility for effective execution and compliance of the records management program by ensuring that management is committed, that resources are allocated, and that practitioners are adequately educated with respect to the program.
7. **Implement the Program**: This includes education and training, and the retention and destruction in accord with the Schedule and Policies. It may also include the acquisition of technology to facilitate the process, including identification, capture, storage, archival, destruction, and reporting.
8. **Implement Regular Audits**: This is to ensure that the records retention program consistently meets all objectives.

APPENDIX 4

# SAMPLE RECORDS MANAGEMENT POLICY PROVISIONS

TABLE OF CONTENTS

## INTRODUCTION

The sample policy statements included herein are a limited representation of actual policy statements in use within various firms of all sizes and operating requirements. While any particular policy statement may apply in any given situation, each policy statement may not represent a "best practice" in any given situation. Accordingly, these samples are presented to educate readers regarding what they might expect to find within various organizations. Determination of suitability of a particular sample, or combination of samples for any particular application, rests solely with the individual decision-maker, after taking into account the unique legal, regulatory, and operating requirements of the organization in which the samples are to be applied.

## 1. STATEMENTS OF PURPOSE AND SCOPE

### SAMPLE NO. 1

The purpose of this Document Retention Policy is to ensure that the Company retains documents only for so long as retention is likely to be useful for business purposes, or is otherwise required by applicable law. By regularly and systematically disposing of outdated documents, we can reduce our storage costs and make more efficient use of documents currently needed. Moreover, in the event of litigation or a governmental investigation or audit, it is desirable to be able to explain that documents no longer in our possession were discarded in the regular course of business pursuant to a formal document retention program, rather than on an arbitrary or ad hoc basis. The regular, periodic discarding of documents pursuant to a formal policy will help avoid any inference that documents that may be relevant to litigation or to an investigation or audit were deliberately destroyed. As discussed in the enclosed policy, should litigation be commenced or reasonably anticipated, or should an investigation or audit be commenced or reasonably anticipated, we will endeavor to save all relevant files until the litigation, investigation, or audit is concluded or we are otherwise relieved of any preservation obligation, even if the files would otherwise have been discarded under our document retention policy.

### SAMPLE NO. 2

As the Company grows, it becomes increasingly important that we safeguard our information, keep critical business documents, and discard materials that are no longer necessary.

### SAMPLE NO. 3

The purpose of the Company's Document Retention Policy (this "Policy") is to ensure retention of records necessary for ongoing business operations, legal compliance, and audit protection, while promoting cost savings, orderly and efficient records management, and protection against unfair allegations of selective document destruction. The law requires that the Company maintain certain types of corporate records, usually for a specified period of time.

### SAMPLE NO. 4

The purpose of the Company's Document Retention Policy is to facilitate the strategic management, on a global basis, of information in all forms, whether electronic or hard copy, from creation to disposal, using generally accepted practices, processes, and systems

SAMPLE NO. 5

The Company's fundamental objective is to retain only those Company Records that are necessary for ongoing business operations, or for compliance with legal, tax, or other regulatory requirements.

SAMPLE NO. 6

The purpose of this Policy is to provide general guidelines for the identification, retention, storage, protection, and disposal of the Company's records consistent with legal and business requirements. Adherence to this Policy will assist the Company in complying with legal requirements and in responding to subpoenas and document demands. Failure to comply with this Document Retention Policy ("Policy") can cause negative consequences, including excess storage costs and the inability to locate records that are needed. All employees are responsible for ensuring that accurate and complete records are identified, retained, stored, protected, and destroyed in accordance with this Policy.

The Company provides its employees with computing and telecommunication resources, including but not limited to, computer hardware/software, Internet access, electronic mail ("email"), telephone, cellular telephone, and voicemail (collectively referred to as computing resources or computer system) for business purposes. Therefore, these resources should be used primarily to further the Company's business objectives.

SAMPLE NO. 7

The purpose of this Policy is to maximize the effectiveness of the Company's use of information assets and to minimize the risk that the Company's records will not be available to meet the business needs of the company, including legal, tax, and other regulatory requirements.

SAMPLE NO. 8

By deleting excess messages, this policy will help increase the capacity of the email system and reduce the risk of misuse of stored messages by deleting excess messages.

SAMPLE NO. 9

These Policies apply to all locations worldwide where the Company and its subsidiaries create or maintain their records (whether stored at company locations, off-site document storage facilities, email, or any other electronic media). They apply to all employees and any other individual or entity that uses the Company's IT Resources. Compliance with this policy will result not only in cost savings to the company, but also in finding and retrieving required records more easily when needed, thereby reducing the need for expensive electronic and manual searching.

SAMPLE NO. 10

The purpose of this Record Retention Policy (the "Policy") is to assure retention of records necessary for ongoing business operations, legal compliance, and audit protection, while promoting cost savings, orderly and efficient records management, and protecting against allegations of selective document destruction.

SAMPLE NO. 11

The Company's Information Systems are intended to help its employees complete their work and protect the integrity of the Company's information. The Company is required to comply with certain regulatory and government agencies that dictate how information is to be stored. The attached policy is designed to meet the following objectives.

- Allow Company employees to work productively from within the office and remotely.
- Maintain Company information within the company in a protected and compliant manner.
- Protect Company employees' privacy by limiting exposure of personal computing equipment to Company-related legal proceedings.
- Protect Company information systems from potential dangers outside the Company network environment.

SAMPLE 12

The Policy applies to records located in homes, storage facilities, or any other location. Such records must be retained or destroyed as required by this Policy.

## 2. GENERAL INSTRUCTIONS TO EMPLOYEES

SAMPLE NO. 1

It is the Company's policy to maintain complete, accurate, and high-quality records. Records are to be retained for the period of their immediate use, unless longer retention is required for historical reference, contractual, legal or regulatory requirements, or for other purposes as set forth herein. Records that are no longer required, or have satisfied their required periods of retention, shall be destroyed in an appropriate manner. However, any and all records that may potentially be used in an official proceeding or that are relevant to a pending or reasonably anticipated legal proceeding or investigation or tax audit will be carefully preserved and maintained for the duration of the proceeding, investigation, or audit in addition to any retention period set forth in this policy.

SAMPLE NO. 2

Please take the time to review this policy and begin implementing it as soon as practicable. Should you have any questions concerning this policy or its application, please direct them to Jane Doe.

SAMPLE NO. 3

Keep all records necessary to conduct the work of your department for as long as they may realistically be relevant or required to be retained under local laws. It is equally important that we promptly delete records we no longer need. Be realistic about the likelihood you'll need records in the future, and don't store records "just in case" you may need them later. Storing unneeded records consumes expensive space and resources and makes it harder to retrieve necessary records.

SAMPLE NO. 4

All employees must fully comply with this Policy and any records retention or destruction policies and schedules circulated within the Company from time to time, provided all employees note the following exception to any stated destruction schedule: part of the Policy is suspending destruction under certain circumstances. If you believe, or the Company informs you, that Company Records are relevant to litigation, or potential litigation (i.e., a dispute that could result in litigation), governmental investigation or potential governmental investigation or existing or potential tax disputes, then you must preserve those records until the Legal Department determines the records are no longer needed. If you believe that exception might apply, or have any question regarding the possible applicability of that exception, please contact the Legal Department.

SAMPLE NO. 5

Destruction of records is permitted only when there is: (1) no improper motive for the destruction of the records; (2) no legal, or regulatory reason to maintain the records and no Hold in place; and (3) such destruction is in accordance with the Retention Schedule.

SAMPLE NO. 6

Each Company Record must be retained in a manner that allows it to be easily retrieved when necessary to meet business needs, including legal, tax, and other regulatory requirements.

SAMPLE NO. 7

User responsibility includes the proper management of drafts, versions and copies. Only the final version of a Company Record should be retained. Drafts and copies should be deleted when the final version is completed, unless there is a specific business need to retain them. In those instances, they should be retained for only as long as the business need continues and no legal obligation dictates otherwise.

SAMPLE NO. 8

Disposal of Company Records must be performed in a manner that assures complete disposal, and protects against unauthorized disclosure during the disposal process at the completion of the retention period.

## 3. POLICIES THAT VARY BY CATEGORY OR TYPE OF RECORD

SAMPLE NO. 1

With respect to various categories of documents that we may have in our files, our policies are as follows:

SAMPLE NO. 2

Keep the following types of records for the specified period after the conclusion of the underlying event (for example, after a customer relationship terminates, after a contract ends, after a platform or feature is no longer offered, or after a tax return is filed):

SAMPLE NO. 3

The specific types of records mentioned here are only examples, not an exhaustive list of the types of records you need to keep. If you aren't sure how long you should keep a specific type of record, check with your manager or send an email to Jane Doe.

## SAMPLE NO. 4

From time to time the Company establishes retention or destruction policies or schedules for specific categories of records to ensure legal compliance, and also to accomplish other objectives, such as preserving intellectual property and cost management. Several categories of documents that bear special consideration are identified below. While minimum retention periods are suggested, the retention of the documents identified below and of documents not included in the identified categories should be determined primarily by the application of the general guidelines affecting document retention identified above, as well as any other pertinent factors. Employees are only permitted to destroy records where there is (i) no improper motive for the destruction of records; (ii) no legal or regulatory reason to maintain the records; and (iii) such destruction is in accordance with any retention schedules circulated by the Company.

## SAMPLE NO. 5

Only the "official" copy or version of a Company Business Record needs to be retained in accordance with the Retention Schedule. Other copies are considered to be informational and should be properly disposed of when there is no longer an immediate need for the information.

## SAMPLE NO. 6

Only the final versions of records should be maintained. Drafts and copies should be purged when the final version is completed, unless there is a specific business need to retain them (and then retained only as long as the business need exists) or pursuant to Hold Orders as indicated below.

## SAMPLE NO. 7

Upon completion of the Project, records relating to the Project which are no longer necessary for ongoing business operations, legal compliance, and audit protection (or pursuant to Hold Orders as indicated below), should be disposed of properly. If you have any questions as to whether certain records should be disposed of, contact the Legal Department as soon as possible.

## SAMPLE NO. 8

Those individuals or working groups seeking a variance from the retention period set forth here must document, in writing, a legitimate business or legal need to retain the record for a different period of time and obtain written approval from the Legal Department thereon.

## SAMPLE NO. 9

All other records not covered by the Retention Schedule must be reviewed on a regular basis—at least once a year—for possible disposal. Non-business records should be discarded when they no longer are needed for business purposes. In general, non-business records should not be retained for longer than three years. There may be instances, however, where there is a need to retain certain non-business records for a longer period of time. Examples are templates or forms used to create other records, or research that may have continuing business value. The retention of these records beyond three years is subject to local management approval and the requirement for annual review.

## 4. EMAIL

SAMPLE NO. 1

As a general policy, the Company automatically deletes all email after 30–60 days. Any important email that needs to be preserved should be printed out before deletion and saved either in a hard copy correspondence file or on the computer desktop in a folder pertaining to the particular subject matter. If saved in a hard copy correspondence file, the email is subject to the general guidelines relating to correspondence. If saved in a computer desktop folder according to subject matter, the folder should be deleted when the matter is concluded, subject to the specific guidelines set forth elsewhere in this Policy.

SAMPLE NO. 2

Emails, drafts, notes, and other short-term materials that are not regularly maintained or necessary for future business operations, or that serve as the basis for a later finished work product should be promptly deleted. Such casually created documents can often be misleading or misunderstood by others in hindsight. For this reason, save selectively, and do not do a mass back-up of old email onto the hard disk drive of your computer.

SAMPLE NO. 3

Email that needs to be saved should be either printed in hard copy and kept in the appropriate file, or downloaded to a computer file and kept electronically or on a disk as a separate file. The retention period depends on the subject matter of the email, as covered elsewhere in this Policy.

SAMPLE NO. 4

The Company's email systems are tools to facilitate communications, and are not for the long-term preservation and storage of Business Records.

SAMPLE NO. 5

If email contains information, either in the body of the message or in attachments, that falls into one of the categories in the Retention Schedule, it must be retained and disposed of in accordance with the Record Retention Policy and Schedule.

SAMPLE NO. 6

The maximum retention period for email that does not fall into one of the Retention Schedule categories is 45 days after the message is sent or received. The 45-day retention period also applies to drafts and attachments, and foldered or archived email messages.

SAMPLE NO. 7

Email retained in accordance with this Policy must be stored in a manner that will facilitate effective search and retrieval as required for business, legal, or tax purposes.

SAMPLE NO. 8

Users must regularly and systematically review email messages to ensure that they comply with email retention, storage, and retrieval requirements.

SAMPLE NO. 9

Email must not be routinely or automatically forwarded to a non-corporate mailbox (e.g., forwarding to your personal email account).

SAMPLE NO. 10

Forwarding company business related email to your external email account, including but not limited to accounts such as Yahoo!, Gmail, MSN, AOL, etc. (any such non-Company email accounts are collectively referred to as "personal email accounts"), is not permitted.

SAMPLE NO. 11

Personal email accounts are not to be used for Company business-related communication, including transferring of Company business-related documents.

SAMPLE NO. 12

The use of personal email archives (PST files) is not permitted.

## 5. EMAIL ETIQUETTE

SAMPLE NO. 1

Email messages should be written in a courteous and professional manner.

SAMPLE NO. 2

Never compose an email that you would not want someone in court to read aloud to a jury. To a judge or jury, an email may just as well be typed on the Company letterhead and sent by regular mail.

SAMPLE NO. 3

Minimize distribution (sending, copying, forwarding, etc.) of email by distributing only to recipients who "need to know".

SAMPLE NO. 4

Do not forward or copy privileged or confidential email to other persons. If you do so, the message may lose its status as privileged or confidential.

## SAMPLE NO. 5

Do not use the Company's IT Resources for:

- illegal purposes;
- personal financial gain;
- gaining unauthorized access to remote computer systems;
- decrypting system and user passwords;
- propagating spam;
- discussing religious or political issues;
- distributing chain letters, copyrighted or otherwise protected materials;
- creating or transmitting offensive material or material that is intended to threaten or harass; and/or
- creating or transmitting content that includes sexual implications, racial slurs, gender-specific comments, or any other comments that offensively address age, gender, race, sexual orientation, religious or political beliefs, national origin, or disability.

## SAMPLE NO. 6

Report any email or Internet misuse to your supervisor or to the Human Resources Department.

## SAMPLE NO. 7

Users must never use Company IT Resources to create, access, transmit, or store any material that would be considered in bad taste, or otherwise inappropriate, offensive, or disrespectful of others (e.g., obscene, lewd, pornographic or violent material, sexually oriented jokes or cartoons, and/or other offensive material related to age, race, color, sex, religion, national origin, disability, or sexual orientation). Users encountering or receiving this kind of material should immediately report the incident to Company management.

## SAMPLE NO. 8

Users must never use Company systems to send or forward electronic "chain letters". These are generally non-business-related messages such as jokes, stories, poems, or solicitations with excessively large distribution lists that can burden system resources and disrupt corporate IT Resources.

## SAMPLE NO. 9

Special caution is urged when using email, instant messaging, or other means of electronic communication to avoid casual or unprofessional communications that may be taken out of context and lead to embarrassment of the individual or the Company, or worse. Remember that electronic communications are often preserved and easily retransmitted by others who may not interpret them as intended.

SAMPLE NO. 10

Organize your email messages like a formal memorandum. For example, you should clearly identify the subject of your email message, write objectively, outline long email messages with letters or numbers, and summarize the purpose of your email message.

SAMPLE NO. 11

To have effective email communication and minimize the need for clarifying follow-up emails, be as objective, complete, concise, and clear as possible when drafting an email message. For example, address the issue at hand without interjecting unneeded emotions, research an issue as thoroughly as possible before sending an email message, and avoid using slang or ambiguous abbreviations.

SAMPLE NO. 12

Users should designate a surrogate for their email accounts who will be able to read and respond to, if necessary, a user's email messages when a user is away for any prolonged period of time. The surrogate feature allows another user to access your account without the need to disclose one's password. All email messages (including responses) created by a surrogate while accessing another user's email account will have a header that indicates the identity of the surrogate creating the message.

SAMPLE NO. 13

Use labels such as "Urgent", "Not Urgent," and "Confidential" in the subject line of email messages, as needed, to help users prioritize responses.

## 6. RETENTION POLICY AND THE LEGAL DUTY TO PRESERVE

SAMPLE NO. 1

All record retention periods are subject to the requirement that an employer preserve records in the event of anticipated or actual litigation. Any records that may be relevant to anticipated or actual litigation must be retained until the final disposition of the case, irrespective of the applicable statutory retention period. A record should be retained if there is any uncertainty regarding whether the record may be relevant to the litigation. In addition, all records concerning harassment and discrimination complaints and investigations should be retained for at least three years following the separation of employment of the individual(s) raising the complaint, irrespective of whether an administrative complaint is ultimately filed.

SAMPLE NO. 2

We sometimes need to keep records for shorter or longer periods because of unusual circumstances like litigation, government investigation, or specific privacy regulations. Notify the Legal Department if you believe such an unusual circumstance exists. Where appropriate, the Legal Department or Finance Department will inform relevant employees of special retention periods.

SAMPLE NO. 3

All documents and files (including computer files and email) relating to a particular transaction or subject matter should be retained once that transaction or subject matter becomes the subject of a threatened or actual litigation claim or governmental investigation. All such documents should then be retained until the litigation or investigation is finally concluded, as confirmed by counsel. For purposes of this policy, threatened litigation should be understood in a broad sense so that once the Company learns, whether formally or informally, that a party may be contemplating litigation against it, or once the Company is contemplating asserting a claim against another party, all files relating to that matter should be retained.

SAMPLE NO. 5

Records may become subject to a "Hold" for a variety of legal compliance reasons. If you have reason to believe that a litigation or investigation is pending or anticipated, please contact the Legal Department for further guidance before disposing of any documents. The Legal Department shall decide whether to issue a "Hold" instructing that records be preserved until the Legal Department removes the Hold instruction.

SAMPLE NO. 6

In certain pending or anticipated litigation and government investigations, "Litigation Holds" are issued by the Legal Staff and Tax Staff requiring that records be preserved until the legal proceeding(s) are concluded (even if the applicable record retention periods have expired and the "Open Tax Years" hold period has lapsed).

## 7. ESI DEFINED AS CORPORATE PROPERTY

SAMPLE NO. 1

Computing resources provided to its employees are the property of the Company. Any information created, modified, transmitted, received, or stored on these resources is the property of the Company. At the end of one's employment relationship with the Company, all computing resources provided during one's employment and any information mentioned above must remain intact and on Company premises.

SAMPLE NO. 2

All email messages created, stored, or transmitted on Company IT systems are the property of the Company, whether originating from internal or external email systems, and may be deleted or disclosed to others at any time without prior notice.

SAMPLE NO. 3

All electronic communications systems (including, but not limited to telephonic and computer-based systems such as voicemail, email, Internet, etc.) and all communication and information transmitted by, received from, or stored in these systems are the property of the Company.

## 8. PERSONAL USE OF INFORMATION TECHNOLOGY RESOURCES

SAMPLE NO. 1

Employees may occasionally use Company computer resources for personal purposes if (a) used responsibly; (b) during their own time; and (c) without incurring any expense or liability to the Company.

SAMPLE NO. 2

Occasional, limited personal use of the Company's IT Resources is permitted if it is reasonable, ethical, and does not interfere with work responsibilities. In general, personal use of Company IT Resources is not appropriate when it interferes with a user's overall productivity or performance on the job, is in conflict with other corporate policies and guidelines for employee conduct, places a burden on Company IT Resources, or otherwise hinders or prevents the Company from conducting its business in the manner deemed optimal by the Company's management.

SAMPLE NO. 3

Computers (laptops and desktops), portable electronic devices such as cell phones, personal digital assistants, "blackberries", and storage media such as USB "thumb" drives, CDs, DVDs, and portable hard drives issued to Company employees or paid for by the Company, as well as access to the Company's network and other information systems, are provided to assist employees in the performance of their jobs and should be used primarily for business purposes. While the Company recognizes that certain users may engage in limited use of corporate information systems including email, telephones, fax, voicemail, and scanning systems for personal and other communications as a matter of convenience, such uses are subject to all policies set forth below.

## 9. NO EXPECTATION OF PRIVACY IN COMPANY ESI

SAMPLE NO. 1

By using Company computer resources, employees understand that they have no expectation of privacy in anything they create, store, send, or receive on the Company's computer system. Passwords are used for security purposes and not for privacy. The Company has the right but not the duty to monitor any and all aspects of its computer system.

SAMPLE NO. 2

Users should have no expectation of privacy concerning their use of Company IT Resources, including email, Company-provided computing equipment, the corporate Intranet, Company-provided access to the public Internet, or other Company IT systems, except where applicable law provides differently. The required use of passwords to gain access to Company IT Resources is for the Company's protection—it does not imply that users can expect that their communications and use of those IT Resources are private. By their use of these systems to the extent permitted by applicable law, users specifically consent to having their use and communications monitored and recorded. This consent only applies to the use of Company IT Resources—it does not apply when a user obtains access to the public Internet outside of the corporate-computing environment or network (for example, when access is not provided by the Company using his/her own personal computer).

SAMPLE NO. 3

The Company has the right to review, audit, or monitor email created, stored, or transmitted on Company email systems in accordance with local law. All email messages and associated records remain the sole property of the Company.

SAMPLE NO. 4

Users have no reasonable expectation of privacy in any information they create, store, send, or receive using Company-issued computers, devices (including without limitation records or other information relating to telephone communications), storage media or the Company network, or other Company information systems to which the users have access.

SAMPLE NO. 5

The Company reserves the right to save, copy, monitor, review, disclose, or make any other use of any such information as the Company if its sole discretion deems appropriate and consistent with its legal obligations. Furthermore, the Company may be required to preserve, collect, search, extract, review, and produce or disclose any information created, stored, sent, or received by any employee in order to comply with legal obligations or for other reasons at any time and with or without notice to the employee.

## 10. CONSEQUENCES FOR NON-COMPLIANCE WITH POLICIES

SAMPLE NO. 1

By continued use of the Company's information technology systems, you agree to abide by the standards and procedures in this policy and any additional policies and procedures that may be implemented by the Company. If you fail to comply with this policy, the Company may take disciplinary action, which may result in your dismissal from employment and legal action against you.

SAMPLE NO. 2

Failure to comply with this Policy and any retention schedules disseminated pursuant to this Policy may result in punitive action against the employee, including suspension or termination. Questions about this policy should be referred to the Company's General Counsel or to its Chief Compliance Officer.

SAMPLE NO. 3

Failure to comply with the Company's Retention Policies may result in the termination of a user's access to Company IT Resources, and, when appropriate, further disciplinary or remedial action, up to and including termination of employment or other contractual relationship.

SAMPLE NO. 4

Failure to retain those records as required by the law could subject you and the Company to penalties and fines, cause the loss of rights, obstruct justice, result in the destruction of potential evidence in a lawsuit, place the Company in contempt of court, or otherwise cause serious problems for the Company.

SAMPLE NO. 5

It is a criminal offense under United States law, punishable by fine or a maximum prison sentence of 20 years, or both, to alter, destroy, mutilate, conceal, cover up, falsify, or make false entry in any record or other document with the intent to impede, obstruct, or influence the investigation or proper administration of any matter within the jurisdiction of a federal department or agency or any bankruptcy case, or in relation to or contemplation of such matter or case. Such investigation or proceeding does not have to be pending or imminent at the time, nor must it be criminal in nature or carried out by a law enforcement agency. Additionally, the same penalty applies to anyone who alters, destroys, mutilates, or conceals a record, document, or other object, or attempts to do so, with the intent to impair the object's integrity or availability for use in an official proceeding. Note that the official proceeding need not be pending at the time of the offense.

SAMPLE NO. 6

It is unlawful to destroy, conceal, or falsify any record for the purpose of obstructing or influencing any lawsuit or other legal proceeding or investigation. Doing so may subject the Company and any offending individuals to civil and criminal penalties including fines and imprisonment.

SAMPLE NO. 7

Failure to comply with the requirement to seek guidance and to preserve records as instructed can result in serious adverse consequences to the Company and to the person(s) involved.

SAMPLE NO. 8

Failure to comply with the requirement to preserve documents and other information as instructed can result in serious adverse consequences to the Company and its employees. Specifically, it is unlawful to destroy, conceal, alter, or falsify any corporate business or other record, document, or object for the purpose of obstructing or influencing any lawsuit or other legal proceeding or investigation. Doing so may subject the Company and any offending persons to severe civil and criminal penalties including fines and imprisonment.

SAMPLE NO. 9

It is unlawful to destroy, conceal, or falsify any records for the purpose of obstructing or influencing any lawsuit or other legal proceeding or investigation. Doing so may subject the Company and any objecting individuals to civil and criminal penalties including fines and imprisonment. In addition, it is a criminal offense, punishable by fine or a maximum prison sentence of 20 years, or both, to alter, destroy, mutilate, conceal, cover up, falsify, or make false entry in any record or other document with the intent to impede, obstruct, or influence the investigation or proper administration of any matter within the jurisdiction of a U.S. federal department or agency or in any bankruptcy case or in relation to or in contemplation of such a case. These criminal penalties may apply even where an investigation has not been formally commenced or is otherwise pending or imminent, and even if the investigation is not criminal in nature. The same penalty applies to anyone who alters, destroys, mutilates, or conceals a record, document, or other object, or attempts to do so, with the intent to impair the object's availability for use in an official proceeding, whether or not pending.

SAMPLE NO. 10

Violation of any preceding policies may result in disciplinary action up to and including termination of employment. Furthermore, if any inappropriate use of the Company's computer equipment, electronic devices, information, or communication systems or networks causes damage or loss to the Company, the Company reserves the right to prosecute responsible parties to the fullest extent of the law.

## 11. SECURITY AND CONFIDENTIALITY CONSIDERATIONS

SAMPLE NO. 1

Information security is the responsibility of every employee and any other individual or entity that uses Company IT Resources. Users must ensure a high level of security in their use of Company IT Resources through appropriate behavior, such as maintaining the confidentiality of passwords, and use of encryption tools for Classified Information. Users must never engage in any activity that would disrupt or compromise the availability, integrity, or security of the Company's information or the Company's IT Resources, or otherwise result in their misuse. Users must immediately report all possible security breaches to Company management or to IT Security.

SAMPLE NO. 2

Users must not download or install unauthorized Internet executables such as games and entertainment software (e.g., MP3 files such as music/songs and movies, peer-to-peer network sharing), screen savers, instant-messaging services, or browser "plug-ins."

SAMPLE NO. 3

Users are prohibited from downloading or installing any software not authorized by corporate IT, including without limitation games and screen savers.

SAMPLE NO. 4

Users are not permitted to install or alter any software on Company-issued or owned computers or devices without permission of the IT Department.

SAMPLE NO. 5

Users are not permitted to usc password protection or encryption on documents and files (including individual Excel worksheets), including without limitation documents and files stored on network file shares, without first obtaining written permission from the Legal Department.

SAMPLE NO. 6

Users are not permitted to install or use encryption software on any Company-issued or owned computer or device without first obtaining written permission from the IT Department.

SAMPLE NO. 7

Employees are obligated to return all records when leaving the Company. This includes the return of any computer or electronic communication systems provided by the Company. Company policy is to retrieve hard drives from individual computers and store them for 14 days before wiping the drives not subject to legal hold or needed for another business purpose.

SAMPLE NO. 8

Upon termination of employment, the Director of Administration will contact the departing employee and request the return of all Company Records in the departing employee's possession, including hard copy and electronic records. The Director of Administration and, if the employee has another supervisor, the employee's supervisor will review, retain, and dispose of those records as appropriate in accordance with this policy.

## 12. DEFINITIONS APPLIED TO RECORDS

SAMPLE NO. 1

Company Records can be any information recorded in any form, such as text, image, or sound. Company Records may be stored or located in any type of media, such as paper documents, microfiche, microfilm, photographs, transparencies, graphs, charts, videos, diskettes, audio recordings, and all forms of electronically stored information.

SAMPLE NO. 2

An Official Record is the official version or copy of a Company Record that is to be retained by the individual or office as identified elsewhere in this Policy and in accordance with the Retention Schedule. Other copies are considered to be "informational", and should be properly disposed of when there is no longer an immediate need for the information.

SAMPLE NO. 3

The corporate records of the Company are important assets. Corporate records include essentially all records you produce within the scope of your employment, whether paper or electronic. Stored information can qualify as a record regardless of the form or medium in which it is created or stored. For example, a record could be a memorandum, email, contract, a voicemail message, computerized desk calendar, appointment book, or expense record.

SAMPLE NO. 4

Electronic communications constitute records subject to this Retention Policy and the Retention Schedule. Like any other records, if an electronic communication contains information (whether in the body of the message or in attachments) that falls into one of the categories in the Retention Schedule, it must be retained and disposed of in accordance with this Policy and the Retention Schedule.

SAMPLE NO. 5

Permanent Records are those that must not be discarded or destroyed, and may generally be characterized as those documents essential to the survival of the Company and recreation of its business in the event of a catastrophe. Permanent Records include records that (1) are essential to continued operations; (2) are essential to the Company's legal and financial status; (3) contain secret processes, formulas, or innovations which are not registered elsewhere or are otherwise related to trade secrets and other confidential matters; (4) are related to the Company's ownership of assets that would otherwise would be difficult or impossible to establish; or (5) are required to be maintained pursuant to a pending or reasonably anticipated legal proceeding or tax audit.

SAMPLE NO. 6

This Policy applies to all Company Records. A Company Record is any documentary material, regardless of physical form, that is generated or received by the Company in connection with the transaction of its business and retained for any period of time. A record that includes both business and personal information, such as an appointment calendar, is a Company Record. Examples of Company Records include (i) writing of any kind, including, for example, correspondence, reports, memoranda, notes, drafts, diaries, and calendars; and (ii) information kept in all media forms including, for example, paper, microfilm, microfiche, tapes, cartridges, diskettes, hard drives, and electronic records, such as email and computer files.

## 13. REMOTE ACCESS

SAMPLE NO. 1

Computer-generated business records, and files created, received, or stored through a home/ remote access connection, are subject to the retention requirements specified in the Record Retention Policy and Schedule. Although users may work on the Company's Business Records at home or other remote locations, they are never to be stored there, unless specifically approved by local Company management. If approved, they must be documented and retained by local management. This is true for all electronic and non-electronic Company Records, whether the record is an original or copy. They must be maintained in accordance with this Policy and the Retention Schedule at a location authorized by the Company organization that is responsible for the record.

SAMPLE NO. 2

Remote access to the corporate network is provided and permitted via VPN. Under no circumstances should VPN software be used on non-Company-issued or owned computers to access the corporate network.

SAMPLE NO. 3

Users are permitted to create, view, edit, or print (including local printers) documents, emails and files using Citrix. Documents; emails and files can be saved to corporate network servers from within Citrix sessions.

SAMPLE NO. 4

When accessing the Company network via Citrix, users are not permitted to store Company-business-related documents, including email attachments and other files, onto computers, devices, or other storage media not issued or owned by the Company.

SAMPLE NO. 5

Users are not permitted to upload files to Citrix from computers or other devices or storage media that are not issued or owned by the Company.

## 14. INSTANT MESSAGING AND BLACKBERRIES

SAMPLE NO. 1

All IM communication, both internal and external, is to be done using Microsoft Office Communicator only. These IM conversations will be logged and retained using the Live Communication Server and may be subject to discovery for litigation purposes. The use of third-party IM services (Yahoo!, AOL, MSN, etc.) is not permitted, unless used through Microsoft Office Communicator.

SAMPLE NO. 2

Blackberry SMS and PIN to PIN messaging will be logged and retained on the Company's Blackberry servers and may be subject to discovery for litigation purposes.

## Appendix 5

# LITIGATION HOLD FOR ESI: CHECKLIST OF KEY STEPS AND SOURCES TO ADDRESS

- **Is litigation reasonably anticipated?**
  - **document rationale for determination**
- **What is the scope of the required litigation hold?**
  - **Who are the custodians with relevant information?**
  - **What are the relevant time periods?**
  - **What is the relevant subject matter?**
  - **What sources and systems are impacted?**
    - **document rationale for determinations**
- **Send notice to affected users/custodians and IT managers**
- **Sources to secure**
  - **Email**
    - **Servers**
      - **Consider whether to suspend routine purge/auto-delete**
    - **Backup Tapes**
      - **Consider whether to suspend recycling**
    - **Archiving Systems**
    - **PCs—desktops and laptops**
      - **Forensic collection?**
      - **Home computers?**
    - **Mobile devices**
    - **Other "local" user storage devices such as portable storage media**
  - **"Business Documents"—word-processing documents, .pdf, spreadsheets, slide presentations, etc.**
    - **File Servers**
    - **Backup Tapes**
    - **Document Management Systems**
    - **PCs—desktops and laptops**
      - **Forensic collection?**
      - **Home computers?**

        - Mobile devices
        - Other "local" user storage devices such as portable storage media
    - Databases and Enterprise Systems—HR, accounting, etc.
    - Voicemail Systems
    - IM
    - Internet Presence
        - Websites
        - Chat rooms, bulletin boards, blogs, etc.
    - Corporate Intranet
    - Third-party custodians of data, such as offsite storage vendors
- Tracking of hold implementation
    - Accurate?
    - Verifiable?
    - Audit trail?
    - Documentation?
- Consideration of appropriate follow-up steps, such as periodic sweeps, reissuance of hold notifications, etc.

APPENDIX 6:

# SAMPLE LITIGATION HOLD PROCEDURE PROVISIONS

TABLE OF CONTENTS

## 1. INTRODUCTORY STATEMENT OF PURPOSE AND INTENT

This document describes certain policies and procedures that the Company uses to address the preservation and collection of electronically stored information ("ESI") under certain circumstances. It also provides certain information regarding the Company's electronic information systems relevant to implementing ESI preservation (the process of implementation commonly is referred to as a "litigation hold") and collection. Typically, the need to execute these steps arises in the context of requests for information or investigations by regulatory authorities or as a result of discovery obligations in civil litigation.

The following contains guidelines subject to adaptation as required by the circumstances of particular cases. They may be updated and revised from time to time as determined appropriate by legal and compliance personnel. Any deviation from these procedures must be approved in writing by the General Counsel or Chief Compliance Officer.

## 2. PRESERVATION OF ESI THROUGH LITIGATION HOLDS

### A. Determination to Implement a Litigation Hold

When it is determined that litigation or government inquiry may be reasonably probable or the Company receives notice of a potential legal proceeding, the first step the Legal Department will take is to investigate and assess whether the circumstances, including without limitation the credibility of any threat, indicate that a legal proceeding is, in fact, reasonably anticipated and thus, that a litigation hold should be initiated. The Chief Compliance Officer or General Counsel must be consulted where it is believed that circumstances may give rise to a preservation obligation. The determination as to whether and why to issue a litigation hold should be documented in a manner that preserves applicable privileges and protections from disclosure, but also in a manner that is sensitive to the fact that the documentation may eventually be disclosed.

### B. Determination of Scope of Hold

Once a determination has been made to preserve information related to a potential or pending legal proceeding—i.e., to implement a litigation hold—the next step is to determine the scope of the hold. This determination involves identifying the appropriate recipients of the hold notice, as well as identifying the subject matter of the information covered by the hold, and any other parameters that may be pertinent to the particular matter, e.g., relevant date ranges or particular types of documents. At this time, the committee that is responsible for electronic discovery, the Electronic Discovery Response Team (EDT), should be involved in all decisions discussed here to determine whether the matter implicates unique sources of ESI that should be targeted for immediate preservation or collection. These determinations and their underlying rationales should be documented in a manner that preserves applicable privileges. Once the initial hold notice has been distributed and initial preservation of relevant sources of ESI has been completed, further discussions with counsel occur with the goal of narrowing or further clarifying the scope of the hold. This can include limiting the custodian list, sources of ESI, the subject matter involved, or relevant date ranges. If required, the sources of ESI that required preservation are then revised, and additional or modified hold notices are distributed to the appropriate recipients.

Our process for preservation of ESI relies to a significant degree on proper identification of custodians—employees or other individuals who may have potentially relevant information. Potentially relevant ESI that is stored on email servers or on local PCs—which include much of the ESI most commonly sought after in litigation—can only be preserved and collected most effectively and efficiently if the custodians are properly identified.

## 3. IMPLEMENTATION OF HOLD

### A. Identifying Custodians and Issuing Hold Notices

A "custodian" of information may be an individual user, or a member of or group within the IT department responsible for certain elements of the information system, a business unit, or any other individual or functional group with access to Company information. To help ensure that custodians of information relevant to a pending or reasonably anticipated legal proceeding comply with legal preservation obligations, those custodians must receive a litigation hold notice from the Company's Legal or Compliance Department. The purpose of this notice is to instruct custodians regarding the nature and scope of a litigation hold as applicable to ESI (and other documents, such as paper files) under their control.

The Sedona Conference Working Group on Electronic Document Retention and Production[1] has identified the following characteristics of effective hold notices:

(a) Identifies the persons who are likely to have relevant information and communicates a preservation notice to those persons;

(b) Communicates the preservation notice in a manner that ensures that the recipients will receive actual, comprehensible, and effective notice of the requirement to preserve information;

(c) Is in written form;

(d) Clearly defines what information is to be preserved and how the preservation is to be undertaken; and

(e) Is periodically reviewed and, when necessary, reissued in either its original or an amended form.

The Sedona Conference Commentary on Legal Holds: The Trigger & The Process, a copy of which is available at http://www.thesedonaconference.org.

Hold notices should also provide a contact for recipients to communicate with where they have questions or need clarification; avoid including details that are irrelevant to the custodians' execution of the preservation instructions, and avoid overstating or stating without qualification the nature of any legal duty giving rise to the notice while emphasizing the importance of compliance.

Additionally, the attorneys (or personnel acting under their direction) responsible for the matter to which the litigation hold relates must provide the IT Department a list of custodians who are subject to the hold. The purpose of this list is to ensure that any routine deletion of ESI from the Company's systems under the control of IT, including but not limited to email, is suspended for those custodians on the list.

## B. Actions by IT to Preserve Electronic Communications

Receipt by the IT Department of a list of custodians triggers a series of actions designed to preserve potentially relevant ESI. These actions work in combination with the efforts of custodians who have received litigation hold notices to satisfy the Company's legal preservation obligations.

### 1. Email Stored on Company Servers

The Company's email system, including applicable retention periods under policy, is described in the Company's Systems Overview. When a particular custodian has email messages that are potentially relevant to a legal proceeding, it is necessary to suspend the normal retention policy for that custodian to ensure that those messages are not lost. To accomplish this, the Company attorney responsible for the matter must send the IT Department the list of custodians subject to the litigation hold for that matter.

When the IT Department receives a list of custodians, it should exempt the custodians on the list from the standard deletion policy. This involves updating the existing or creating a new Policy for the identified custodians' mailboxes to allow for indefinite message retention for all folders.

This process should be implemented as soon as possible upon identification of custodians to avoid regularly scheduled deletion, unless alternative timing is requested by the responsible Company attorney in writing.

[1] The Sedona Conference is a group of judges, lawyers, and technology professionals who issue "white papers" on electronic preservation and discovery issues; these white papers have been cited frequently by courts and historically have played an influential role in the development of the law of e-discovery.

Email messages in the mailboxes of custodians subject to the litigation hold are then retained indefinitely, until the Company attorney responsible for the matter communicates to the IT Department otherwise. If any of these custodians are named as custodians in a new matter, that matter will be added to a list of matters maintained by the IT Department for which the employees are subject to a hold. If a custodian is on the exemption list for multiple matters and one matter ends, the exemption remains in effect, and will remain in effect until the last matter concludes. As a result, many custodians—particularly custodians at the highest levels of the Company—may have email messages stored on the Company's servers that are far older than the standard retention period.

The Company will not retain email of former employees unless those employees were subject to a litigation hold at the time they left the Company. In the absence of a litigation hold, the Company deletes former employee email from the servers approximately 14 days after the employee leaves the Company. If the former employee was subject to a litigation hold at the time he or she departed, the Company retains the former employee's mailbox on the email servers until such a time that a legal preservation duty terminates.

### 2. Email Stored on Backup Tapes

The Company's backup tapes may contain unique email messages that are no longer stored on the Company's Exchange servers, because a backup tape may contain messages that were deleted during the 14-day sweep. For example, were the IT Department to examine the email stored on email servers for an employee not subject to a litigation hold on a Friday (sweep day), it would find messages no more than 14 days old in his/her inbox.. The schedule and functioning of the Company's backup systems are described more fully in the Company's Systems Overview.

Unique messages may also be present on the Company's backup tapes because employees not subject to litigation holds are free to delete messages from their mailboxes, and a message that an employee has deleted from the server may have been present on the server at the time one of the backups was made. For example, upon examination of an employee's Inbox stored on the Company's email servers, a message that was 14 days old, but deleted by the employee one day prior to examination, would not be present on the server. It would, however, be present on each of the daily backup tapes except the one made on the day of deletion by the employee.

The oldest daily backup tape will have the great majority of unique messages for a custodian that is present on the Company's backup tapes, because tapes made more recently contain a smaller subset of the messages deleted from the Company's servers in the 14-day sweep.

Handling of backup tapes should be discussed and resolved with the IT Department as soon as possible, because everyday backup tapes are overwritten. Where it is decided to preserve information from email backup tapes, the IT Department may restore the mailboxes of relevant custodians from the backup tapes if instructed to do so by legal or compliance personnel.

Note that backup tapes may be held in the Company's litigation inventory pertaining to past or existing matters. This inventory must also be considered in determining if relevant information may exist on backup tapes that have been retained for different matters.

## 4. ACTIONS BY IT TO PRESERVE OTHER ESI

### A. ESI on PCs or Other Local Storage Devices

User laptops and/or desktop machines are to be preserved in a forensically-sound manner to involve write-protected copying and a verified forensic image, unless otherwise advised by the responsible attorney. Once this copy is completed, in effect a snapshot in time exists for the local machine and it can be placed back into use and/or circulation with employees under most circumstances. The Legal Department will determine when such methods are not necessary after analyzing and balancing a number of criteria including without limitation the nature of the pending or anticipated legal proceeding, the potential exposure to the Company, the potential for loss of relevant information, and the costs involved.

Normally, the Company does not retain the information saved on the PCs or other local storage devices of employees who leave the Company. Rather, the Company re-images the PCs of former employees to facilitate deploying such computers to current employees. If the former employee was subject to a litigation hold at the time the employee left the Company, the hard drive of the machine is removed, stored, and recorded by the IT Department until the litigation hold is released.

### B. ESI on File Servers

Generally, group shares or directories (department shares) and user shares or directories identified for preservation should be collected "logically" by a forensic team utilizing safeguards to ensure that no metadata is changed on the source server during the collection phase and that the data retains all metadata as it is collected.

### C. ESI in Company Databases

The Company has hundreds of databases that contain a wide range of information. Depending on the nature of a matter, some of the Company's databases may be sources of relevant information. Any such databases must be identified and litigation hold procedures identified and implemented for those databases that are impacted. It may be necessary to secure access to databases for outside counsel and experts or the government, and generate reports from databases for production.

### D. ESI on Voicemail

Voicemail messages stored on voicemail servers are not subject to retention limits. Therefore, voicemail messages may remain on the servers until collection. Generally, call logs are retained on the voicemail server for a 24-hour period and then purged automatically. If a legal determination is made that these call logs are subject to preservation requirements, the logs must be exported from the system that same day to ensure that the logs are not purged during that night's deletion process.

## 5. PROCEDURES FOR COLLECTION OF ESI

Certain matters, typically civil litigation, may allow for Company IT staff to "self collect" and perform ESI collection using internal resources. The specific methodologies and steps to be employed under such circumstances are dependent on the nature and location of the relevant ESI and are detailed below. In the event of a government inquiry or other matter where the evidentiary integrity of the electronic evidence collection may come under scrutiny or where the risk of compromising the evidentiary value of the data is deemed unacceptable, collection should involve an independent expert with appropriate experience and technology to perform the operation in a minimally invasive, efficient, and forensically sound and defensible manner. Additionally, it is imperative that proper chain of custody controls and thorough documentation meeting or exceeding forensic industry standards is created to support the authenticity of the ESI and the transparency of the collection process.

### A. Actions by IT to Collect Electronic Communications

#### 1. Email Stored on Company Servers

Occasionally timing or other considerations make it impractical to narrow the scope of a litigation hold at least for purposes of its initial implementation. In those instances, a backup of the entire email server(s) will be made and the backup tape will be retained in the Company's litigation inventory.

However, where the scope of the hold is more focused and particular custodians can be targeted, a procedure should be performed for identified custodians to capture their "live" mailbox. Specific "switches" and options should be selected by the practitioner/technician in an effort to preserve deleted email and "double-deleted" email messages, as described in more detail below . . .

### 2. Email Stored on Backup Tapes

Backup tapes from email servers will be physically inventoried based on labels and/or information provided by IT personnel or backup operators. This information will also be cross-referenced against tape rotation policies in an effort to isolate tapes that fall within an identified date range. Once the tape population is identified, a chain of custody documentation is initiated and unique evidence IDs are assigned based on a tape or group of tapes' backup date.

A trusted, confidential magnetic media specialist should be used for backup tape-restoration efforts. This partner should be fully vetted and subject to non-disclosure and confidentiality agreements with the Company or its representatives . . .

## B. Actions by IT to Collect Other ESI

### 1. ESI on PCs or Other Local Storage Devices

For specified custodian PC and/or laptop hard drives, specified steps will be performed to capture the appropriate data in a forensically sound manner.

For each custodian hard drive a unique evidence ID control number will be generated. This number will correspond to the data from the hard drive throughout the lifecycle of the matter.

For any computer hard drive data collection, the individual performing the collection will note the make, model, and serial number of both the computer and the resident hard drive. This information will then be detailed on a chain of custody and collection log form which will also provide information pertaining to the date of collection and the methodologies and software(s) employed.

The following details the collection steps for a typical hard drive acquisition in a *forensically sound* manner . . .

### 2. ESI on File Servers

Following the transmission of a litigation hold notice, the IT Department interviews the affected custodians and identifies those file servers to which the affected custodians had access as well as which sections of the file servers the custodians used. Then, all relevant file server data associated with that custodian will be collected as described below.

A unique Evidence ID will be allocated to each custodian data source that is collected during a logical-level acquisition (e.g., a custodian home drive or a network share). An Acquisition Record will also be completed for each data source that is allocated a unique Evidence ID on the server. The ID used should be unique across all matters at the Company and be clearly displayed on the destination media. The Acquisition Record should detail the following . . .

The information above should be entered into an evidence-tracking database that records the details and circumstances surrounding the collection of each piece of evidence. In addition, a proper chain of custody tracking must also be maintained at each "handoff" of evidence from one storage location or evidence custodian to another.

### 3. ESI in Company Databases

As explained above, the methods of collecting electronic information from the Company's many databases differ depending on the database. Relevant variables include the size of the database, the nature of the information stored in the database, and the application used to store the information. Collecting information from the Company's databases involves close coordination with the IT Department.

## Appendix 7

# SELECTED TOPICS FOR DEPOSITIONS OF CORPORATE REPRESENTATIVES REGARDING FACTS IMPACTING ESI AVAILABILITY TO EXAMINING PARTY

TABLE OF CONTENTS

## INTRODUCTION

- Given the central role of ESI in litigation, the discovery process frequently includes examination into the systems, policies, procedures and practices that influence what ESI is preserved and produced. Authority for depositions on these kinds of facts is often found, for example, in Rule 30(b)(6) of the Federal Rules of Civil Procedure, which permits depositions of corporate representatives on topics identified by the requesting party. We will not attempt to explore the legal parameters of such depositions here, but rather lay out, at a high level, some suggestions as to topics that might be covered by the attorney charged with conducting such an examination before trial.
- As a generic outline, the topics presented here are more general than would be the case in a real deposition, one that would deal with specific facts and most likely some documentation provided in advance of the deposition. Of course, the art of examining a witness is largely in the follow-up—listening to the answer and probing it. Potential witnesses on the ESI topics appearing below should think carefully about the additional questions their answers are likely to raise and how they should answer them.
- By no means are the topics presented below intended to be comprehensive. There are many more topics that could be explored and questions asked depending on the particular situation in which the deposition occurs. Likewise, there are many different ways to ask these questions. Rather, these topics and questions are intended to assist the attorney planning for the deposition by providing some directional guidance, and to assist those preparing for these types of depositions with some insight into what might be covered.
- Note that not included here are the generic topics that are not specific to an examination on ESI sources and discovery issues, such as questions relating to witness background and preparation.

## DOCUMENTATION RE: SOURCES OF ESI

- Most organizations will have some form of documentation regarding their information systems and related policies and procedures. If discovery of these types of documents has not occurred through written discovery requests or other disclosure mechanisms, the examining attorney may wish to probe what is available and request production. Ideally, such documents would be produced in advance of the deposition and would be available for use as exhibits, but in practice this does not always happen.
- Documentation, especially documents that were not prepared for litigation purposes, can provide insight and understanding into a party's sources of ESI. There are too many possible types of documentation to identify here, but examples could include graphical representations, such as network diagrams or "data maps", lists or inventories of applications, servers and databases, applications inventories, and reports from asset-tracking systems showing what equipment was issued when and to whom.
- The examiner should also find out what personnel are responsible for creating and maintaining any of the documentation, as well as the process for doing so.
- An IT organization chart is a very useful document to have. Without having the kind of information represented in such a chart, the examiner should ask the witness to identify which IT personnel are responsible for each source or system.

## ELECTRONIC MAIL – GENERAL

- Does everyone at the company have a corporate email account or only certain categories of employees?
- If the latter, which categories or personnel?
- What email system does the company use (for example, Microsoft Exchange, Lotus Notes, Other)?
  - What version?

- When was it installed?
- [Address legacy systems if relevant.]
- What functionality is available to users? Specifically:
  - can they use offline mode (in Exchange) or equivalent?
  - can they store .psts (in Exchange) or otherwise archive locally or elsewhere?
  - can they use automatic forwarding to third-party accounts, e.g., Yahoo!Mail or "gmail"?
  - are they restricted by any policy or technical means from use of the company email system for non-business communications?
  - are they restricted by any policy or technical means from use of non-company email accounts for business communications?
  - [Note that if the answer is "yes" the means of restriction should be probed and, if appropriate, the steps taken to monitor and enforce compliance with any applicable policies]
- Does the company apply a mailbox size limit?
  - What is it?
  - What happens when a user reaches the limit (e.g., are they able to continue to receive or send mail)?
- Does the company deploy spam or antivirus protection?
  - If so, what tools are deployed and how are they configured?
  - What happens to quarantined emails? Where are they stored?
- [Note that several other sections below return to email topics in connection with, for example, servers, backups, mobile devices, etc.]

## PUBLIC FOLDERS

- Does the company use public folders? [Public folders are locations on servers set up to facilitate collaborative sharing of information among users granted access to the folder.]
- If the answer is yes, the examiner should probe how the folder is used and access controlled, as well as retention practices, e.g.:
  - Is there a policy governing how public folders are to be used?
  - Can users move email messages to which they want other users to have access to a public folder?
  - Are the folders accessible by multiple employees?
  - What is the process for creating a new public folder?
  - How are permissions and access controlled?
  - What retention rules or practices apply to public folders, if any?
  - [Note applicability of other sections below, e.g., servers and backups.]

## REMOTE ACCESS

- Many companies provide means of remote access so that users can work efficiently from outside the office. The nature and use of the access provided can impact the existence and location of ESI, among other things. Accordingly, the examiner should determine how any remote access is handled.

- For example, the examiner should determine whether users can access the company servers via Outlook Web Access (OWA) or some equivalent via a Web browser or by using a Virtual Private Network (VPN).

## SERVERS

- Servers are one of the fundamental sources of most ESI collections. There may be multiple different types of servers playing various roles, but typically email servers and file servers are a primary focus of electronic discovery.
- Does the company routinely purge or "auto-delete" any information from servers? (Note that this is a fairly common practice for email servers.)
  - If so, what is purged? [Note that very often routine purging is limited to certain folders, such as Inbox, Sent, and Deleted Items; very often emails the user moves to personal folders are outside the scope of the purge.]
  - How is the purge implemented technically and procedurally?
  - On what schedule does the purge occur?
  - Are there any exceptions to the regular purge?
  - How is the purge administered by IT personnel?
- What types of files are stored on the company's file servers? [Note that file servers normally contain "business documents" such as word processing documents, slide presentations, and spreadsheets.]
- Is access restricted or controlled in any way?
- Are there file shares or group shares?
  - How are these organized?
  - Who has access?
- What is the retention schedule for files on file servers?
- How is file server content organized?
- How is it accessed by users?
- [Note backup section below.]

## BACKUPS

- What systems and sources are backed up?
  - Servers?
  - Laptops?
  - Other?
- How are the backups made, i.e., what is or are the backup system(s) in use and how are they configured (hardware and software)?
- What is the schedule for backups?
- Are they full or incremental?
- Are tapes used?
- What type of tapes?

- Are the tapes recycled?
- Where and how are they stored?
- How are the tapes labeled, inventoried, and/or organized?
- What information is available about the content of the tapes from reasonably accessible records?
- What is required in terms of tools, resources, and cost to search the tape content?

## EMAIL ARCHIVING SYSTEMS

- Does the company use an email archiving system?
  - If so, what system?
  - How is the system configured?
  - What data does it save?
  - What data does it discard?
  - Where does it save data?
  - Who administers the system?
  - How is data extracted from the archive?
  - How long has the archive been in use?
  - Were any emails predating the installation of the archive system migrated to the archive?

## HARDWARE

- What hardware is issued to users of interest?
  - Desktops?
  - Laptops?
  - Storage devices or media? [Note that some companies prohibit the use of "thumb" drives or other storage devices by policy; if that is the case here, the examiner should probe the monitoring and enforcement of compliance with such policies.]
  - Mobile devices?
    - What are the criteria for issuing mobile devices?
    - Are they completely synchronized with servers?
    - Is SMS or PIN-to-PIN messaging enabled/permitted? [Note that data from such communications may reside on the device itself but not on the servers.]
- Is there an asset-tracking system that reflects this information?

## DOCUMENT MANAGEMENT SYSTEMS

- Does the company use a document management system to store, manage, and/or search documents on file servers or elsewhere?
  - If so, what system and how is it configured?

- Where is the data stored?
- How can relevant ESI be identified and be extracted from the system?
- What retention rules are applied to the system?

## LEGACY SYSTEMS

- The examiner should explore what systems were in use prior to the current systems and consider whether the timing may indicate the existence of ESI in legacy systems based on the time period relevant to the lawsuit.
- If any such legacy systems are identified, the examiner should follow the trail of the potentially relevant ESI in such systems—determining whether it is still being stored and if so in what manner.

## DATABASES AND ENTERPRISE SYSTEMS

- Organizations of any significant size will have multiple systems using databases to store a variety of ESI. Examples would include customer relationship management systems, financial and accounting systems, human resources systems, engineering systems, etc. The list is endless depending on the particular industry and business in question. At very large companies this list might include hundreds or even thousands of different systems.
- This "structured" data is often overlooked in the excitement to find the smoking gun in the haystack of emails. But for many types of cases, such as those involving allegations of accounting fraud, or allegations of patterned employment discrimination to name a few examples, such database systems are critical. They also create unique challenges for electronic discovery on a variety of levels.
- The examining attorney needs to first determine what the corporate landscape looks like for these types of systems. Depending on the number of systems involved, the examiner may need to approach this landscape by exploring categories of systems as opposed to individual systems or instances of systems. Then the examiner can narrow the examination to focus more detailed questions on the systems containing ESI that is potentially relevant to the case.
- The examiner should find out, for example:
  - What types of ESI are stored in the system?
  - How does information enter the system?
  - How does the system process that information?
  - Where does the system store the ESI?
  - In what format is the ESI stored?
  - What database technology may underlie the system (for example, Oracle or SQL)?
  - What reports can the system generate?
  - How is the system backed up?
  - Is the system audited? When? How? What documentation reflects the audits?
  - Who has access to the system and what rights do they have to manipulate or view ESI in the system?

## VOICEMAIL SYSTEMS

- Does the company provide the use of a voicemail system?
- If so, what type?

- Which categories of employees have voicemail?
- In what format does the system store voicemails?
- [Note that in many of today's "unified messaging" systems, the voicemail system is connected with the email system, and voicemails are stored as .wav files which can be transmitted via email; in other cases the system sends notification to a user that a voicemail has arrived but accessing the voicemail requires using the telephony system.]
- What are the retention rules applied to voicemails?
- Is the voicemail system backed up? [See backup section.]

## INSTANT MESSAGING

- Does the company provide employees use of an instant messaging ("IM") system?
  - If so, identify and describe the system, who has access, what parameters are in place and functionality enabled, etc.
- Does the IM system allow communications with users external to the company (who are using other IM systems)?
- What data does the IM system generate and what does it retain (e.g., logs, full content of chats, etc.)?
  - Can it be configured to retain additional data?
  - If so, what is involved in doing so?
- Does the company permit employees to use third-party IM applications via the corporate network (for example, Yahoo!Messenger)?
- If such use is restricted, is this done by policy or technical restriction?
  - If by policy, how is compliance with the policy monitored and enforced?
  - If technically, how is the restriction achieved?

## THIRD-PARTY CUSTODIANS

- Many companies outsource elements of their IT operations or records management. The result is that relevant ESI may be in the possession of those third parties, thus requiring additional steps to ensure proper preservation and collection. One common example is storage of backup tapes for disaster recovery purposes, but many companies outsource practically their entire IT function. Parties are not free to ignore relevant ESI simply because it is in the hands of a vendor, but it can be easily overlooked until it is too late.
  - Does the company outsource any of its IT or records management functions?
  - If so, what functions?
  - What ESI is retained by the vendor?
  - What retention policies are applied to that ESI?

## INTRANET AND INTERNET

- It is almost hard to imagine a business of any significance without some presence on the Internet. The forms this presence can take are many, including for example, websites, blogs, chat rooms, and bulletin boards.

In many cases information from these sources is relevant. Accordingly, in these cases it is critical that the examiner understand the details of the company's Web presence, including the content as well as the retention policies applied to the resultant ESI.

- Many companies also maintain an Intranet for the use of corporate employees. More often than should be the case, the corporate Intranet is not subject to strong central control and business units are free to set up their own areas on the Intranet with content that is not reviewed for compliance in advance of or even after posting. The examiner should understand the rules of the road—or lack thereof—for the corporate Intranet, including without limitation the process for the posting of content, the degree of access permitted to various users, and the retention policies applied to Intranet ESI.

## GENERAL DOCUMENT RETENTION POLICIES AND PROCEDURES

- Does the company have a document retention policy?
- If so, is it written?
- When was the policy established? [Note that if relevant given the time period of the matter, the examiner will have to track the evolution of the current policy by discovering the prior policy and what changes the retention policies underwent over the time period in question.]
- Is there a retention schedule that accompanies the policy?
- How does the company try to ensure compliance with the policy?
  - Does the company monitor for compliance? How? Is this monitoring documented?
  - What does the company do when it finds non-compliance?
  - Has this ever happened? With what result? Are there records of this or these incidents?
  - Are employees trained on the policy and how to comply?
- What steps does the company take to ensure the confidentiality and security of its data?
- What group or groups and which individuals are responsible for formulating and implementing the document retention policies?

## IT USAGE POLICIES

- Does the company have a set of policies governing employee use of the company's IT asset? What are they? Are these written?
- Do these policies address permitted storage devices and locations?
- Do they address whether home computers or other non-company-issued devices may be used for business purposes?
  - How does the company monitor and enforce compliance with these policies?
  - Who is responsible for formulating and implementing the policies?

## FORMER EMPLOYEES

- What are the company's policies and procedures with respect to IT assets and ESI held or stored by users who have left the company?

- What happens to their computers when they leave?
- What happens to other devices that may store ESI?
- What happens to ESI they have stored on servers?
- What happens to their access rights and permissions?

## LITIGATION HOLD PROCEDURES

- Does the company have policies and procedures governing compliance with legal preservation duties, i.e., "litigation holds"?
- What are they? [Note: the examiner should make sure that all sources are addressed by the procedures. It may be necessary to confirm this for each item on the list. For example, the examiner should find out what procedures have been established for handling email, "business documents" on file servers, computer assets of departed employees, backup tapes, etc.]
- Are these policies written?
- Who decides whether and when a hold should be implemented?
- Are these determinations documented along with the rationale?
- Who determines the scope and parameters of any litigation hold?
- Are these determinations documented along with the rationale?
- How is specific ESI that may be subject to a hold identified?
- Are electronic search methods and technology used?
- If so, what are they?
- What testing is done to ensure correct identification?
- Does the company send hold notices to employees or third parties with ESI that is potentially relevant to reasonably anticipated or pending legal action?
    - Are these based on a standard form that the company uses?
    - How does the company transmit the notices?
    - Does the company transmit notices to each individual custodian with potentially relevant ESI?
    - Are recipients required to acknowledge receipt of and compliance with hold notices? Are there records of such acknowledgements?
- Are employees trained on how to implement litigation holds over ESI?
- Does the company use any specific hardware or software tools to implement litigation holds?
- Does the company monitor and enforce compliance with litigation holds?
    - How?
    - What records does the company keep of such activity?
- Does the company follow up on hold notices issued to individual custodians? How?
- Who was/is involved in formulating and implementing litigation hold policies and procedures, and what are/were their respective roles regarding the same?

## COLLECTION POLICIES AND PROCEDURES

- Does the company have policies and procedures governing the collection of ESI?
- What are they? [Note: as above, the examiner should make sure that all sources are addressed by the procedures. It may be necessary to confirm this for each item on the list.]
- Are these policies and procedures written?
- How does the company monitor for and enforce compliance?
- Who formulated these policies and procedures?
- Who carries out collections?
  - What training and/or certification do they have?
- How do they decide what to collect?
- What hardware and software tools do they use and how?
- What testing is done to verify proper collection?
- What elements of the collection process are documented and how?
- How is the chain of custody managed?
- How does the collection process attempt to ensure the integrity of ESI as evidence?
- What safeguards are in place to prevent alteration of metadata?

## THE INSTANT LITIGATION—CHRONOLOGY OF EDISCOVERY STEPS PRESERVATION

- At this point the examiner may wish to explore what the company did in the case at hand to comply with its various preservation and discovery obligations, in light of the information about sources, systems, personnel, policies, and procedures acquired through the above-outlined avenues of questioning.
- This would include detailed questioning about any actions taken to comply with the duty to preserve ESI relevant to the case, including without limitation who was involved in such actions, when they took such actions, how they identified ESI for preservation, and what documentation exists concerning such actions. For example:
  - When did the company decide that it had an ESI preservation duty in this case?
  - Who was involved in making that decision?
  - Was the decision and the rationale for it documented?
  - When did the company decide on the scope of the duty?
  - What did it decide to preserve?
    - Which custodians?
    - For what time periods?
    - Were keywords used?
    - What sources of ESI were targeted?
  - Who was involved in making that decision?
  - Was the decision and the rationale for it documented?
  - Was a hold notice sent to custodians?
    - To whom?

        - How?
        - What did it say?
        - Were they asked to confirm receipt, understanding, and compliance?
        - Did any of them ask questions about the notice?
        - What was done to follow up and ensure compliance?
        - Was all of the above documented?
    - The examiner should ask about what specifically was done to preserve each source of ESI, including:
        - What steps were taken;
        - Who performed the preservation steps;
        - When they did so;
        - What hardware/software tools were used; and
        - What documentation of the efforts exists.
- Were custodians interviewed to determine what sources of ESI might exist?
    - What were they asked?
    - Who conducted the interviews?
    - When?
    - Is there documentation of these interviews?
- Were electronic searches conducted to identify ESI for preservation?
    - What sources were searched electronically?
    - What types of files did the search target?
    - How was the search executed?
        - Was the protocol documented?
        - Who performed the searches?
        - Were keywords used? If so, what were they?
        - What technology was used to execute the searches?
        - What steps were taken to verify that the search captured results accurately?
        - [Additional probing of the limitations of any search technology might be performed, including how the search addressed problematic files, such as password-protected files.]
        - What records of the searches were kept?

## COLLECTION

- Was the ESI collected the same ESI as what was preserved?
- If not, why not and what was the discrepancy?
- How was the collection performed? [Note that this may need to be asked for each source of ESI.]
- Was the process documented? How?
- Who performed the collections and what are their qualifications to do so?

- What hardware/software tools did they use?
- Was metadata preserved intact through the collection methods used?
- What documentation was kept regarding the chain of custody?
- Were there sources from which ESI was not collected?
  - Which sources?
  - Why?
  - Were there types of files that were not collected?
  - Were any efforts made to recover deleted ESI?

## POST-COLLECTION

- The examiner should track chronologically the progress of the ESI from the point of collection to production. For example:
  - What was done with the ESI after it was collected?
  - If further "culling" and/or "processing" was performed on the ESI, what was done, what technology was used, and who performed the culling and/or processing?
- Was there a process for handling processing "exceptions" and if so, what was it? If not, what happened to the exception files?
- How was the review for production carried out?
  - Who conducted the review?
    - Were the reviewers attorneys?
    - Was any of the review outsourced to contract attorneys?
    - If so, were any of these attorneys outside the U.S.?
  - What review procedures were followed?
  - What technology was used to conduct the review?
    - How does it work?
    - What checks were done, and what documentation exists to verify completeness and accuracy?
  - Was sampling used as any part of the review process?
- What checks were done, and what documentation exists to ensure that all documents designated for production were copied to the production media?

## EVIDENTIARY QUESTIONS

- The examiner may wish to lay the groundwork for future analysis of evidentiary admissibility issues. For example, questions may be asked to ascertain whether or not it is appropriate to consider certain documents business records under a hearsay exception. The examiner should research the criteria for admissibility under the applicable law and ask questions designed to assist an analysis of whether those criteria have been met.
- The chain of custody questions outlined above would be examples. Another example would be to ask whether the document in question is a record that employees are required to keep as part of their job responsibilities, which is a potentially important factor under the aforementioned business records analysis.

# BIBLIOGRAPHY


## BOOKS

Becker, Bob and Kimball, Ralph and Mundy, Joy and Ross, Margy and Thornthwaite, Warren. *The Data Warehouse Lifecycle Toolkit, 2nd Edition*. New Jersey: John Wiley & Sons, Inc., 2008

Cohen, Adam I. and Lender, David J. *Electronic Discovery: Law and Practice*. New York: Aspen Publishers, 2007

Date, C. J. *Database in Depth: Relational Theory for Practitioners*. California: O'Reilly Media, 2005

Derfler Jr., Frank and Freed, Les. *How Networks Work, Seventh Edition*. Indiana: QUE Publishing, 2005

Farmer, Dan and Venema, Wietse. *Forensic Discovery*. New Jersey: Addison-Wesley, 2005

Henderson, Harry. *Encyclopedia of Computer Science and Technology*. New York: Facts On File, Inc., 2003

Husman, Goran. *Exchange 2000 Server On Site*. Paraglyph Press, 2001

Neilson, Greg. *Lotus Domino Administration In A Nutshell*. California: O'Reilly Media, 2000

Nelson, Sharon D. and Olson, Bruce A. and Simek, John W. *Electronic evidence and Discovery Handbook: Forms, Checklists and Guidelines*. Illinois: American Bar Association, 2006

Preston, W. Curtis. *Backup & Recovery*. California: O'Reilly Media, 2007

Preston, W. Curtis. *Using SANS and NAS*. California: O'Reilly Media, 2007

Ranier, Jr., R. Kelly and Turban, Efraim. *Introduction to Information Systems: Supporting and Transforming Business, Second Edition*. New Jersey: John Wiley & Sons, Inc., 2008

Turban, Efraim and Leidner, Dorothy and McLean, Ephraim and Wetherbe, James. *Information Technology for Management: Transforming Organizations in the Digital Economy, 5th Edition*. New Jersey: John Wiley & Sons, Inc., 2005

Weiss, Steven A. and Coale, David. *e-Discovery*. Illinois: American Bar Association, 2007

Wiegand, Greg, ed. *Encyclopedia of Technology Terms*. Indiana: QUE Publishing, 2002, Updated 2008. Internet: www.whatis.com

## ARTICLES/PAPERS/REPORTS

Andrews, Whit, *Information Access Technology, 2007*. September 5, 2007, Gartner, Inc.

Austin, D. Douglas, *Managing Microsoft Exchange and Outlook Files Throughout the Discovery Life Cycle*, Internet: http://my.advisor.com/doc/19273

Battle, Jenifer A. L. *Saving ESI With 'Litigation Hold' Letters*, July 13, 2007. The Legal Intelligencer

Battle, Jennifer A. L. *Saving ESI With 'Litigation Hold' Letters*, Law.com, July 13, 2007 Internet: http://www.law.com/jsp/legaltechnology/pubArticleLT.jsp?id = 1184231195691

Bayer, David et al. *Litigation Support Tools and Techniques*, 2006, Houston, International Legal Technology Association

Boehning, H. Christopher and Toal, Daniel J. *Cost-Shifting and Accessible Data in EDD*, June 28, 2007. New York Law Journal

Bradley, Tony. *Archiving and Retaining Communications*, March 30, 2007. Processor Magazine

Brandon, John. *Control The Flow of Enterprise Email*, April 20, 2007. Processor Magazine

Brown, Matthew. *Enterprise Search Platforms, Q2 2006*, June 13, 2006, Forrester Research

Brownstein, Mark. *A New Storage Paradigm*, November 2, 2007. Processor Magazine

Bulk, Frank. *Have Phone, Will Travel*, October 8, 2007. Information Week

Chickowski, Ericka. *Deduping Your Way to Storage Efficiency*, January 26, 2007. Processor Magazine

Chickowski, Ericka. *Virtual Tape Array vs Virtual Tape Library*, May 25, 2007. Processor Magazine

Chin, Kenneth and DiCenzo, Carolyn. *E-Mail Active Archiving, 2007*. May 16, 2007, Gartner, Inc.

Chivvas, John. *Discovering E-Discovery*, October, 2006. Rough Notes Magazine

Chivvas, John. *The Evolution of Document Management*, September, 2007. Rough Notes Magazine

Cohen, Adam I. *How New Technology Reduces the True Cost of e-Discovery*, Law Journal Newsletter, Volume 25, Number 2, May 2007

Cohen, Adam I. *Understanding e-Discovery Risks*, 2007, FTI Consulting, Inc.

Conry-Murray, Andrew. *Virtualization Smackdown*, October 15, 2008. Information Week

Conry-Murray, Andrew. *Web 2.0 And Legal Discovery*, April 19, 2008. Information Week

Conry-Murray, Andrew. *Where To Start With ILM*, February 27, 2008. Information Week

Dolan, Michael and Olivas, Dario. *Legal Process Outsourcing of First Level Document Review*, Tusker Group, Internet: http://www.sourcingmag.com/content/c060918a.asp

Dreger Jr., Richard S. and Moerschel, Grant P. *The Data Warehouse Revised*, May 26, 2008. Information Week

Fletcher, Meg. *E-Discovery Falls Hardest On Insurance Industry*, May 2007, Business Insurance Europe

Fonseca, Brian. *E-discovery Rules Still Causing IT Headaches*, January 7, 2008. Computerworld

Fort, Ann G. *Rising Costs of E-Discovery Requirements Impacting Litigants*, March 20, 2007, Fulton County Daily Report

Gain, Bruce. *Cradle-To-Grave Data Administration*, September 21, 2007. Processor Magazine

Gain, Bruce. *Going The Array Way: Disk-Based Centralized Storage Has Become A Value Proposition for SMEs*, September 7, 2007. Processor Magazine

Gain, Bruce. *Know When To Retire Storage Tape Media*, July 20, 2007. Processor Magazine

Garretson, Cara, ed. *Can An iPod Bring Down Your Company?* April 9 2007. Network World

Ginevan, Sean. *Get The Message*, October 8, 2007. Information Week

Gruman, Galen. *How To Do Storage Virtualization Right*, September 11, 2007, CIO Magazine

Haber, Lynn. E-Discovery: Reducing the Cost of Review, Semantec Corporation, February 14, 2007. Internet: http://www.devx.com/symantec/Article/33749

Haig, Robert L. *Making the Case for Change*, April 2008, ABA Journal

Harler, Curt. *How To Archive Email*, September 21, 2007. Processor Magazine

Hoover, Nicholas J. *The Ultimate Answer Machine*, August 6, 2007. Information Week

Jacoby, Conrad J. *E-Discovery Update: Recognizing Hidden Logistical Bottlenecks in E-Discovery*, LLRX.com, April 24, 2007

Jander, Mary, ed., *Managing Tape in the Age of Disk*, July 20, 2007, Byte and Switch

Jander, Mary. *Managing Tape in the Age of Disk*, July 20, 2007. Byte and Switch

Jaskiewicz, Stanley P. *E-Lawyering Requires Rethinking Technology and Law*, Internet Law & Strategy, March 16, 2007, (The Estrin Report) Internet: http://estrinlegaled.typepad.com/my_weblog/2007/03/elawyering_requ.html

Jaskiewicz, Stanley. *Follow the Mail: Don't Let Your Employees' Multiple E-Mail Boxes Become An Electronic Nightmare*, July 10, 2007, e-Discovery Law & Strategy, Internet: http://infogovernance.blogspot.com/2007/07/follow-mail-legal-technology.html

Kendler, Preggy Bresnick, Ed. *Virtual Roundtable: The Age of e-Discovery*. Insurance + Technology, March 2007, CMP Media

Lamont, Judith. *Taking Control of the e-discovery Process*, KM World Magazine, Jul 10, 2007, Internet: http://www.kmworld.com/Articles/Editorial/Feature/Taking-Control-of-the-e-discovery-process-36894.aspx

Leahy, Ted. *Records Management: A Sleeping Giant*, March 2006. Business Finance

MacKinnon, Chris A. *A Systematic Approach To VoIP*, February 2, 2007. Processor Magazine

MacKinnon, Chris A. *Server Virtualization Performance*, August 3, 2007. Processor Magazine

Marko, Kurt. *Proactive Archiving: Technologies Designed To Preserve Information & Meet Regulatory Requirements*, March 28, 2008. Processor Magazine

Marko, Kurt. *What's Up With Centralized Storage: Overview and Issues To Consider*, April 13, 2007. Processor Magazine

Martin, Richard. *Red Shift*, August 20, 2007. Information Week

McNabb, Kyle. *Enterprise Content Management Suites, Q4 2007*, Forrester Research, November 9, 2007

Millard, Elizabeth. *IM and Texting Are Here To Stay*, October 12, 2007. Processor Magazine

Millard, Elizabeth. *Smaller Players in the Backup Market*, January 26, 2007. Processor Magazine

Moguli, Rich and Ouellet, Eric and Proctor, Paul E. *Content Monitoring and Filtering and Data Loss Prevention, 2Q07*. April 13 2007, Gartner Inc.

Newman, David. *Key Issues for Enterprise Information Management*, April 3, 2007, Gartner Inc.

Nicola, Matthias and Martin Sommerlandt and Zeidenstein, Kathy. *From Text Analytics To Data Warehousing*, IBM Corporation 24 Apr 2008, Internet: www.ibm.com/developerworks/db2/library/techarticle/dm-0804nicola

Ortiz Jr., Sixto. *Say Goodbye To Tape: Moving From Tape To Disk-Based Backup*, July 27, 2007. Processor Magazine

Perry, Christian. *Virtualization Venture*, September 21, 2007. Processor Magazine

Reichman, Andrew. *Storage Resource Management is Knocking: Open the Door*. May 8 2007. Forrester Research

Robb, Drew. *Managing and Protecting Data In Virtual Environments*, October 12, 2007. Processor Magazine

Robb, Drew. *Tips For Smoother Email Archiving*, April 18, 2008. Processor Magazine

Sawyer, John H. *Incident Response: Security Triage and Treatment*. 2006. TechTracker, CMP Media

Skogstad, Emma Jane. *Taming the Perfect Storm: Record Management in the Information Age*, February 2, 2006. APQC

Tero, Vivian, *State of Play: Litigation Readiness of the Corporate IT Infrastructure*. May 8 2008. IDC

Toigo, Jon. *Managing Enterprise Storage*, Oct. 22 2007, InformationWeek

Villars, Richard L. *The Economic Impact of File Virtualization: Reducing Storage Costs and Improving Management Efficiency*. May 2007. IDC

Vorro, Alex. *e-Discovery: A Way To Paperless Organization*, April 1, 2008, Insurance Networking News and SourceMedia, Inc.

Withers, Kenneth J., *Annotated Case Law on Electronic Discovery*, Federal Judicial Center, July 5, 2006, Internet: www.fjc.gov/public/pdf.nsf/lookup/ElecDi09.pdf

Wittmann, Art. *Data Deduplication: Did You Say 20% Or 20 Times?* May 19, 2008. Information Week

Yegulalp, Serdar. *USB Flash Drives Mobilized*, June 23, 2007. Information Week

## INTERNET REFERENCE SITES

AIIM International (Enterprise Content Management Association) http://www.aiim.org
American Bar Association (Resources for Lawyers) http://www.abanet.org/
ANSI (American National Standards Institute) http://www.ansi.org
ARMA (Association for Information Management Professionals) http://www.arma.org
CGOC (Compliance Governance Oversight Council) http://www.cgocouncil.com/about/index.html
EDD Blog Online (Information source and discussion forum for e-Discovery issues) http://www.eddblogonline.com/
e-Discovery Law http://www.e-Discoverylaw.com
EDRM (E-Discovery Reference Model and forum for legal and e-Discovery practitioners) http://www.edrm.net
Federal Judicial Center (Materials on Electronic Discovery) http://www.fjc.gov/public/home.nsf/autoframe?openform&url_l = /public/home.nsf/inavgeneral?openpage&url_r = /public/home.nsf/pages/196
FindLaw for Legal Professionals (e-Discovery articles) http://technology.findlaw.com/
FirstGov.Gov (U.S. Government Public Central Resource Site) http://www.firstgov.gov
IEEE Computer Society http://www.computer.org
International Council on Archives http://www.ica.org
International Journal of Digital Evidence (Discussion forum in the field of digital evidence hosted by Utica College) http://www.utica.edu/academic/institutes/ecii/ijde/index.cfm
ISO (International Organization for Standardization) http://www.iso.org
IT Management Resource Centers (Information and discussion forum for variety of IT functional areas and issues) http://www.itmanagement.com/
Law.Com, Legal Technology (e-Discovery articles and blogs) http://www.law.com/jsp/legaltechnology/edd.jsp
Litigation Support Vendors Association (not-for-profit forum for major software companies covering e-Discovery) http://www.lsva.com/pn/
LLRX.com (Law and technology Web journal for legal community) http://www.llrx.com/
Lotus Notes (IBM Home Page for Lotus Notes) http://www.306.ibm.com/software/lotus/products/notes/
Microsoft Products (Home Page for All Microsoft Products) http://www.microsoft.com/en/us/default.aspx
NAGARA (National Association of Government Archives and Records Administrators) http://www.nagara.org
NIST (U.S. National Institute of Standards and Technology) http://www.nist.gov
Sedona Conference (Forum for legal and e-Discovery practitioners) http://www.thesedonaconference.org/
Society of American Archivists http://www.archivists.org
TAWPI (The Association for Work Process Improvement) http://www.tawpi.org
U.S. National Archives and Records Administration http://www.archives.gov

# GLOSSARY

## A

**Adobe Acrobat**—From Adobe Systems Incorporated, Acrobat is the leading program for creating and viewing PDF files—available in a free version and Professional version that enables file conversion, search, tagging, and other functions, and allows use of third-party add-ons.

**Animation File**—A file containing software that puts various graphic elements in motion for viewing by users.

**Application Fabric**—Software driven capability to create a scalable and robust virtual computing environment on top of existing infrastructure.

**Application Server**—A server dedicated to processing applications, such as, for example, accounting systems. Also see *Server.*

**Application Service Provider (ASP)**—Third party that provides hosting services for a variety of information processing functions, and within e-Discovery, a portion or all of the functions related to the e-Discovery lifecycle. Also see *Hosting* and *Service Bureau.*

**Archival Storage**—Long-term storage of essential information under strict environmental and security parameters, but not requiring immediate access.

**Attachments**—Attachments fit two categories—True Attachments and Physical Attachments. True attachments are created by an author or custodian and referred to in the cover or parent document, such as an email with an attachment for example. Physical attachments are bound, clipped, or stapled without any reference by the author or custodian to the attachment. Also see *Unitization.*

**Audio File**—A file containing analog or digital sound elements, which can be played (heard) through an output device.

**Auditability**—The transparency, openness, or receptiveness of a system or process to being examined, with inherent features such as logs that facilitate the examination process.

**Audit Log/Trail**—Chronological record of selected information such as computer user activity for example that might include logins, logouts, files accessed, actions performed, and communications in and out.

**Automated Litigation Support (ALS) Systems**—ALS Systems are the application of specialized software programs to facilitate execution of functions within the e-Discovery lifecycle. ALS Systems are considered essential to the effectiveness of performing required functions and achieving objectives within the e-Discovery lifecycle.

## B

**Backup Storage**—Exact copy of ESI stored separately from the original to serve as a source for recovery in the event of a system problem or disaster.

**Backup Tape**—Magnetic tape used to store backup copies of ESI.

**Bandwidth**—An expression, usually in megabits per second (mps), of the throughput (speed and volume) of a network connection.

**Bates Number**—A unique serial number electronically impressed on every page of a document collection. Often used in conjunction with a suffix or prefix to identify the producing party, the case, or other relevant information. Bates numbering was originally done by manually stamping the numbers onto hard copy originals.

**Best Practices**—Methods generally accepted and promulgated within an industry as being superior over others.

**Bibliographical or Objective Coding**—Recording objective information, such as date created, author, recipient, and copies, from electronic documents and associating that information with a specific electronic document.

**Block-level Deduplication**—Process of eliminating duplicate content within the file, as opposed to eliminating duplicate files. Also see *Deduplication* and *SIS (Single Instance Storage).*

**Blowback**—A hard copy set of documents printed from digital images, and usually produced in a batch from a coded database that enables automatic sorting and grouping of the documents.

**Boolean Search**—Use of logical operators such as ''and'', ''or'', and ''not'' to include or exclude terms from a search. Also see *Proximity Search.*

**Bridge**—Network peripheral device for connecting various network segments. Also see *Hub.*

**Broadband**—Designation for communication networks, such a fiber optics, having higher throughput than other networks.

**Burn**—Copying files to a removable media, usually a CD or DVD.

**Byte**—Consists of 8 bits as the basic capacity measurement for most computer data, and increases in increments of 1,000 expressed as Kilobyte, Megabyte, Gigabyte, Terabyte, Petabyte, Exabyte, Zettabyte, and Yottabyte. Also see Chapter 5, Overview of File and Storage Systems, for *Table of Storage Capacity.*

## C

**Cartridge**—See *Tape Cartridge.*

**Case Deduplication**—Eliminates duplicate documents within a case. Also see *Deduplication.*

**Case Management Services**—A type of litigation support service to help prepare lawyers, law firms, and legal departments to try a case. Specific services may include interviewing witnesses, document review, and case preparation.

**Case Management Software**—Litigation collaboration software that helps law firms and third parties prepare for and manage a case.

**CD (Compact Disc)**—A type of optical disc storage media that includes read only (CD-ROM), write once then read only (CD-R), and write multiple/read multiple (CD-RW).

**Certificate**—Electronic affidavit vouching for the identity of the transmitter. Also see *PKI Digital Signature.*

**Chain-of-Custody**—Documentation and testimony regarding the possession, movement, handling, and location of evidence from the time it is obtained to the time it is presented in court; used to prove that evidence has not been altered or tampered with in any way; necessary both to assure admissibility and probative value.

**Checksum**—A value created and stored with a block of data to ensure that the data is stored or transmitted without error.

**Child**—See *Parent/Child.*

**CIO**—Chief Information Officer.

**Clawback Agreement**—Agreement between parties to a litigation outlining procedures to protect against waiver of privilege or work product protection due to inadvertent production of documents or information.

**Client**—Any computing device that requests a service of another computer system. A *Thin Client* is a wired or wireless device that depends on a host for application processing. A *Thick Client* is a wired or wireless device that may request a service of another computer system, but also has its own computing capability.

**CMS**—Content Management Systems are collaboration systems used to manage the creation and communication of corporate documents.

**Coding**—The inclusion of bibliographical information about each document into an automated litigation support program so that an affidavit or list can be produced in compliance with applicable rules. Coding also enables sorting and grouping in line with relevancy and privilege review. Coding usually includes the following basic information: Author, Bates Number, Date, Document title and type, and Recipient.

**Coding Manual**—Document providing instructions and information related to the coding function performed within the review process of e-Discovery. Also see *Coding.*

**Collection**—Process of harvesting ESI from various sources for processing and review phases e-Discovery.

**Compliance (Management)**—Process of adhering to policy, legal, or regulatory requirement.

**Compound Document**—Collection or combination of more than one document or elements into one document. May be composed from different applications, and embed objects or linked data to include images, text, animation, or hypertext for example.

**Compression**—Process for reducing the size of files to reduce storage space and bandwidth required for access and transmission.

**Computer Forensics**—See *Forensics.*

**Computer Memory**—See *RAM.*

**Concept Search**—Taking into account the context within which search words appear to ascertain meaning. Also see *Search.*

**Container File**—A single file containing multiple documents and/or files (pst, nsf, Zip) that can be ripped or decompressed to determine volume, size, and record count, or to be processed for litigation review and production.

**Content Comparison**—A method of deduplication that compares file content to image or paper and ignores metadata. Also see *Deduplication.*

**Contextual Search**—Searching ESI whereby the surrounding text is analyzed to determine relevancy. Also see *Search.*

**Correlation Search**—A statistical method (Latent Semantic Indexing and Analysis) for finding the underlying semantic relationship of terms and their correlation, whereby the presence of one or more terms could confer significance to a document. A common example would be the relationship of words like law, lawyer, attorney, and lawsuit as representative of a shared meaning. Correlation search enables grouping and clustering of ESI into meaningful categories.

**COTS**—Commercial Off-The-Shelf Software.

**CSO**—Chief Security Officer.

**Culling**—Removing documents from collections to be produced or reviewed. Also see *Harvesting.*

**Custodian**—The owner or person responsible for safekeeping of ESI.

## D

**Data**—For practical purposes, the building blocks of ESI. Technically, data also includes elements that reside in many places within computing and storage devices, not accessible to users, such as program code, for example. Also see *Data Element* and *ESI.*

**Data (Database) Administrator**—IT person responsible for maintaining databases.

**Database**—The term database commonly refers to a collection of records and the software (database management system) used to manage user interaction. Technically, a database and a database management system are separate entities. There are a variety of database structures from which ESI is obtained, including Data Warehouse, Dimensional, Flat, Hierarchical, Network, Object, and Relational. (See Chapter 8, Databases, for a definition of each type of database.)

**Database Server**—A server optimized for database transactions.

**Data Deletion**—See *Deleted Data.*

**Data Element**—A combination of characters or bytes referring to one separate piece of information, such as name or address.

**Data Sampling**—Method of examining a statistically representative portion of ESI to determine how much of a universe of ESI is responsive.

**Data Warehouse**—Special form of large-scale dimensional database optimized for intensive queries of diverse business data elements analyzed and used to derive business insights and intelligence.

**DEB (Digital Evidence Bag)**—A standardized and encrypted or otherwise protected electronic container to preserve and transfer evidence in a form that prevents deliberate or accidental alteration. The container provides metadata related to the contained information.

**Deduplication**—Deduplication is a software or hardware-based process for identifying exact or near-duplicate files within a collection, and only storing the original and any changes to the original. This eliminates file redundancy, reduces storage volume, and reduces the time required in discovery of ESI. Vertical deduplication locates duplicates within the records and information of a single custodian, while horizontal deduplication applies globally across all custodians. Also see *Near Deduplication, Block-level Deduplication*, and *Single Instance Storage*.

**Deleted Data/File**—ESI residing on media space that has been designated as available for reuse. The deleted ESI remains intact until it is overwritten. Deletion may be automated or manual and intentional or unintentional.

**Deliverable**—A project management term used to describe a tangible work product.

**Digital Fingerprint**—Fixed-length hash code that uniquely represents the binary content of a file. Also see *Hash*.

**Digital Signature**—See *Certificate* and *PKI Digital Signature.*

**Dimensional Database**—See *Database.*

**Directory**—A simulated file folder or container used to organize files and directories in a hierarchical or tree-like structure.

**Disc Drive**—See *Hard Drive.*

**Disc Mirroring**—Process for protecting ESI by storing an exact copy of ESI on a second storage media during storage of the original ESI. Also see *Mirroring*.

**Document Classification**—Using a field bibliographical coding to group documents into categories such as correspondence, memo, report, and article for example.

**Document Lifecycle**—Phases inclusive of the functions to create, communicate, modify, store, retrieve, and destroy.

**DoD 5015**—Department of Defense standard for records management.

**Dots per Inch (DPI)**—DPI is a measure of the resolution of an image file, which governs the clarity with which it displays on screen. DPI also refers to the accuracy of the OCR process. Standard resolution for litigation support is 300dpi.

**DSL (Digital Subscriber Line)**—Technologies that provide digital data transmission over the wires of a local telephone network.

**DVD (Digital Video Disc)**—A type of optical disc storage media that can be written to and read from. DVDs are faster, have larger capacity, and support more data formats than CDs.

## E

**e-Discovery**—The preparation, preservation, collection, processing, review, and production of evidence in electronic form in response to business, regulatory, or legal requirements. e-Discovery is also sometimes referred to as EDD (Electronic Data Discovery).

**e-Discovery Process Lifecycle**—Phases inclusive of the functions: Preparation, Search/Collection, Processing, Culling, Review/ Analysis, and Production/Presentation.

**e-Discovery Readiness Program**—The process and initiatives (projects) to ensure adequate preparation for and optimization of the e-Discovery process.

**e-Discovery Response Team**—Team formed to execute e-Discovery requirements in response to investigation or litigation.

**e-Discovery Vault**—A secure, central repository for storage of discovered ESI, that is accessible by authorized users.

**Electronic Appeal Book**—A digital file containing a factum, appeal book, evidence, and transcripts used in the appeal process. Often created using the PDF format, electronic appeal books are popular with judges and counsel because they allow for hypertext linking from the factum to the evidence, among other features.

**Email (Electronic Mail)**—An electronic messaging system for communicating information and attached documents to one or more parties. Emails consist of addresses, header information, the message body, attachments, and metadata.

**Email Administrator**—IT person responsible for maintaining email systems.

**Email String/Thread**—Series of emails linked together by email responses and forwarding, often treated as a single document.

**Encryption**—A protection process using complex algorithms to render the contents of a message or file unusable or unintelligible to computers or persons not authorized to use/read it.

**Encryption Key**—A data value that is used to encrypt and decrypt data.

**Endorser**—A small printer in a scanner that adds a document-control number or other endorsement to each scanned sheet.

**ePaper**—Electronic version of a document, usually in PDF or TIFF file format.

**ESI (Electronically Stored Information)**—ESI is the term adopted in Rules 26(a)(1), 33, and 34 of the Rules of Civil Procedure, Amended December 2006, to include any type of information that can be stored electronically, and to acknowledge that electronically stored information is discoverable. It is intended to be broad enough to cover all current types of computer-based information, and flexible enough to encompass future changes and technological developments.

**Evidentiary Image**—See *Forensic Copy.*

**Exabyte**—See *Byte.*

**Exchange Server**—A server running Microsoft Exchange messaging and collaboration software. It is widely used by enterprises using Microsoft infrastructure solutions. Among other things, Microsoft Exchange manages email, shared calendars, and tasks.

## F

**Federated Search**—An enterprise-level search across multiple sources via single query from a single user interface. Also see *Search.*

**File**—Collection of ESI stored under a specified name on storage media.

**File Conversion**—Changing data or a file from one format to another. For example, converting native files from their original source format to an image-based format such as PDF or TIFF.

**File Deletion**—See *Deleted File.*

**File Format/Extension**—Three characters (usually) following a file name, to designate the type of file, which defines how it is stored and used. See the Appendix, File Formats Used Worldwide.

**File Level Binary Comparison**—Method of determining duplicate files using the digital fingerprint of the files while ignoring metadata. Also see *Deduplication.*

**File Server**—Computing device optimized to store files for access by multiple users.

**File System**—Combination of software and logical structures used to organize and manage storage and access to ESI on storage media.

**File System Metadata**—System generated metadata stored externally from the ESI and used by the system to track ESI. Also see *Metadata.*

**Filename**—Name of a file excluding root drive and directory path information.

**Filtering**—See *Search.*

**Fingerprinting**—See *Forensics* and *Hash.*

**Flat File Database**—See *Database.*

**Flash Drive**—See *USB Drive.*

**Forensic Capture/Copy**—A method of preserving the original state of a physical storage media, and copying the entire contents of the media to preserve files and folders, and all other information on the media, including deleted files, file fragments, metadata, and other data. Forensic capture applies compression and encryption for protection and to guard against allegations of spoliation.

**Forensics**—The scientific examination and analysis of ESI while residing on storage media or after being retrieved from storage media, in a manner that conforms to legal requirements for evidence collection for use in a court of law.

**FRCP (Federal Rules of Civil Procedure)**—Rules that govern civil actions brought in U.S. federal district courts. Many states enact similar rules.

**Full Text Search**—Search of ESI for specific words, numbers, and/or combinations or patterns. Also see *Search.*

**Fuzzy Search**—Searches allowing and finding close approximations of words, such as misspellings for example, often to overcome errors during OCR scanning. Also see *Search.*

## G

**Gigabyte (GB)**—See *Byte.*

**GIR Analysis**—Gap-Impact-Risk Analysis follows a situational assessment to provide essential information for decision making. Also see *Situational Assessment.*

**Governance**—Formal oversight of and direction to a process or program by one or more senior persons with authority.

**Grid Computing**—A form of virtualization to optimize unused computing resources in which a central resource manages a range of geographically dispersed disparate computers to perform a variety of computing tasks when the computers are not otherwise being used.

## H

**Hard Disk Drive (HDD) Cartridge**—Small, removable device containing a hard disk. Cartridge fits into a docking station connected to computer via USB port.

**Hard (Disk) Drive**—Storage device consisting of one or more spinning magnetic media platters on which data can be written and erased.

**Harvesting**—The process of retrieving and collecting ESI from storage devices/media for processing and loading to Automated Litigation Support (ALS) Systems.

**Hash**—A relatively small, unique number representing the unique digital "fingerprint" of data, resulting from applying a mathematical algorithm to the set of data. The fingerprint may be called hash, hash sum, hash value, or hash code. Used to validate the authenticity and/or integrity of data.

**Hierarchical Database**—See *Database.*

**Hosting**—Provisioning of applications, storage, and Internet access by a third party.

**HTML (HyperText Markup Language)**—Document presentation format used on the Internet that applies tags to enable Web browsers to display text and images.

**HTTP (HyperText Transfer Protocol)**—Underlying protocol used by the Internet to define how messages are formatted and transmitted, and what actions Web servers and browsers should perform in response to various commands.

**Hub**—Network device that connects multiple computers and network peripherals together.

**Hybrid Search**—Enables search and analytics of structured and unstructured data from single interface without requiring change in formats. Also see *Search.*

**Hyperlink**—Underlying code—represented on screen by underlining words or highlighted graphics—within a document that redirects to another location when clicked on by a user. Documents that include hyperlinks to navigate within the document are called HyperText.

## I

**Identification**—One of the first steps in the e-Discovery process, finding discoverable and relevant ESI within various sources.

**ILM (Information Lifecycle Management)**—The program and methodologies for understanding, organizing, and managing the governing framework and technology infrastructure in which information is processed.

**Image File Formats**—Document images can be saved using different file formats, including JPG, GIF, PDF, single-page TIFF, or multi-page TIFF. ALS Systems can usually handle a variety of different formats.

**Imaging**—See *Scanning.*

**Index**—A technique used in information systems to enable faster and more efficient search and retrieval of information in files and databases, typically consisting of a separate file or database of key data elements (dates, names, keywords, etc.), parsed from a source, with pointers to the original source.

**Information Asset (Source) Management**—The inventory and tracking of custodians, and the IT devices and ESI related to them.

**Instant Messaging (IM)**—Form of electronic communication involving immediate text correspondence between two or more online users.

**Integrated Platforms**—For e-Discovery, those software products that combine several e-Discovery solutions into one software suite.

**Internet**—Worldwide, publicly accessible series of interconnected computer networks permitting communication among users.

**Intranet**—Private network that uses Internet-related technologies to provide services internal to an organization or defined infrastructure.

**IP (Internet Protocol) Address**—Unique address that electronic devices use to identify and communicate with each other on a computer network using the Internet Protocol. Also see *TCP/IP.*

**iSCSI**—See *SCSI.*

**ISDN (Integrated Services Digital Network)**—All digital network that can carry data, video, and voice.

**ISP (Internet Service Provider)**—Business providing access to the Internet for a fee. ISPs may be a source of ESI evidence through files stored on their servers. Also see *Hosting* and *Service Bureau.*

**IT (Information Technology) Infrastructure**—The people, processes, and hardware, network, and software components collectively used for information processing and management within an organization.

## J

**Journal**—Chronological record of data processing operations. Journals may be used to reconstruct previous or updated versions of a file. In database management systems, journals are records of all stored data items that have values changed as a result of processing and manipulation of the data.

**Journaling**—Copying of sent and received emails in native format to a secondary storage device for retention or preservation.

**JPEG**—Compression algorithm commonly used for still images.

**Jukebox**—Mass storage device that holds and loads multiple optical discs into a drive.

## K

**Keyword Searching**—The use of key words and Boolean techniques to search for documents containing relevant information. Also see *Search.*

**Kilobyte (KB)**—See *Byte.*

## L

**LAN (Local Area Network)**—A group of computers at a single location that are connected via wired or wireless networks. Also see *Network.*

**Lead Date**—The date of a parent document, or if no parent, the document's own date. Lead date is used in a database as an option to enable chronological sorting of documents by parent, so that any attachments remain in chronological sequence.

**Legacy Data**—ESI residing on outmoded or replaced storage devices for which little or no processing capability or knowledge remains within the organization, or which has become too costly to maintain effectively.

**Legacy System**—Outmoded IT components for which little or no processing capability or knowledge remains within the organization, or which has become too costly to maintain effectively.

**Legal (Litigation) Hold**—Communication issued as a result of current or reasonably anticipated litigation, audit, legal, or regulatory matter that suspends the normal disposition or processing of ESI. Hold orders or Hold notices may also be referred to Preservation, Suspension, or Freeze orders or notices.

**Linking**—The ability within an ALS System to connect evidence, transcripts, notes, pleadings, Web sites, and other documents to each other with hypertext links.

**Load File**—A data file is a critical deliverable from the scanning/coding function that establishes links between records in a database and the document image files to which each record pertains. Without a correctly structured load file, documents and their respective database records will not be in sync.

**Lotus Domino**—IBM's enterprise-level server product that hosts Lotus Notes and Web server capabilities.

**Lotus Notes**—IBM's enterprise-level collaboration suite that provides email, calendars, custom application development, database, and Web services.

**LRP (Litigation Response Plan)**—Developed to guide e-Discovery process.

## M

**MAID (Massive Array of Idle Disks)**—A disc-based storage architecture designed to capture the idle storage capacity of tens of thousand of discs, with a focus on increasing reliability and reducing access times and cost when compared to tape.

**Maintenance Programs**—Applications that run at scheduled intervals according to predefined rules to maintain ESI and IT infrastructure components.

**MAN (Metropolitan Area Network)**—Usually the limited use of fiber-optic to connect buildings within specific areas of a city.

**MD5 (Message-Digest)**—Algorithm meant for digital signature applications where a large message has to be compressed in a secure manner before being signed with the private key. Also see *Hash.*

**Meet-and-Confer**—Meeting between counsels under Rule 26 of FRPC.

**Megabyte**—See *Byte.*

**Metadata**—Metadata provides information about other information sources—origins, usage, authenticity, and characteristics that provide additional meaning and context, and accordingly is considered discoverable evidence. Also, vendors may add metadata as a result of processing, most of which is used for process reporting, chain-of-custody, and ESI accountability. See Chapter 6, Native Files and Metadata.

**Metadata Comparison**—Comparison of specified metadata as the basis for deduplication without regard to content. Also see *Deduplication.*

**Metrics**—Units of measurement, and specifically within e-Discovery, those discernable units, such as documents, files, etc., that lend themselves to quantification.

**Mirror Image**—See *Forensic Capture.*

**Mirroring**—Duplication of ESI for backup or to distribute Internet or network traffic among several servers with identical ESI.

**MPEG (1-4)**—Various standards applied to compression/decompression of full motion video to digital.

**Multimedia**—Combinations of video, audio, text, and graphics in digital form.

## N

**NAS (Network Attached Storage)**—Self-contained computer connected to a network, with the purpose of supplying file-based data storage services to other devices on the network.

**Native Files**—The original form in which a document or file is created by a software application. Two good examples are spreadsheets and word processing documents. Native files contain the content that users see, such as text and spreadsheet numbers, and information (metadata) about the document that users normally do not see, such as author and creation date.

**Native File Review**—A process that requires opening the document in the application in which it was created, or in a special application capable of supporting native file review.

**Natural Language Search**—Use of plain language without requiring special connectors or precise terminology. Also see *Boolean Search.*

**Near Deduplication**—Identification, tagging, or grouping files that do not have the same hash values, but are similar with minor differences in content and/or metadata. An example would be the various threads in an email distribution.

**Near-Line Data/Storage**—Use of offline storage to retrieve information in near real time for online use via robotics moving storage media (tape cartridges or optical discs) from storage library to read/write device. Also see *Offline Data/Storage.*

**Network**—Two or more computers and other devices connected together for the exchange and sharing of ESI and resources.

**Network Administrator**—IT person responsible for maintaining networks.

**Network Database**—See *Database.*

**NIST (National Institute of Standards and Technology)**—Federal agency that works with industry to develop and apply technology measurements and standards.

**NIST List**—Hash database of computer file types developed by NIST to identify those generated by a system and those generated by a user.

**Node**—Any device connected to a network.

**Normalization**—Database normalization is a technique for designing relational database tables to minimize duplication of information to safeguard against logical or structural problems. In the e-Discovery process, normalization involves reformatting certain data elements to a standardized form, such as the date and time stamp of a specific volume of ESI to a specific time zone to enable a process such as deduplication.

## O

**Object Database**—See *Database.*

**Objective Coding**—Manually reviewing a document and completing database fields, such as Bates number, author, recipient, cc, date, title, type, source, characteristics, and keywords. Objective coding, unlike subjective coding, does not require the coder to exercise discretion or be familiar with a particular case in order to correctly code the document. Also see *Coding.*

**Offline Data/Storage**—ESI storage in a system outside the online network (network in daily use), and only accessible by means of the offline storage system, which usually requires manual intervention. Also see *Near-Line Data/Storage, Online Data/Storage*, and *Storage.*

**OLE (Object Linking and Embedding)**—A feature in Microsoft applications that allows each section of a compound document to call up its own editing tools or special display features. This allows for combining diverse elements in compound documents. Also see *Compound Document.*

**Online Review**—Use of an ALS System by one or more persons to perform one or more of the review functions.

**Online Data/Storage**—ESI storage in active systems used in day-to-day operations.

**Ontology**—Collection of categories and their relationships to other categories and to words, and often used to find related documents when given a specific query.

**Open Source**—A class of software that is publicly available, usually under license drafted by the Open Source Initiative (OSI), an organization devoted to promotion of publicly available software.

**Operating System (OS)**—Software that directs the overall activity of a computer, network, or system, enabling all other software programs and applications to operate.

**Operational Storage**—Storage of information in active use for day-to-day operations. Also see *Online Data/Storage.*

**Optical Character Recognition (OCR) and Optical Word Recognition (OWR)**—OCR and OWR are computerized processes that generate a searchable text file from a digital image or picture file when it is scanned. As their names imply, OCR recognizes characters, and OWR recognizes words. OCR software compares the shape of letters in the image with its library of fonts and then generates the appropriate digital letter. Accuracy of OCR is largely dependent on the quality of the original document. OWR uses multiple OCR engines and compares results to a built-in dictionary. OWR is more accurate than OCR especially on older or poor-quality originals.

**Outlook**—Microsoft program that includes email, task management, and a calendar. All data is saved in a single PST file on the user's hard disc drive.

**Outsourcing**—Outsourcing refers to the shifting of work from one organization to another, including from within an organization in one country to an organization in another country. Within the e-Discovery lifecycle, Coding is the function most generally outsourced to reduce costs. Also see *Service Bureau.*

**Overwrite**—To manually or automatically record or copy new data over existing data, permanently deleting the original data.

## P

**Parent/Child**—A hierarchical arrangement in which a subordinate entity is the child of a superior entity. An example would be Microsoft's file system tree structure, where one folder is the parent and folders under the parent are child folders. Also, in e-Discovery, parent refers to the first, or cover, document and child refers to documents attached to the first or cover document.

**Parsing**—Transforms input text into a data structure suitable for later processing, while capturing the implied hierarchy of the input. Data may be parsed from one source of ESI to another.

**Pattern Recognition/Matching**—Pattern Recognition technology searches ESI for like patterns and flags, and extracts the pertinent data. Pattern matching technology compares one file's content with another file's content.

**PCI (Peripheral Component Interconnect)**—Small printed circuit board that can be inserted into an expansion slot of a computer motherboard to add functionality to a computer system.

**PDA (Personal Digital Assistant)**—Mobile handheld device containing common applications for organizing schedules and work.

**PDF (Portable Document Format)**—Software from Adobe Systems Incorporated that converts single or multi-page documents into Adobe's proprietary format that captures the document's original formatting features and enables display across a variety of computer platforms. PDF provides security, navigation tools, search, and other features that facilitate document exchange. If the optional security features are not activated, content from.

**PDF/A**—The International Standards Organization (ISO) PDF specification for the long-term preservation of archived documents.

**PDF Conversion**—Converting documents in another file format to PDF.

**Peripheral**—Any accessory device attached to a computer, such as a disk drive, printer, modem, or to a network, such as router, or switch.

**Petabyte (PB)**—See *Byte.*

**PKI (Public Key Infrastructure)**—A security arrangement that enables computer users without prior contact to be authenticated to each other, and to use the public key information in their public key certificates to encrypt messages to each other.

**PKI Digital Signature**—A method for providing authentication of any message using the Public Key Infrastructure. A document or file may be digitally signed using the party's private signature key, creating a digital signature that is stored with the document. Anyone can validate the signature on the document using the public key from the digital certificate issued to the signer. Validating the digital signature confirms who signed it, and ensures that no alterations have been made to the document since it was signed.

**Pointer**—A pointer is an index entry in the directory of a disc (or other storage medium) that identifies the space on the disc in which an electronic document or piece of electronic data resides, thereby preventing that space from being overwritten by other data. In most cases, when an electronic document is "deleted," the pointer is deleted, that allows the document to be overwritten, but the document is not actually erased.

**Point Solutions**—Standalone software or hardware products that address a single solution.

**Presentation Process**—Phase of the e-Discovery Lifecycle devoted to developing trial presentations.

**Preservation**—The process of ensuring retention and protection from destruction or deletion of all potentially relevant ESI. See also *Spoliation.*

**Preservation Letter/Notice/Order**—See *Legal Hold.*

**Print Server**—Server dedicated to delivering printing services via the network.

**Private Network**—A network connected to the Internet but isolated by security measures allowing use of the network only by authorized users.

**Privileged ESI**—The compilation of ESI identified and logged as responsive and/or relevant, but withheld from production on grounds of privilege.

**Privilege Review**—Privilege review is often a combination of automated search and filtering combined with reading selected documents to determine and flag those considered privileged and to be excluded from production.

**Production ESI**—The universe of ESI identified as responsive to requests and not withheld on the grounds of privilege, and exchanged via electronic media. Also see *Quick Peek.*

**Production Number**—See *Bates Number.*

**Production Process**—Phase of the e-Discovery Lifecycle devoted to "packaging" relevant ESI for delivery.

**Project Management**—Formal methodology for managing resources to achieve objectives.

**Project Plan**—One of the first deliverables under project management—defines project components and how the project will move forward. Also see *Deliverable.*

**Proximity Search**—For text searches, the ability to look for words or phrases within a prescribed distance of another word or phrase.

**PST File Format**—Used by the Microsoft Outlook program. Also see *Outlook.*

## Q

**Quality Control**—Formal method of controlling processes to ensure expected results.

**Query**—Access to a database to retrieve information.

**Quick Peek**—A production of ESI made available to the opposing party before being reviewed for privilege, confidentiality, or privacy, under stringent guidelines and restrictions to prevent waiver.

## R

**RAID (Redundant Array of Independent Discs)**—A method of storing information on servers that usually combines multiple hard drives into one logical unit thereby increasing capacity, reliability, and backup capability.

**RAM (Random Access Memory)**—Hardware in a computer that retains memory on a short-term basis and stores information while the computer is in use.

**Raster Image (Bitmap)**—A data structure representing a generally rectangular grid of pixels, or points of color, capable of being displayed via various media.

**Record**—Information, regardless of medium or format, that has value to an organization.

**Records Management**—Human and automated processes related to influencing the lifecycle of records in accord with business, regulatory, and legal purpose.

**Redaction**—The "blacking out" of information in documents to be produced. Redaction is usually accomplished in an ALS System by overlay so the original document image is not altered. Redactions should be permanent on documents included in final production.

**Relational Database**—See *Database.*

**Relevancy Screening**—The review of documents prior to scanning to eliminate irrelevant documents, using search tools that can filter out irrelevant files by criteria such as date range, custodian, folder, or in the case of emails, by date, author, or recipient.

**Removable Storage**—See *Offline Data/Storage.*

**Residual Data**—Term generally referring to any information not serving a current useful purpose on a computer or storage media that may be recoverable using forensics techniques.

**Restore**—The act of transferring ESI from a backup medium to an online system, and possibly recreation of the original hardware and software operating environment.

**Review**—One of the functions within the e-Discovery lifecycle whereby potentially responsive ESI is examined and evaluated for selection of relevant ESI, including assertion of privilege or confidentiality for example.

**Rip**—Extraction of ESI individual files from container files, such as individual emails from collections of emails, in such a way as to preserve ESI integrity of metadata, authenticity, and ownership.

**ROM (Read Only Memory)**—Permanent hardware memory that can be read but not written to or changed, usually on a chip containing firmware (software on a chip) for starting the computer and running certain imbedded system programs.

**Root Directory**—The top level in a hierarchical file system.

**Routers**—Specialized computers with a wide range of capabilities and processing power for directing wired or wireless network traffic.

**Rule 26 Automatic Disclosure of ESI**—Parties in litigation must provide a copy (or description by category and location) of ESI that will support that party's claims and/or defenses.

**Rule 26 Enhanced Meet-and-Confer Requirements**—Parties must meet and confer at the outset of the case to discuss their plans and proposals regarding the conduct of the litigation, including any issues relating to preservation, disclosure, or discovery of ESI, including the form in which ESI should be produced and claims of privilege, or protection as trial-preparation material.

**Rule 26 Inadvertent Production of Privileged Information**—If discovery information is subject to a claim of privilege, or protection as privileged trial-preparation material, the party making the claim may notify any party that received the information of the claim and the basis for it. After being notified, a party is required to promptly return, sequester, or destroy the specified information and any copies it has and is not permitted to use or disclose the information until the claim is resolved.

**Rule 26 Production of Information "Not Reasonably Accessible"**—A party need not provide discovery of ESI from sources that the party identifies as "not reasonably accessible because of undue burden or cost." The party being asked to produce ESI bears the burden of demonstrating the information is not reasonably accessible because of undue burden or cost. Even if that showing is made, the court may nonetheless order discovery from that party if the requesting party shows good cause.

**Rule 33 Production of ESI In Response To Interrogatories**—Provides the option to respond to an interrogatory by specifying and producing the business records, including ESI, which contain the answer.

**Rule 34 Production of ESI In Response To Requests For Production Of Documents**—Provides the option to respond to an interrogatory by specifying and producing the business records, including ESI, which contain the answer.

**Rule 37 Safe Harbor Provision**—Remedies for a party's failure to respond to, or cooperate in, discovery. Amended Rule 37 provides that, absent exceptional circumstances, a court may not impose Rule 37 sanctions on a party for failing to provide ESI lost as a result of the "routine, good faith operation of an electronic information system."

**Rule 45 Subpoena**—For third parties to produce designated documents, electronically stored information, or tangible things in that person's possession, custody, or control; or permit the inspection of premises.

## S

**Safe Harbor**—See *Rule 37.*

**Sampling**—Sampling refers to the process of testing a database or a large volume of ESI for the existence or frequency of relevant information as an aid in determining whether to perform more extensive searches.

**SAN (Storage Area Network)**—SANs make all dedicated storage devices available to all servers on a LAN or WAN, with the servers acting as pathways from users to the storage devices, thus freeing the servers for business applications.

**SAS (Serial Attached SCSI)**—See *SCSI.*

**Scanning**—Converting text and images of a page of a paper document into a computer file as an image, as readable text, or as a combination of both.

**SCSI (Small Computer System Interface)**—Industry standard connection between computers and peripherals, such as hard discs, CD-ROM drives, and scanners. iSCSI, an advanced form of SCSI, allows two hosts to negotiate and then exchange SCSI commands using IP networks, thus enabling storage area networks (SAN). iSCSI requires no dedicated cabling and can be run over existing switching and IP infrastructure.

**Search**—The use of various automated methods for identifying and finding potentially relevant ESI.

**Search and Collection**—A phase of the e-Discovery Lifecycle devoted to finding and acquiring potentially relevant ESI.

**Searchable PDF**—A PDF document that retains the formatting and looks of the original document, and can be text-searched using Acrobat or third-party search tools.

**Server**—A computer on a network that contains ESI, applications, or other services shared by multiple users of the network on their client PCs. See Chapter 3, Overview of the Information Technology Infrastructure.

**Service Bureau**—Company that provides services such as scanning and coding to the litigation market. Also see *ASP*, *Hosting*, and *Outsourcing*.

**SHA-1 (Secure Hash Algorithm)**—Used for computing a condensed representation of a message or file that enables confirmation of whether or not separate files are exact duplicates. Also see *Hash*.

**Single Instance Storage (SIS)**—A system's ability to keep one copy of a file that multiple users or computers share. SIS helps eliminate duplication and increase efficiency. SIS is frequently implemented in file systems, email server products, backup, and other storage-related solutions. Deduplication, when applied to ESI storage, achieves greater volume reduction than SIS. Also see *Deduplication*.

**Situational Assessment**—Examination to determine the current state in relation to the desired state, and to uncover any problems related thereto. Usually followed by a gap-impact-risk (GIR) analysis. Also see *GIR Analysis*.

**SMS (Short Message Server)**—Gateway for enabling messaging between devices.

**Spoliation**—The deliberate or inadvertent modification, loss, or destruction of evidence by a party who has been put on notice of litigation but has failed to take appropriate steps to preserve potentially relevant information.

**SQL (Structured Query Language)**—Worldwide standard language for retrieval and management of data in relational database management systems, and for sharing data among large interconnected databases.

**SSD (Solid State Disk)**—Very small memory/storage device for mobile and other small devices.

**Steering Committee**—A group of stakeholders formed to provide governance and guidance to major programs.

**Steganography**—The practice of hiding a message or file within a larger file or an image or audio file in such a way that others cannot discern the presence or contents of the hidden message. Steganography can be used for purposes such as digital watermarking (fingerprinting) for copyright protection, and to maintain confidentiality. Steganography can also be used for illegitimate purposes such as theft or concealment of data or hiding illicit images.

**Storage**—Placement of information on a storage device for day-to-day use (operational storage) or for disaster recovery (backup storage) or for long-term retention (archival storage).

**Storage Device**—Any device, such as a disc or tape drive serving as the host for storage media, capable of storing ESI.

**Storage Media**—A medium for storing ESI, including magnetic tape, discs, CDs, DVDs, and solid state electronics for example.

**Structured ESI**—Information organized by computer program in a consistent manner to allow manipulation usually via database structures that enable sorting, searching, and reporting for example. Also see *Unstructured ESI*.

**SSD**—Solid state disc in the form of USB stick or memory card.

**Subjective Coding**—High-level legal analysis of documents in an ALS System that relates each relevant document to one or more appropriate legal or factual categories or issues as defined by the lead attorney.

**Suspension Notice**—See *Legal Hold*.

**Synchronization**—The ability to merge two or more copies of a database together, preserving rather than overwriting the latest changes made in any copy.

**System Administrator**—IT person responsible for developing and/or maintaining core infrastructure systems, as opposed to business applications.

**Swap File**—A file used to temporarily hold information for programs that are running. Swap file information temporarily remains after programs are terminated and may be retrieved using forensic techniques.

**Switch**—Network peripheral that joins multiple computers together within a LAN, with limited intelligence to direct data to the correct recipient computer.

## T

**T1 and T3 Lines**—High speed, high bandwidth leased communication connections to the Internet.

**Tape Cartridge**—A plastic housing for a tape reel and the preferred mechanism for use in tape-based storage systems.

**Tape Drive**—A hardware device used to store or backup ESI on a magnetic tape.

**Tape Recycling**—Process of overwriting tapes with new data, usually on a fixed schedule involving tape rotation.

**Tape Restoration**—Process for harvesting ESI from tapes for e-Discovery or because tapes are damaged, obsolete, or difficult to maintain, and storing harvested ESI on alternative media.

**Task/Resource Schedule**—A project management form used to define the timeline for tasks and people to complete deliverables. Also see *Deliverable*.

**Taxonomy**—Categorization or classification based on a predetermined system, and applied in ESI retrieval to find documents that are related to a query by identifying other documents in the same category or classification.

**Temporary File**—Files temporarily stored on a computer by Internet browsers and office applications to enable faster screen display. Forensic techniques may reveal computer usage through examination of temporary files.

**Terabyte**—See *Byte*.

**Text Messaging**—Sending/receiving short messages (160 characters or less) between mobile devices or computers.

**Text Mining**—Process for finding value in text—categorization, clustering, patterns, concepts, relationships, novelty—using a variety of techniques such as parsing the input text, along with the addition of some derived linguistic features and the removal of others, and subsequent insertion into a database. Also see *Data Mining*.

**Thick Client**—See *Client*.

**Thin Client**—See *Client*.

**Thread**—Usually refers to a series of communications on a particular topic such as might take place with emails, bulletin boards, or messaging systems.

**TIFF (Tagged Image File Format)**—A widely used graphic file format for storing bit-mapped images with different compression formats and resolutions.

**Transactional File System**—Specialized file system enabling high volume transactions with fault tolerance, transaction roll back, and audit logging—typically used in financial systems.

**Transcript Formats**—Discovery and trial transcripts available electronically that can be searched, annotated, linked, and organized into brief reports in ALS Systems and in dedicated transcript management programs.

**Transparency**—The inherent feature of a process or system to be easily externally viewed or audited.

**Trial Presentation**—The display of evidence via computer display at a hearing rather than by way of multiple photocopies. Full-featured ALS Systems have built-in trial presentation features.

**True Attachments**—See *Attachments* and *Unitization*.

## U

**Unallocated Space**—An area of storage media, such as a hard drive, that does not contain normally accessible information. Unallocated space usually results from file deletion since the file is not actually erased but is only rendered inaccessible through normal means. Until the unallocated space is used for new ESI, the "deleted" ESI can be retrieved using forensic techniques.

**Unitization**—The identification of document boundaries, as well as the linking of cover documents and their attachments in an ALS System. Document boundaries and linking must be determined prior to scanning according to their relationship or the rules established by the litigation manager.

**Unstructured ESI**—Information not easily readable by machine or suitable to a database structure, such as email content, and audio or video files and unstructured text such as the body of an email or word processing document. Also see *Structured ESI*.

**USB Drive**—Small removable storage device that uses flash memory and connects via a USB port.

## V

**Validation**—Various automated processes used to ensure the accuracy of scanned images and coded information, and to verify the accuracy of attachment ranges and dates.

**Verbatim Coding**—Extracting data from documents in a way that exactly matches the information as it appears in the documents.

**Vertical Deduplication**—A process through which duplicate documents or information are eliminated within a single custodial or production document set. Also see *Deduplication*.

**Virtualization**—An IT architecture and device management scheme that makes disparate devices appear and operate as one large pool of resources; applicable to computers, servers, or storage devices.

**Voice Mail**—Recording in a file of analog or digital voice message.

**VoIP (Voice over Internet Protocol)**—Transmission of voice across an Internet connection, often with limited attachments such as images and video.

**VPN (Virtual Private Network)**—A secure network designed using public communication transmission to connect nodes for access only by authorized users.

**VTL (Virtual Tape Library)**—Disc-based storage system that emulates some of the characteristics of tape arrays.

## W

**WAN**—Wide Area Network.

**Web Repository**—A Web Repository is part of an ALS System made available for users to perform required functions of document review via secure connection to the Internet, with no local software required other than a Web browser.

**Web Server**—Server specialized for transactions via the Internet.

**Workflow**—The automation of a function or process whereby ESI or tasks are passed from one user to another for action according to predefined rules.

**WORM Discs**—WORM (Write Once Read Many) discs are primarily used to archive information that must not be altered.

## X

**XML (Extensible Markup Language)**—Specification for enabling users to define their own elements to facilitate sharing structured data across different information systems, particularly the Internet.

## Y

**Yottabyte**—See *Byte.*

## Z

**Zettabyte**—See *Byte.*

# INDEX

*References are to chapters (Ch.) and section numbers.*